SYSTEMS ANALYSIS
AND PROJECT MANAGEMENT

McGRAW–HILL SERIES IN MANAGEMENT

Keith Davis, *Consulting Editor*

SYSTEMS ANALYSIS
AND PROJECT MANAGEMENT

DAVID I. CLELAND

Associate Professor of Management
Air Force Institute of Technology
Wright-Patterson Air Force Base, Ohio

WILLIAM R. KING

Associate Professor
Graduate School of Business
University of Pittsburgh

McGRAW-HILL BOOK COMPANY   New York   St. Louis
San Francisco   Toronto   London   Sydney

SYSTEMS ANALYSIS
AND PROJECT MANAGEMENT

Library of Congress Catalog Card Number: 68–17179
ISBN 07-011309-2

7890 KPKP 79876543

TO

Velma, David,
Jennifer and Matt Cleland
and
Fay, Jim-Jim,
Suzie and Ceze King

PREFACE

Management theory and practice have undergone radical changes in the past two decades. Perhaps nowhere else is this so evident as in the management activities involved in maintaining an adequate defense capability for the United States. The management tasks involved in efficiently and effectively utilizing $60 billion to $70 billion annually—a sum exceeding the gross national product of most of the world's nations—are enormously complex. So too, however, are the potential benefits of improved management.

In the early 1960s, new approaches to managing the defense system began to be implemented under Secretary of Defense Robert McNamara. The benefits achieved through these innovations have led to the introduction of these modern management approaches in other government departments, as reflected in President Lyndon B. Johnson's directive in 1965 "to immediately begin to introduce a very revolutionary system of planning and programming and budgeting through the vast Federal Government." [1]

Concurrent with these management revolutions in government have been similar changes in business and industry. The advances in technology and the increased complexity of a "demand-creation" economy have outmoded many of the management theories and techniques which were developed for a "demand-satisfaction" environment. Recognizing this, industry has applied many of the modern management ideas adopted by the government.

The major changes in the government and civilian environments have involved both the strategic planning and the execution functions of management. In *strategic planning*—deciding what should be done—the manager must select, from the myriad of available alternatives in each decision situation, one that will be good for his organization. In the *execution* process, he

[1] As reported in *Time*, Sept. 3, 1965, p. 20.

must ensure that effective implementation actions are taken so that his decision is carried out and the organization's goals are achieved.

The modern analytical approach to the strategic planning aspect of management is most often termed *systems analysis*. In the execution process, similar ideas are applied under the label *project management* (or, alternatively *systems management, program management,* or *product management,* depending on the environment). Hence the title of this book—*Systems Analysis and Project Management.*

The current emphasis on systems analysis and project management emanates from a recognition of the duality of the manager's role. Whatever his level, the manager is faced with both strategic decision-making tasks and those which involve organizing and controlling the execution of those decisions. In many contexts, one or the other of these two functions may predominate, but both are there, and one suspects that those managers who do not view their role in this dual context may be ignoring a potentially important aspect of their responsibility.

This book is an attempt to present the modern ideas of systems analysis and project management in a form which will demonstrate their essential unity and their applicability in a wide variety of industrial and governmental management environments. The modern organization, be it governmental, educational, or industrial, is confronted with a continuing stream of potential projects. Whether the projects involve urban renewal programs, transportation systems, new products, corporate merger possibilities, or the acquisition of new equipment or facilities, their impact will be felt throughout the organization. Individuals at various levels of the organization will be called on to provide information and assistance to those who analyze and carry out the projects. Thus, a basic understanding of the strategic decision-making processes involved in comparing and evaluating these project proposals, and of the efforts necessary to effectively carry out those which are selected for implementation, is necessary at all levels of the organization.

Those who work directly in decision-making or project-management roles should be particularly interested in the book. Moreover, those who must interact with systems analysts and project managers should find that the book provides the basis for communication between practitioners of systems ideas and those who must function in an environment in which these ideas are becoming increasingly important. In particular, the introduction of planning-programmig-budgeting concepts into the executive branch of the government has made it essential that government personnel at all levels be conversant with these modern ideas.

For students of business and engineering management, the book provides a framework for the integration of traditional management theory with the newer concepts of operations research and project or systems theory. The areas of apparent conflict between traditional management thought and the modern systems ideas should be the source of stimulating discussion.

The level of quantitative or mathematical sophistication of each of these audiences should be adequate for an understanding of the book. The emphasis is on the underlying concepts and methodology and not on the specialized mathematics, and no special mathematical competence is required of the reader. The text material itself is suitable for an upper undergraduate and a graduate course in management. It is presumed that the student or practitioner using this book has been exposed to the rudiments of management theory, but no detailed knowledge is necessary.

The growing body of literature reflecting the awareness of the dynamics of management practices by contemporary academicians and practitioners has been drawn on extensively. There are sufficient footnotes and recommended readings so that the instructor can structure his presentation around the background of his students.

The format of the book is simple. Part 1 deals with the underlying concepts and forces which have motivated the modern management revolution. Parts 2 and 3 deal, respectively, with the strategic decision phase of management and the execution phase of management.

Part 1, Basic Systems Concepts, provides the foundation for both the planning and the execution phases of modern management. That foundation is the systems approach.

In Part 2, the strategic decisions involved in the planning aspect of management are discussed in terms of the decision-making process. The emphasis in this part is on the analysis of the decisions using the systems approach.

In Part 3, consideration is given to the execution of decisions as a major part of the manager's responsibility. Here, the recognition that the value of the rigorous thought provided by systems analysis can be negated by ineffective execution forms the basis for discussion of the economic, social, political, and human aspects of project management.

We should like to acknowledge those who gave of their time, energy, and knowledge to aid us in this effort. Particularly, Bill Converse and Lloyd Dunlap, who provided opportunity and encouragement during the writing process, Keith Davis and John Mee, who perused the manuscript, Dave Dellinger, who critiqued our ideas in both verbal and written form, and Janet Wheeler and Betty Holt, who assisted and monitored our production of the manuscript with their usual diligence and humor. Our thanks also go to those, too numerous to mention, who gave us permission to reproduce, adapt, or draw on their work for use in the book. Of course, in all cases we have given our own interpretations to the thoughts and works of others, so that all opinions expressed are solely our responsibility and do not necessarily reflect the opinions of others or of our organizations.

As always, we acknowledge the contributions of our families, whose sometimes negative direct impact on the completion of the work is always far outweighed by their positive indirect influence.

David I. Cleland

William R. King

CONTENTS

9   The Organizational Chart: A Systems Viewpoint   196

10   Project Authority   225

SYSTEMS ANALYSIS AND PROJECT MANAGEMENT

PART 1

BASIC SYSTEMS
CONCEPTS

CHAPTER 1

The Systems Concept in Management

The work of management has been
recognized as a distinct type of
endeavor which performs such
activities as objective-setting, decision-
making, policy formation, planning,
organizing, motivating, controlling,
and innovating. Although there may
be some slight difference among the
management scholars and authorities
on the terminology used to identify
the sub-functions, the basic concepts
are very similar.[1]

Within this century, the United States has developed a thriving economy
which is unparalleled in history. Now, much of the rest of the world is
emulating this development. The revolutionary changes in technology which
have fostered these achievements are apparent to all. However, not so
obvious are the radical changes in management which have paralleled the
technical innovations.

The emergence of the professional manager is one significant indication
of the changes which have occurred in management thought and practice.
The professional manager is one who, while not necessarily sharing in the
ownership of the enterprise, nonetheless seeks to manage the human and
nonhuman resources in a fashion which is consistent with the goals of others
—be they the owners or society.

The problems of management have confronted military, government, and

[1] John F. Mee, *Management Thought in a Dynamic Economy,* New York University
Press, New York, 1963, p. xix.

business leaders since antiquity. Only in the twentieth century, however, has there evolved a systematic examination of management thought whose objective is to codify empirically developed principles into a theory of management. Because the world is changing, the theory is imprecise and still incomplete; hence, it must be constantly revised and modified.

The meaning of management

Management is the process concerned with the achievement of objectives. It may be described in a number of ways, e.g., as the task of creating the internal environment for organized efforts to accomplish group goals. In coordinating group activity, the manager plans, organizes, staffs, directs, and controls. Ralph C. Davis of Ohio State University defines management as "the function of executive leadership anywhere." [2] Other definitions of management are fundamentally the same, and most contain certain universal elements:

> Management is a distinct process dealing with group activity.
>
> An objective is involved.
>
> The objectives are achieved through establishing salient relationships between human and nonhuman resources.
>
> The manager does not necessarily perform things for himself, but accomplishes objectives through others in the group situation.
>
> Decision making is pervasive in the management process.

Analysis of these elements indicates that scholars agree quite well as to the functions and nature of the management process.

Functions of the manager

Management is a distinct skill, apart from the technical skills involved in an organization. The management process is composed of identifiable functions or homogeneous activities. While some disagreement exists among current academicians and practitioners as to what the manager's functions are, abundant evidence reflects that there are two major functions of management: *planning* and *execution*.

PLANNING AND EXECUTION   The more abstract of the two major phases of management is planning. As it is used in this book, the term subsumes two common interpretations of planning. First, there is the concept of planning

---

[2] Ralph C. Davis, *The Fundamentals of Top Management,* Harper & Row, Publishers, Incorporated, New York, 1951, p. 6.

which incorporates the "process of preparing for the commitment of re- sources in the most economical fashion, and, by preparing, of allowing this commitment to be made less disruptively." [3] This interpretation of planning is usually referred to as *long-range* planning since it involves explicit con- sideration of the (sometimes distant) future.

The process of *strategic decision making* is also taken to be an element of planning. Strategic decision making usually involves consideration of the alternative allocations of resources which may allow the organization to pursue its goals.

The relationships of the long-range planning and strategic decision-making phases of the planning function can be readily illustrated in the marketing context. Long-range marketing planning encompasses the consideration of alternative ways of achieving the goals of the firm.[4] Thus, if the future pat- tern of per-share corporate earnings is the relevant measure of the degree of attainment of the corporation's objectives, the future goals might be achieved by penetrating new markets, introducing new products, expanding sales of existing products, etc. The strategic decisions of the company en- compass specific consideration of alternative ways of achieving these desired states. For instance, the firm might wish to consider the relative worth of a new product versus an expanded advertising outlay to promote an existing product, or it might desire to choose a "best" new product. In either case, strategic choices—those related to corporate goals—are being made.[5]

The execution function of management also involves several different sub- functions. The most important of these are organizing, motivating and con- trolling. *Organizing* has to do with the procurement of human and nonhuman factors, the grouping and alignment of personnel and physical resources, and the delegation of authority and responsibility within the organizational struc- ture. The organizing process must recognize that a complex system of informal relationships exists in any group activity. This informal organization is a network of personal and social relationships existing along with the formal organzational structure. The informal organization emphasizes people and their roles as determined by their peers, in contrast to the formal organiza- tion, which emphasizes functions, positions, and specific grants of authority and responsibility.

Motivating has to do with the face-to-face leadership situation between superiors and subordinates and between peers and associates. *Controlling* is

[3] E. Kirby Warren, *Long-range Planning: The Executive Viewpoint*, Prentice-Hall, Inc., Englewood Cliffs, N.J., 1966, p. 21.
[4] See Mark Stern, *Marketing Planning: A Systems Approach*, McGraw-Hill Book Company, New York, 1966, for an extensive discussion of planning in marketing.
[5] See William R. King, *Quantitative Analysis for Marketing Management*, McGraw- Hill Book Company, New York, 1967, for a discussion of strategic decision making in marketing.

the process of making events conform to plans, i.e., coordinating the action of all parts of the organization according to the plan established for attaining the objective.

The manager performs all these functions—planning (in either the long-range planning or the strategic decision-making context, or both), organizing, motivating, and controlling—more or less continuously and regardless of his organizational level, although the emphasis placed on each function is different at the different organizational levels. The operational manager who is charged with the responsibility for accomplishing a specific mission, for example, is most concerned with the control function in performing the mission itself. A staff official who is charged with the development of the overall plan of a project is more involved with the planning function than with organizing or controlling. Indeed, Drucker holds that ". . . planning and doing are separate parts of the same job; they are not separate jobs. There is no work that can be performed effectively unless it contains elements of both . . . advocating the divorce of the two is like demanding that swallowing food and digesting it be carried on in separate bodies." [6]

Authority and responsibility patterns

Authority and responsibility form the legal framework of management. Authority is defined as the right derived from some legitimate source to direct the efforts of others. It is the power to act. Ultimate formal auhority, as derived in the industrial establishment, flows from the Constitution of the United States, through the particular state constitution, to the corporate charter. This is the *legal authority* attached to an organizational position, and it is an important source of power. Such authority does not, however, in the absolute sense, give one the right to make someone else do something. It does provide the superior with inducements in the form of penalities and rewards (promotions, job assignments, etc.) which give him real and meaningful power over subordinates.

In the absolute sense, a manager's authority must come from the acceptance and respect accorded him by his subordinates. Formal authority can be delegated, but no one can delegate influence. The organization can only ensure that the manager is provided with environmental conditions conducive to the acceptance of his authority by subordinates. In the long run, his most meaningful authority may be that derived from the alliances he is able to build within his environment and the conflicts he can resolve within his organization.

[6] Peter F. Drucker, *The Practice of Management*, Harper & Row, Publishers, Incorporated, New York, 1954, p. 284.

The development of management thought

In the traditional framework of management, what the manager does is fundamental and universal, regardless of the nature of the organization, be it military, ecclesiastical, or industrial. All managers, regardless of their organizational level, perform certain basic functions directed toward accomplishing predetermined goals. Proper execution of these functions is both an art and a science; as an art, it requires that the manager use skill acquired through experience; as a science, it requires that he use knowledge that has been systematized and formulated.

Science and art are complementary in both the management discipline and the management process. One may have a sound theoretical knowledge of management and yet fail as a manager because he lacks proficiency in the art of the discipline, particularly in the art of managing activities requiring close and continuing contacts with people. Management is a distinct field that requires knowledge and skills apart from the technical skills involved in the work, such as engineering, accounting, production, and procurement. Today's manager is concerned with developing an underlying theory or philosophy of management so that he can be provided with a broad framework for making and executing decisions in his environment.

The cornerstone of traditional management theory is a set of *principles*—those fundamental maxims explaining certain phenomena and constituting the framework around which a theory is built. Some of these principles are easily recognized, while others are still hypothetical and require verification and codification. Indeed, even well-accepted principles are sometimes disregarded in practice. For instance, dual subordination may exist in an organization, and the hasty critic may conclude that there is no validity to the principle of unity of command. In fact, though the concept that each employee should receive orders from only one superior may be violated in one organization, it still may be applicable to many others.[7]

The changing management environment

The complexity of modern industrial and governmental enterprises, with the consequent increase in the quantity and complexity of managerial decisions, has outmoded some principles of traditional management. There is a greater degree of uncertainty involved in the present "demand-creation" economy than there was in the "demand-satisfaction" economy of yester-

---

[7] The unity of command principle is credited to Henri Fayol. Doubtlessly, it can work well in small organizations where the management process operates solely through superior-subordinate relations. In more complex organizations, its validity is open to doubt.

year, so that the delineation of the best alternative in any of the decision problems faced by managers is more difficult than ever.

The payoffs from good decisions and good execution are also greater than ever before. The most vivid illustrations of decisions involving great uncertainty, potentially huge payoffs, and severe complexity are those involved in the awarding of government research and development contracts. Weapons systems costing billions of dollars are no longer uncommon, and the planning required to obtain and implement a contract for the development of such a system is of a fantastic magnitude and complexity. Yet, even when the contract is gained and the basic development completed, the uncertainty of reward is not lessened, for such contracts are increasingly being written on an incentive basis, rewarding or penalizing the contractor according to the level of performance of the finished product. Thus, the aerospace contractor cannot emphasize the preaward planning phase of his task and do a "good-enough" job of execution. The pressure is on him for good planning *and* execution, and if he fails to achieve both, he may find that he has suffered a financial loss on what appeared to be a lucrative government contract.

It would be foolish, however, to argue that management became complex last night or at any recent point in time—or, indeed, over the past two decades. The increase in complexity has been a gradual one, resulting directly from our ever-expanding society. Our present-day perception of the degree of this increase in complexity is amplified by the relatively slow concurrent development of new techniques for handling ever more complex problems.

One significant factor which has come into play almost overnight has served to focus the attention of managers on their need for objective analysis and new management ideas. That factor—the moronic [8] electronic computer, with its associated fast data-processing equipment—has proliferated itself to the extent that the data which are available to the manager are almost inexhaustible. Virtually instantly, the modern manager can have at his fingertips data on sales, costs, and profit margins; only a few years ago, the cost of garnering such an amount of data from the reams of diverse reports on which they were originally compiled would have been prohibitive.

Faced with this complexity and availability of data, coupled with the knowledge that the techniques necessary to make use of them are becoming

---

[8] The adjective "moronic" is applied to the computer by the authors in a defensive reaction to the widespread association of the word "brain" with it. Whatever the capacity of the computer as we know it may be, it is in no sense a brain, but merely a fast and efficient processor which must be ordered to perform each and every action in a degree of detail which would normally be associated with the intellect of a submoron.

available to his competitors, the manager has had little real choice but to undertake scientific analysis of problems which lie outside the scope of his judgment and intuition and to organize for the execution of decisions in fashions which are consistent with this new decision-making framework.

Science and management

The functions of management will always involve such difficult-to-quantify elements as establishing objectives, coordinating the efforts of groups of human beings, and motivating individuals to seek the goals of the organization. Traditionally, the preeminence of art in management was recognized to the extent that science was virtually neglected. The basic functions of management—planning (deciding what should be done) and execution (doing it)—have been analyzed scientifically only in the twentieth century. The pioneer of scientific management was Frederick W. Taylor, who introduced basic analytic methods into factory management early in the century. Taylor's classic statement, "knowing exactly what you want to do, and then seeing that they do it in the best and cheapest way," introduced the era of scientific management at the shop level. Taylor's main concern was with the efficiency of workers and managers in the actual production functions of a factory, however, and this preoccupation with the operations level probably led to his neglect of the problems of management at higher organizational levels. Koontz and O'Donnell at the Graduate School of Business Administration, University of California, Los Angeles, credit Henri Fayol, a French industrialist, with being the father of modern management theory. Fayol's now classic book, *Administration Industrielle et Générale,* published in 1916, was not translated into English until 1929; no English translation was published in the United States until around 1949.[9] This book presents a clear perspective of the management process. According to Koontz and O'Donnell: [10]

> A study of Fayol's monograph, with its practical and clear approach to the job of the manager and its perception of the universality of management principles, discloses an extraordinary insight into the basic problems of modern business management.

Its examination and treatment of the organic functions of management are, in the main, still valid after several decades. Others have contributed to the development of management principles and theory, but the works of Taylor and Fayol remain as the classics.

[9] Harold Koontz and Cyril J. O'Donnell, *Principles of Management,* 3d ed., McGraw-Hill Book Company, New York, 1964, p. 17.
[10] *Ibid.*

Systems and the systems concept [11]

One major idea lies at the root of the modern, scientific approach to management. That idea—the systems concept—has had a substantial impact on both the planning and the execution functions of management. This effect is best illustrated in the planning context by the increasing emphasis which is being placed on the scientific analysis of managerial decisions. Increasingly, managers are relying on decision analysts, who may call themselves "operations researchers," "systems analysts," or "management scientists," to aid in the selection of best strategies from the myriad which are typically available. And, as they do, the basic framework by which decisions are made shifts away from the traditional pattern.

In the execution phase of management, the manager has also become increasingly independent of traditional management thinking and principles. In an effort to "get the job done," pragmatists have evolved new management approaches which are best exemplified by the current emphasis on project management [12] in executing plans and decisions.

A *system* may be defined literally as "an organized or complex whole; an assemblage or combination of things or parts forming a complex or unitary whole." The value of the systems concept to the management of an enterprise can be seen in terms of two elements of the manager's job. First, he desires to achieve *overall effectiveness* of his organization—not to have the parochial interests of one organizational element distort the overall performance. Second, he must do this in an organizational environment which invariably involves *conflicting organizational objectives*.

To demonstrate this, consider the corporate viewpoint involved in the simple decision involving which products are to be produced and in what quantities. The production department of the enterprise would undoubtedly prefer that few products be produced in rather large quantities so that the number of costly machine setups necessary to convert from production of one product to production of another would be minimized. Such a policy would lead to large inventories of a few products. The sales personnel, on the other hand, would want to have many different products in inventory so that they could promise early delivery on any product. The financial manager, recognizing that large inventories tie up money which could be invested elsewhere, would want low total inventories. The personnel manager would desire constant production levels so that he would not constantly

---

[11] Some of the material in this section is adopted with permission from a paper by one of the authors. See William R. King, "The Systems Concept in Management," *Journal of Industrial Engineering*, May, 1967, pp. 320–323.

[12] Sometimes referred to as "systems management" or (in the marketing context) "product management."

be hiring new workers for short periods of peak production and laying them off in slack periods. One could go on to identify the objectives of almost every functional unit of an organization relative to this simple tactical decision problem. Obviously, all these objectives conflict to a greater or lesser degree—low inventory levels versus high inventory levels, many products versus few products, etc.

The same kind of situation can exist at every other level of the enterprise. The production department must constantly balance the speed of production with the proportion of rejects and the proportion of defective products which are not detected. The marketing function becomes involved when defective products cause complaints and lost sales. Indeed, wherever the "labor" has been divided in an organization, the management task of effectively integrating the various elements is paramount, and this can be effectively accomplished only if the manager adopts the systems approach to the "system" which is his domain.

The systems concept or viewpoint is the simple recognition that any organization is a system made up of segments, each of which has its own goals. The manager realizes that he can achieve the overall goals of the organization only by viewing the entire system and seeking to understand and measure the interrelationships and to integrate them in a fashion which enables the organization to efficiently pursue *its* goals.

Of course, this means that some functional unit within an organization may not achieve its parochial objectives, for what is best for the whole is not necessarily best for each component of the system. Thus, when a wide variety of products are produced in relatively small quantities, the performance of the production department may appear to be falling off; yet if this leads to greater total revenues because no sales are lost, the overall impact may be positive. This simple realization is the essence of the systems viewpoint, which has led to more effective management decisions and to organizing for the efficient execution of those decisions.

Systems and planning

The systems concept in management decision making virtually necessitates the use of objective analysis of decision problems. The human mind can comprehend only so much, and the systems viewpoint requires consideration of the many complex interrelationships between problem elements and the objectives of numerous functional units. Moreover, even if the manager were able to reduce these complexities to manageable proportions by abstracting out all but the salient aspects, he would have no guarantee that his subjective decision process was either logical or consistent.

The increasing requirements of the systems viewpoint, coupled with the previously noted changing environment, have resulted in the use of objective scientific analysis in solving decision problems. The fields of operations research, management science, and systems analysis have contributed to this end through the application of scientific methods to management decision problems. Practitioners in each of these fields rely on models—formal abstractions of real-world systems—to predict the outcomes of the various available alternatives in complex decision problems.

Because these models are usually symbolic, it is possible to reduce complex relationships to a form that can be put down on paper and, using techniques of logic and mathematics, to consider interrelationships and combinations of circumstances that would otherwise be beyond the scope of any human being. Models permit experimentation of a kind which is unavailable in many environments; one may experiment on the model describing a system, rather than on the system itself.

Of course, this does not mean that the decision maker cedes his responsibility for making decisions to some mystical scientific process or that his judgment and intuition do not play a major role in decision making. Because of the nature of the mathematics which are available, models have one of the "deficiencies" of the human brain; that is, they consider only a part of the real-world decision problem. Other parts are omitted because they are relatively unimportant or simply because they cannot be handled using existing techniques. The difference between explicit models and subjective decision making using nebulous "models" which exist in the manager's mind is one of degree. The process is similar, but explicit models formalize salient characteristics and relationships which may be blurred in the mind of a man. Explicit consideration is given to those aspects of the real world which should be included in the model and those which should be abstracted out. Men tend to include in their mental models the first (or last) aspects which occur to them and to exclude others which stretch the bounds of their comprehension. Moreover, once the explicit model has been constructed, the objective approach has the guarantee of logic and consistency, which are not necessarily features of judgment and intuition.

The role of the manager's judgment and intuition is simply refocused by the systems approach. They are directed toward those aspects of problems which are best handled subjectively. The factors in an objectively viewed decision problem which must be handled subjectively are usually separate and distinct. This permits calm, expert judgment on each aspect, rather than gross judgments encompassing wide varieties of disciplines and areas of experience.

Moreover, the manager's judgment is still of paramount importance in the process of integrating the results of objective analysis with the predicted effect of unconsidered problem elements and arriving at a decision based on the totality of available information.

In effect, the systems approach to planning may be viewed as a logically consistent method of reducing a large part of a complex problem to a simple output which can be used by the decision maker in conjunction with other considerations in arriving at a best decision. It permits him to focus his attention on the aspects of the problem which are most deserving and to restrict the attention which he allocates to those things which are best handled by systems analysis. Such an integration of science and intuition permits consideration of the interrelationships of functional activities. In simple terms, it enables the manager to get the "big picture" in its proper perspective, rather than requiring him to devote attention to relatively minor aspects of the total system.

Systems and execution

Not only has the systems concept caused great changes in the planning, or strategic decision-making, portion of the manager's function, but it has also caused revolutionary changes in the fashion in which decisions are executed. The most striking example of this is the emergence of the project manager.

The *project manager* may be defined as that individual who is appointed to accomplish the task of integrating functional and extraorganizational efforts directed toward the development and acquisition of a specific project. The project manager (or systems manager) is confronted with a unique set of circumstances and forces with each project, and these circumstances and forces channel his thought and behavior into somewhat singular patterns of response.

The project manager's position is based on the realization that modern organizations are so complex as to preclude effective management using traditional organizational structures and relationships. Traditional philosophy is based on a vertical flow of authority and responsibility relationships and emphasizes only parts and segments of the organization. It does not place sufficient importance on the interrelationships and integration of activities involved in the total array.

The need for this new way of thinking evolves naturally. Top management cannot be expected to comprehend all the details and intricacies involved in the management of each activity, whether it is a weapons system under development, a product being marketed, or a client being serviced. Functional units are properly more concerned with their function than with individual products or projects. Thus, the need for a manager who can cut across traditional functional lines to bring together the resources required to achieve project goals is clear.

Just as the systems viewpoint necessitates consideration of the combined effect and interrelationships of various organizational functions in the manager's planning task, so too does it require integration of these functions at the execution level. The project manager is able to operate through the various functional managers in directing the resources which are involved in effectively carrying out a project. Thus, he can focus his attention on project goals, rather than on parochial production goals or marketing goals, and he serves as the instrument for implementing decisions in terms of the same structure in which they are made—the system.

In practice, the project-management structure is superimposed on the functional organization of the company and provides a focal point for the decision-making and execution phases of a particular project. The nature of the job of managing a large project forces the integration. Today's project manager faces an interlaced managerial activity encompassing broad spectrums of authority and responsibility. Management relationships have become so complex that unless someone is in control of the situation, vast amounts of resources can be exhausted before it is possible to effect a necessary retrenchment or redirection.

Summary

The general framework of this book has been outlined in this chapter. The major functions of management—planning and execution—will be treated in the subsequent two parts. The objective of the discussion will be to integrate the modern ideas of systems analysis and project management into a framework of traditional management theory. Organizational theory and management principles provide a basic guide for planning, organizing, and controlling the human and nonhuman resources involved. The truly significant result of this integration is the realization that the systems aspects of management cannot be separated from foundations of traditional management theory. A new breed of manager has been created to meet the challenges and problems of this new management situation—one who combines the talents of the traditional manager with an analytic capability and the talents of the project manager to become a *total* manager, capable of coping with the decision-making, functional, and project aspects of the job.

The important point to stress is the essential unity of the traditional and modern approaches. Systems analysis does not supplant an intuitive approach to planning. Rather, the two approaches are complementary. In the same way, the concepts of traditional and project management complement each other; they are not two distinct approaches to the execution function.

Taken together, the traditional and modern concepts of planning and execution form an integrated whole. Management relationships and problems change as new theories and techniques are formulated. Principles of management appropriate in one environment may not be appropriate in another. No doubt, new ideas of management will evolve as we become more knowledgeable concerning the structure and dynamics of our industrial society. The modern manager must maintain his pragmatism and utilize both traditional and modern thinking in making and executing his decisions in this environment of high risk and uncertainty. His management philosophy must change with the patterns in management, for only a management philosophy which is developed on such a base is adequate for today's complex management tasks.

Recommended readings

Cleland, David I.: "Why Project Management," *Business Horizons,* Winter, 1964.

Davis, Keith: *Human Relations at Work,* McGraw-Hill Book Company, New York, 1962.

Davis, Ralph C.: *The Fundamentals of Top Management,* Harper & Row, Publishers, Incorporated, New York, 1951.

Drucker, Peter F.: *The Practice of Management,* Harper & Row, Publishers, Incorporated, New York, 1954.

Gaddis, Paul C.: "The Project Manager," *Harvard Business Review,* May–June, 1959.

King, William R.: "The Systems Concept in Management," *Journal of Industrial Engineering,* May, 1967, pp. 320–323.

Koontz, Harold: "Making Sense of Management Theory," *Harvard Business Review,* July–August, 1962.

—— and Cyril J. O'Donnell: *Principles of Management,* 3d ed., McGraw-Hill Book Company, New York, 1964.

Warren, E. Kirby: *Long-range Planning: The Executive Viewpoint,* Prentice-Hall, Inc., Englewood Cliffs, N.J., 1966.

Ways, Max: "Tomorrow's Management: A More Adventurous Life in a Free Form Corporation," *Fortune,* July 1, 1966.

PART 2

SYSTEMS ANALYSIS FOR STATEGIC DECISIONS

CHAPTER 2
Systems Analysis

Ultimately all policies are made . . .
on the basis of judgments. There is
no other way, and there never will
be. The question is whether those
judgments have to be made in the fog
of inadequate and inaccurate data,
unclear and undefined issues, and a
welter of conflicting personal opinions,
or whether they can be made on the
basis of adequate, reliable information,
relevant experience, and clearly
drawn issues. In the end, analysis is
but an aid to judgment. . . . Judgment is supreme.[1]

The application of the systems concept in the planning function of management has come to be labeled "systems analysis." At the outset, however, one
should recognize that a semantic "jungle" exists; i.e., different people use
different terms to express the same thing. For example, many managers and
analysts use the terms "systems analysis," "operations research," "operations
analysis," "cost-effectiveness analysis," "cost-benefit analysis," etc., synony-
mously. Others attempt to distinguish among the fields of inquiry which each
of these terms denotes.

If one is less concerned with precise definitions than with understanding
the systems approach and knowing what people do under the guise of one
or more of these terms, this semantic entanglement presents little difficulty.
All the endeavors which any practitioner would label with one of these
terms have common elements; the main differences are in the *scope* of the
analytic activity. Here, we shall find that it is useful to concentrate on the

[1] Alain C. Enthoven, as quoted in *Business Week,* Nov. 13, 1965, p. 189.

process—the methodology—rather than the scope. Hence, we can view the essential elements of operations analysis, systems analysis, cost-effectiveness analysis, etc., simultaneously—since, indeed, they are identical in their salient features—and leave precise definitions to those who practice in particular environments and who may find it useful to attempt to define these terms.[2]

To understand the methodolgy called "systems analysis," it is first necessary to have an understanding of problems, for the goal of systems analysis is the solution of the decision problems which face the planner.

Decision problems

Any decision problem, whether within the confines of an organization or in the daily life of an individual, involves several important elements.[3] First, someone or some group must be faced with the problem—the *decision maker*. The term "decision maker" as used here should not be interpreted to mean a forceful dynamic activist, as opposed to one who procrastinates. The scientific meaning of the term implies nothing about the personal qualities of the person who may fill the role. In the scientific sense, *a decision maker is an entity, either an individual or group, who is dissatisfied with some existing state or with the prospect of a future state and who possesses the desire and authority to initiate actions designed to alter this state.*

For example, the marketing vice-president who is dissatisfied with a downward sales trend is potentially a decision maker in the scientific sense. He must, of course, actually possess both the desire and the authority to alter promotional expenditures or take other actions designed to increase sales if he is to function as a decision maker.

The decision maker's desires to achieve some state of affairs—his *objectives*—are the reasons for the existence of a problem. These objectives have (or should have) some relationship to the overall strategic objective of the firm. The strategic objective provides the policy framework and criteria from which ancillary objectives are formulated. The objective becomes the focal point from which strategic decisions are made.

Often, objectives are expressed as a wish for either the attainment of a

[2] For a discussion of the relationship between the scopes of these activities, see E. S. Quade, "The Limitations of a Cost-Effectiveness Approach to Military Decision-making," RAND Corporation, P–2798, Santa Monica, Calif., September, 1963.

[3] Similar problem elements have been discussed by C. W. Churchman, R. L. Ackoff, and E. L. Arnoff, *Introduction to Operations Research*, John Wiley & Sons, Inc., New York, 1957, chap. 5.

new state, such as higher profits, or the retention of an existing one, such as "our image as the industry's leader." Usually, however, the objectives of the decision maker are expressed as some combination of achievable goals and retentive constraints on the pursuit of those goals, e.g., to maximize profits while simultaneously maintaining an image level.

To pursue his objectives meaningfully, the decision maker must have available to him *alternative actions* which can promote the state of affairs he wishes to achieve. These available alternatives, together with a *state of doubt* as to which one is best, constitute the heart of any decision problem.

Perhaps the most common error made by potential decision makers (those dissatisfied individuals with authority to act) who base their thinking solely on subjective experience, judgment, and intuition is that they fail to recognize the existence of alternatives. Theirs is the failure to perceive and consider alternatives which have never been used before and which are therefore likely to be beyond the scope of experience and sound subjective evaluation. In effect, the potential decision maker who is dissatisfied but recognizes no alternatives to present methods abdicates his responsibility, since the existence of alternatives implies the potential existence of a problem. The failure to recognize the alternatives, and hence the problem, has the same result as would a conscious choice of the *status quo* from among a range of possible alternatives.

The significant aspect of the decision maker's failure to consider alternatives is that it is perfectly natural. Everyone's judgment is conditioned by his range of past experience, and most of us do not conduct our daily lives in a fashion which is conducive to the generation of new alternatives. Thus, if the decision maker takes the same approach to organizational problems that he does to personal ones, he is unlikely to be fully aware of the range of alternatives which may be available.[4] What he needs in the organizational context is a set of concepts and procedures which will aid him in defining and developing alternatives. The idea and techniques of systems analysis provide such a basis.

We shall investigate these basic concepts and techniques later. At this point, we shall simply note that the decision maker must constantly be on the alert for decision problems which may appear from nowhere with the development of new techniques or policies. It should always be borne in mind that one never really shirks a decision, since the state which may be retained by the apparent avoidance of alternatives is itself an outcome of

[4] We shall not investigate the implications of this statement concerning the way in which we should conduct our personal lives. It is generally true that most people conduct more detailed analyses of organizational decisions than of personal decisions. Whether they should do so or not depends on personal values rather than organizational values.

the unrecognized problem. As such, it is always a prime candidate for subsequent comparison with outcomes which might have been realized from unrecognized alternatives.

When problems are thought of in this general way, it becomes clear that the concept of a problem encompasses both the long-range planning and the strategic decision-making aspects of the manager's planning function. So, too, does the general idea of a problem include the tactical problems which must be faced in the execution phase. In this discussion we shall focus on the planning phase, but most of the concepts are equally applicable to the tactical decisions necessary to "get the job done."

Solutions to decision problems

To formally solve a decision problem, it is necessary that the decision maker choose the *best* of the available alternatives. In very simple decision problems, this is equivalent to saying that he should choose an alternative which leads him to a state which is at least as good as all other states. In more complex problems, the idea of a best alternative is somewhat more subtle. We may define a *problem solution* as the best of a set of alternative actions.

This apparently simple and straightforward statement has tremendous practical ramifications. What is meant by "best," for instance? How is the best alternative to be found? Is the alternative we consider best necessarily the same one our superior would choose? We shall investigate such questions as these in the remainder of this chapter and in subsequent chapters.

The concept of searching for and selecting the best alternative, however defined, is itself subject to controversy at the practical level. Professor Herbert Simon of the Carnegie Institute of Technology has proposed in his *principle of bounded rationality* that people seldom attempt to find the best alternative in a decision situation.[5] Rather, they select a number of good-enough outcomes and an alternative which is likely to achieve one of them. In searching for a new product, for instance, the marketing executive makes no attempt to enumerate all possible products so that he can select the best one; rather, he decides what he wishes to achieve with a new product and selects one which is likely to satisfy his desires.

This descriptive concept (how people *do* act) has normative implications (how people *should* act), for one might argue the irrationality of complete rationality; i.e., the completely rational man should evaluate all alternatives and choose the best one, and yet it would be irrational to do so if this would involve the expenditure of vast amounts of time and money.

[5] This principle is discussed extensively in D. W. Miller, and M. K. Starr, *Executive Decisions and Operations Research*, Prentice-Hall, Inc., Englewood Cliffs, N.J., 1960.

Of course, the idea of selecting a best alternative is questionable in another respect. Not only might it be irrational to try to investigate every alternative, but in most complex problems, it is also impossible to do so. Our understanding of the underlying structure of most complex systems is incomplete, and we are often unable to understand the interrelationships of all the factors bearing on the decision problem in question. To expect optimization in such a state of knowledge would be utter folly. In fact, as we shall illustrate, one view that may be taken of systems analysis is that it simply helps the decision maker to better understand the structure of the problem.

The systems-analysis process

Systems analysis is a scientific process, or methodology, which can best be described in terms of its salient problem-related elements. The systems-analysis approach involves:

1 Systematic examination and comparison of those alternative actions which are related to the accomplishment of desired objectives
2 Comparison of alternatives on the basis of the resource cost and the benefit associated with each alternative
3 Explicit consideration of uncertainty

Examination and comparison of alternatives

The process of examining and comparing the alternatives which are deemed relevant to the accomplishment of objectives is not as simple as it might at first appear. At one level, there is the problem of examining a prescribed set of actions. For example, when a corporation attempts to compare several potential new product ideas in order to select the best one, or when the Air Force compares several proposed designs for a counterinsurgency aircraft, the range of alternatives to be considered is rather well defined.

On the other hand, it may be necessary or desirable to invent new alternatives. If the obvious alternatives are all inadequate to achieve a given qualitative objective, it will be necessary to develop new ones.[6] Often the obvious alternatives will achieve an objective but will involve a prohibitive cost, so that new alternatives are necessary. In either case, the new alterna-

[6] The great decision makers of history have often been so regarded because of their ability to see beyond the range of alternatives presented to them. Solomon, for example, pretended to choose an alternative which he had invented (to have the child's body severed.) In reality, he chose an alternative involving the gathering of information (in the form of the reactions of the women claiming to be the baby's mother). So, too, did Charlemagne invent an alternative by accepting the crown from the Pope's hand and placing it on his head. He thus avoided the two poor alternatives presented to him—to be crowned by the Pope or to refuse to be so crowned.

tives to be considered may simply be different combinations of the same controllable aspects. For instance, if the objective is to give the United States some defined capability to move men and supplies and if the basic alternatives considered are land, sea, and air transport, it may not be possible to achieve a given capability with any one mode. Fast air transport might not be able to move sufficient quantities, land transport is obviously restricted when bodies of water are encountered, and sea transport is restricted to water, but some combination of the three might very well serve to achieve a capability for land and sea movement in the desired quantity. Of course, this is obvious, and no rational person would conceive that only one of the media of transport—land, sea, or air—should be considered exclusively. Yet, this is exactly the general sort of thing which has sometimes been done in the past in planning for the achievement of objectives along parochial lines.

AN ILLUSTRATION FROM GOVERNMENT   Consider the following hypothetical situation. Suppose that the United States Army decided that in order to fulfill its assigned mission, it must be able to transport a given quantity of men and supplies to any point in a given area within some prescribed time period. For example, its objective might be to move a regiment to the Near East in three days and to support the regiment there for a three-month operation. Because of the three-day stipulation, this role must obviously be performed by the Air Force, which then decides the best airplane to meet the requirement and, having done so, initiates the acquisition process.

The relevance of this hypothetical situation to the examination and evaluation of alternatives becomes apparent when one enumerates what has been considered and what has not been considered in the process. First, the transportation of the men and supplies by water *has* been considered—at least implicitly. It has been recognized that no water transport could move troops and supplies from a United States base to the Near East in three days. Air transport, of course, has been considered also, but what has not been considered is some *combination* of air and sea transport.

As soon as this point is raised, it becomes apparent that air transport can fulfill the function of getting the troops there quickly, with sufficient supplies to sustain them for some period of time, and that water transport can then come into play to move supplies for the long-term support of the operation. And, we know intuitively that the air fleet required for the initial movement would be considerably smaller than that required to meet the full, long-term requirement. Of course, water-transport capability is also required in the latter situation. But it is not at all clear which alternative is best, and if the initial procedure had been followed and the requirement placed immediately on the Air Force, the latter alternative would probably not even have been considered because the Air Force (properly so) has its own interests and range of activity, and it would not normally recommend that the Army seek out the Navy to provide a service which it could provide itself.

To extend this hypothetical illustration further, we might point out that there are doubtlessly other alternatives which should be considered. For instance, the United States could permanently store supplies aboard victory ships and harbor them in Italy or Greece.[7] This would presumably permit faster sea movement and, consequently, require a smaller transport fleet. Or, we could simply store supplies in warehouses in friendly Near East locations. The range of alternatives is endless, and even though one cannot consider every possible one, consideration should be given to the *objectives* and not to some *requirements* emanating from basic objectives.

Of course, if none of the obvious alternatives will achieve a prescribed objective or if they are all too costly, it may be necessary to invent new alternatives which go beyond simple combinations of aspects of the basic ones. In our hypothetical situation, this would probably require the participation of engineers and scientists, for it is unlikely that the systems analyst would be qualified to make technical innovations in transportation. For example, one alternative which might be considered in this case is the use of a "hydrofoil," a vehicle which is supported by a cushion of air and which can move across both water and land. A fleet of large hydrofoils might provide the best alternative, but since the capacity of most existing versions is small, the feasibility of this alternative would warrant close investigation—both technically and economically.

AN ILLUSTRATION FROM INDUSTRY   In the case of a company's examination of new product alternatives, the analogous line of thought is apparent. The search for a new product begins with the generation of ideas. The ideas may reflect changes in existing products which are redesigned to make them appeal to new or expanded markets, or they may involve entirely new classes of products. Usually, there is some attempt to relate the product idea to some perceived need and(or) some resource of the organization in question. Therefore, one might examine each product idea in terms of questions such as:

1   Can the present production facilities be utilized?
2   Can present raw materials be utilized?
3   Can it be distributed through the present organization?
4   Does it make use of the know-how of our present organization?

[7] The authors emphasize that the problem and the alternatives discussed here have no relationship to any which may have been considered by any government agency. They are purely conjectural. Their purpose is to illustrate the variety of consideration which must be given to alternatives if the systems concept is to be applied.

However, there are no simple good or bad answers to such questions. In general, positive responses might appear to be favorable for most companies. Products which fit into the existing raw-material, production, and distribution scheme would appear to be preferable to those which do not. Hence, an oil company might consider products which use oil as a raw material, require refining, and can be sold through service stations to be preferable to products not meeting these criteria. In fact, however, the list of potential products meeting all these criteria is rather limited. As a result, several major oil companies have broadened this limited view of raw materials, production facilities, and the distribution organization to include their clerical and managerial resources and correspondence with credit-card customers. One result has been the marketing of travel insurance policies. This new product utilizes many of the human resources already available to the companies as "raw material" and "production capacity." In addition, the sale of these policies through existing postal correspondence with credit-card customers represents a broad view of distribution facilities. The possibility of direct insurance marketing through the standard outlets—the service stations which sell the company's brand of gasoline and oil products—has also not been omitted from consideration.

This example illustrates how a broader view of the function of an organization can lead to feasible new product ideas. The oil company thinks of itself as being in the travel business rather than the oil business. The result is travel insurance and arrangements with food processors to distribute hot meals to weary travelers at their service stops. The insurance company, on the other hand, thinks of itself as being in the finance business rather than the insurance business and begins to invest its capital in new ventures and to develop new insurance policies to meet the changing needs of an affluent society.

In any case, the answers to questions concerning the feasibility of new product ideas, such as those posed, should be interpreted in two ways. First, are the definitions of the present organization broad enough? Second, do positive responses to the questions really reflect preferences which are consistent with the organization's objectives? If diversification is a primary organizational goal, positive answers to questions concerning the compatibility of a new product with the existing system might reflect negatively on the product idea. Rather than the more restricted view of always finding alternatives which fit in well with the existing system, the primary overall consideration must always be: *What are the objectives of the organization, and how compatible is the alternative with them?*

INTERDISCIPLINARY TEAMS   Both of these illustrations lead one to the conclusion that the generation of alternatives other than those which are obvious or those which are obvious combinations of basic alternatives is not a simple task which can be handled by a single individual. To generate feasible transportation alternatives requires a variety of technical skills, as does the generation of new product alternatives. Usually, no single individual possesses all the requisite skills.

The concept of an interdisciplinary team has been found to be beneficial in this and other phases of systems analysis. An interdisciplinary team is a working group made up of people with varying backgrounds and skills each of whom brings his own point of view and experience to bear on the problem, often with results which are significantly superior to those which a single individual might be expected to produce.

In addition, the nature of most significant decision problems implies alternatives which have psychological, sociological, and physical aspects. Hence, what better way to study complex systems made up of interrelated parts than with teams made up of individuals who can bring their knowledge of the related disciplines to bear?

BRAINSTORMING   One device which has been used successfully in one form or another in generating new alternatives is the technique called "brainstorming." In a brainstorming session, a group is called together and encouraged to discuss possible new alternatives, say, new products or fruitful areas for new products. "Out-of-the-blue" thinking aloud is encouraged. No critical analysis of ideas is permitted, although it is hoped that each "wild" idea may lead to another and perhaps eventually to a radical idea which has merit. The interaction of the individual members of the group is believed to have a stimulating effect. Often during later analysis, although most of the recorded ideas which have been put forth in the brainstorming session are discarded as impractical, a few ideas which merit study are uncovered. Some who have participated in apparently fruitless sessions have felt that, at the very least, the sessions served to open new avenues of thought in the minds of individuals who might later produce meritorious ideas.[8]

---

[8] Pseudosophisticates may consider the technique of brainstorming to be old hat. Nonetheless, the pragmatist will find that the basic idea is both useful and used (although the term "brainstorming" may not always be applied). A good illustration of its utility is the important role it plays in the operations of the Van Dyck Corp., which specializes in devising new products for clients such as Olin Mathieson, J. C. Penney, and Textron. *Business Week* (July 2, 1966, pp. 52–54) describes Van Dyck's brainstorming sessions as follows: ". . . the staff bats around ideas, and scrawls them down on scraps of paper, which are tossed into a huge fishbowl. . . . Any idea goes in if it has aroused even a glimmer of response from the group. Later on, a two-man team—always one engineer and one industrial designer—cull out the most promising candidates."

The basis for comparison

In order to determine which of several alternative ways of accomplishing some objective is the best, they must be evaluated and compared on the basis of costs and benefits.

Costs are the resources—dollars, people, machines, etc.—which, when allocated to one alternative, cannot be used for other purposes. *Benefits* are those worthwhile elements which are derived as a result of some action.[9] Thus, if an advertising manager decides to spend $100,000 on TV "spots" (the cost) and this results in $300,000 in additional sales revenue (the benefit), both aspects describe the overall *worth* of the alternative. And although there is an apparent single measure which one might apply to evaluate this alternative—benefit minus cost—it is clear that another alternative including the expenditure of $110,000 and resulting in an increased revenue of $310,000 might not be equally good, even though both have a benefit-cost difference of $200,000.

We shall go more deeply into a discussion of the appropriate combination of costs and benefits to use in evaluating alternatives later. Here, the important point is that both aspects must be considered.

That this principle seems obvious does not mean that it is always applied. Consider, for example, the following excerpt from an address by Alain C. Enthoven, Assistant Secretary of Defense for Systems Analysis, in which he discussed the pre-1961 operations of the U.S. Department of Defense: [10]

> The Department of Defense was organized in such a way that military requirements were determined by the Services, the Joint Staff and JCS quite independently of costs, while on the other hand, we had a financial management system for determining budgets without any explicit reference to military requirements or military effectiveness. The forces and the budgets, or, in other words, the effectiveness and the costs were considered on completely separate wave lengths. The system did not recognize the cost effectiveness principle.

The principle referred to by Enthoven may be stated simply as follows: In order to determine the overall worth of an alternative, both cost and benefit (effectiveness) must be considered. He continued his description of cost-effectiveness analysis with an illustration of how a failure to *explicitly* consider costs and benefits in planning may lead to very poor results when cost constraints must be met: [11]

[9] Often termed "effectiveness" in the context of military systems analysis.
[10] Alain C. Enthoven, address before the Aviation and Space Writers Convention, Miami, Fla., May 25, 1964.
[11] *Ibid.*

Suppose that I want to buy a house and, instead of using the cost effectiveness approach, I do it in the more traditional way. First, I determine my housing requirements without any consideration of costs. I count up the rooms I require: I need a bedroom for myself, one for each of my children, and one for my parents or other guests who come to visit us occasionally. I need a study because I occasionally bring some of my work home with me and need a quiet place to work. My wife needs a sewing room. I need a pool in the basement because my doctor has told me that I must swim every day if I don't want to have another operation on my back. Now, you might laugh when I say that I have to have a pool in my basement, but I can validate that requirement. I can argue for it very convincingly. I can produce a Doctor's certificate, and you can't prove to me that I don't need that pool. Moreover, I work at the Pentagon and I work long hours. Therefore, I need to live within five minutes drive of the Pentagon. When I put this all together, I find that I have established a requirement for a house that costs a hundred thousand dollars. Having done that, I review my financial situation and find that I am only able to spend about $30,000. So what do I do? If I am operating under the old concept, I take the $100,000 design and I slice off 70 percent of it and what's left is my house.

Now, clearly that's not a very sensible way to design a house, I might find that I left off the bathroom, or included the bathroom, but left off the plumbing that is required to make it work. Yet that's a pretty fair description of the way that the Department of Defense did its business. We found in 1961 that we had Army Divisions without adequate airlift or other means of mobility and with far from adequate supplies of equipment. We had tactical air wings without supplies of non-nuclear ordnance, and numerous other similar problems. In effect, we had bought a lot of houses without the bathrooms or the plumbing.

Thus, as Enthoven describes, if one does not take explicit account of costs and benefits, but rather thinks solely in terms of requirements, he is likely to be left holding the bag. If it takes a $100,000 house to meet my requirements and I can afford only a $30,000 house, I clearly should not just "chop off" some features of the $100,000 house until it costs $30,000. Rather, I should begin to plan with the $30,000 in mind. Enthoven described this process as follows: [12]

The rational economic way of buying a house, or of buying a defense program is to consider alternative balanced programs each of which yields the most effectiveness possible within a budget that corresponds

[12] *Ibid.*

approximately to the availability of our resources. If I think that I have about $30,000 to spend on a house, I should consider several alternative houses each optimized for my purposes within financial limits such as $28,000, $30,000, $32,000, and perhaps $34,000 and then I should ask myself whether the extra advantages associated with the more expensive houses are worth the extra financial sacrifices I would have to make to pay for one. It's altogether possible that they might be. For example, a larger house might have a recreation room, and this might enable me to economize elsewhere on recreation.

Of course, the use of costs and benefits (effectiveness) as bases for evaluating and comparing alternatives is not a new idea. The *application* of this basis is relatively new, however.

Uncertainty

Most organizational decision problems which are of the complexity of those faced by strategic planners in government and industry involve great uncertainty. Strategic planning and decision making necessarily involve consideration of the future course of events, and the future is inherently uncertain. Virtually all decision making—whether it is subjected to formal analysis or not—involves the uncertain future, of course. The important aspect of the systems-analysis approach is that it gives *explicit* consideration to uncertainty. Many approaches to decision making—whether subjective or objective—do not have this characteristic. The common assumption in these is one of certainty—that each action leads uniquely to a specified outcome. A simple example will serve to illustrate the implications of the certainty assumption.

Suppose that two people are available to be assigned to two tasks—one to each. Table 2-1 gives the anticipated time which each person will require to

Table 2-1   Anticipated time (hours) required by two people in two tasks

		Tasks	
		1	2
People	A	②	4
	B	3	⑥

accomplish each task; i.e., person A will take two hours to perform task 1 (if he is assigned to it), and person B will take three hours to do it (if he is assigned to it). The decision maker in this situation has two alternatives:

Alternative 1: (Assign A to 1 and B to 2)
Alternative 2: (Assign A to 2 and B to 1)

These two alternatives involve the selection of either the two circled entries in the table (alternative 1) or the two uncircled entries (alternative 2).

The total number of man-hours required to perform both tasks is eight (i.e., $2 + 6$) in the case of alternative 1 and seven in the case of alternative 2. Hence, the second alternative appears to be best on this basis. However, if we recognize that the entries in the table are *predictions* of uncertain future events, we may wish to reconsider this evaluation. In deciding on the superiority of the second alternative, we have assumed that we know precisely (with certainty) that each person will perform each task in a given amount of time. In fact, probably neither of the people has performed the tasks so often that we could confidently predict the time that will be required. Suppose, for example, that the second task is of such a nature that we (unknowingly) always overestimate the required time by 100 percent. If this were so, the true table corresponding to Table 2-1 would be Table 2-2 (assuming that we are perfectly accurate in estimating for the first task).

Table 2-2   Actual time required by two people in two tasks

		Tasks	
		1	2
People	A	2	2
	B	3	3

From Table 2-2, it is clear that we have no basis for a preference between the two alternatives; both are identical in terms of the information and criterion. Of course, there may well be other factors we would wish to consider, but no such information is given here.

The point, then, is that even with formal analysis, it is easy to fall prey to the certainty assumption, and such an assumption can lead to very poor results. In this example, it really does not matter which alternative we choose, since both are equal in every way. However, we must recall that the decision maker does not have knowledge of this sort; i.e., he never has available to him anything other than imperfect information of the kind contained in Table 2-1. Information such as that shown in Table 2-2 is always unknown to him.

The problem of the decision maker and the decision analyst is to take prior account of the inherent uncertainty in strategic decisions. Systems analysis attempts to provide a vehicle for doing this, and although it is much easier to talk about considering uncertainty than it is to actually do it, explicit consideration of uncertainty is one of the basic reasons for the success of the systems-analysis approach.

The role of systems analysis

From the preceding discussion, one might reasonably infer that a strong "sales pitch" is being made for systems analysis. Indeed, this is the case, but in order not to make the mistake of the supersalesman who leaves his customers dissatisfied, we should carefully consider the role played by systems analysis, the limitations of systems analysis, etc.

Should all problems be analyzed?

First, we must consider the sort of problem to which systems analysis is applicable. Is it applicable to all decision problems?

The answer is that while it is conceptually applicable to the strategic problems encountered in the planning phase of management, to the tactical problems of the execution phase, and indeed to any problem, be it organizational or one of the day-to-day personal problems which we all face, a reasonable person would not wish to apply systems analysis to all problems.

Some problems are relatively simple in nature and need not be subjected to extensive analysis of any sort. The decision maker who is standing in the middle of a street with a car bearing down on him at 60 miles per hour is in a problem situation; he wants to avoid injury, and he has at least two alternatives—to run to the right curb or to run to the left curb. Any prolonged contemplation or analysis on his part, however, will lead to an outcome which is clearly not the one he desires. The need in this situation is for a quick and accurate decision of the variety which is the forte of some traditional managers and which is the very cornerstone of combat management in the military, where battles may be won or lost simply as a result of initiative rather than the choice of the best alternative. In such "time-sensitive" tactical military contexts, the speed with which the decision is made is critical; i.e., the eventual outcome depends more on the speed with which action is taken than on the specific alternative which is chosen. A tactical commander in such a situation must therefore necessarily rely largely on a framework of experience and intuition to solve his decision problems.

In strategic decision problems—in either the military or the civilian sphere—the environment is more "knowledge sensitive"; i.e., the eventual outcome is usually influenced much more by the chosen alternative than by the speed of action. This sort of decision involves great uncertainty, a myriad of alternatives, and the employment of resources in a time frame which extends into the (perhaps distant) future. If analytic resources are available, the "Damn the torpedoes; full speed ahead" philosophy, which can lead to brilliant military accomplishments, is quite inappropriate to the environment in which the alternatives are new products to be marketed, various antimissile systems to defend our nation, or programs to aid the poverty-stricken.

Of course, there are other sorts of decisions—between the time-sensitive and knowledge-sensitive extremes—which also do not require extensive analysis. Routine decisions made on a day-to-day basis within the framework of established policy exemplify those decisions which require neither inordinate haste nor the expenditure of significant analytic resources. In the several chapters dealing with the planning function of management, we shall concentrate on those knowledge-sensitive strategic decisions which clearly warrant analysis. In Part 3, attention will be given to decisions involved in the execution process of management.

Quantitative and qualitative analysis

Since systems analysis is an outgrowth of traditional scientific method, and since measurement in science is quantitative in nature, systems analysis itself has come to be viewed as quantitative. While it is true that systems analysts often draw upon mathematics as an aid in formulating and solving problems, the complementary role of quantitative and qualitative analysis should be made clear. In fact, since sound qualitative analysis was being performed before most quantitative analysts were born, there is some need to justify the use of quantitative approaches in decision making.

To justify the use of quantitative analysis as an aid to decision making which is preferable to witchcraft or coin tossing, one must argue on some basis other than the inherent "goodness" of science. Science, like everything else in this complex world, has both positive and negative aspects and therefore is not justified simply by the fact that it exists.

One can, of course, point to the successful applications of the scientific method to military and industrial decision problems and argue the likelihood of further success as greater knowledge is gained. Indeed, the gains achieved in the past as a direct result of scientific analysis are impressive, and perhaps this is sufficient evidence to warrant further attention.

To proceed a bit further along a pragmatic line, one might recognize that the same objective input information is available to the scientific analyst as is available to the witch, the gambler, or the "intuitive" decision analyst. The scientific approach has the additional virtue of guaranteed logic and consistency, and the totally subjective process has no such guarantee. In addition, if one views the scientific process as serving as a complement to the subjective processes of the decision maker, nothing is lost and something may be gained by making use of it.

Another value of scientific analysis is its reproducibility. Scientific analysis is a logical process which is well suited to being carried out with pencil and paper (and sometimes slide rule, desk calculator, or electronic computer). In any event, the assumptions, logical steps, and conclusions are always clearly spelled out and recorded. Thus, the analysis may always be resurrected, after the decision to which it contributed is made and the results observed, and the *analytic procedure itself can be evaluated.* If this "testing" proves the worth of the analysis, the same procedure can be applied again with greater assurance that the results will be desirable. A purely qualitative approach has no such permanent value aside from its contribution to the trial-and-error learning process of the individual.

However, the importance of judgment in decision making is not reduced by the potential significance of scientific analysis. One of the primary features of the scientific approach is its degree of abstraction—the omission of certain aspects of the real-world problem which the decision maker faces. These omissions mean that only a part of the real-world problem is treated scientifically. The decision maker must then integrate the results of scientific analysis with the significant intangibles which are not part of the formal analysis in order to arrive at a best decision. In doing so, he must call upon the same levels of judgment, intuition, and experience which are used by the traditional manager. The difference between the two approaches is that the scientifically oriented decision maker distinguishes between subjective analysis and objective analysis and applies each to the areas in which it is most useful.

Human morale is a good example of the kind of factor which is often difficult to incorporate into formal analysis. In any decision problem, the impact of an action on the morale of the people involved may well have as much to do with the organization's effectiveness as anything else, or perhaps more. Yet impact on morale is difficult both to measure and to evaluate. In such a case, the analyst might formulate and solve a problem without giving consideration to the morale level of the organization. It would then be the province of the decision maker to integrate this solution with his judgment concerning its impact on morale and to determine an alternative which he considered to be best overall. This may or may not be the same alternative that the formal analysis produced. The value which the analysis had, however, was that it considered everything other than morale and allowed the decision maker to focus his judgment on that element which required judgment. If the analysis had not been performed, the decision maker could easily have been so concerned with the obviously important factors that he would not have given much attention to the one element—morale— which could not be adequately handled on any basis other than human judgment.[13]

The view which we shall take of strategic decisions and of the role which scientific analysis should play in them is therefore a simple one. The process of scientific analysis is viewed as a logical and consistent method of reducing a large part of a complex decision problem to simple outputs which the manager can use, in conjunction with other factors, in arriving at best decisions. It permits him to focus the analytic resources which are at his disposal on the aspects of the problem where they are most effective. He is therefore able to efficiently utilize both scientific and nonscientific analysis to best advantage. Such an integration can hardly be worse than, and is potentially far superior to, a purely subjective approach to decision making.

Optimization

The formal solution of a decision problem involves the determination of the best available alternative. The process of seeking the best is called *optimization;* i.e., best alternatives are optimum alternatives.

[13] Even the state of morale in an organization is amenable to some degree of scientific analysis through a morale survey. In today's large organizations, the human relations environment is too awesome for an executive to learn how employees feel simply by observing them and then making an intuitive value judgment about the state of their morale. In a morale survey, checklists, attitude surveys, or similar devices are used to gather and interpret the data and place a numerical value on the results. Appraisal then involves the exercise of judgment about what the measurements mean in light of the total organizational situation. See, for example, Williard V. Merrihue and Raymond A. Kotzsell, "ERI: Yardstick of Employee Relations," *Harvard Business Review,* November–December, 1955; and Keith Davis, *Human Relations at Work,* McGraw-Hill Book Company, New York, 1962, chap. 5.

In many complex decision problems involving great uncertainty, the "state of the art" of systems analysis is such that optimization cannot be meaningfully achieved or even sought. In other words, even though we think in terms of achieving best alternatives, we often cannot do so.

Alain Enthoven eloquently states the importance of judgment in decision making in the quotation which introduces this chapter. If only because *all* judgment cannot be quantified, systems analysis necessarily cannot seek global optimization. Only a part of a problem is even quantified, and if one is led to believe unquestioningly that the solution to the abstract model which has been analyzed is also necessarily the solution to the real-world problem, he is doomed to failure.

Moreover, since the systems dealt with by systems analysis are complex, the *structure* of the system may not be well understood. Perhaps the best illustrations of this come from the areas of government fiscal policy and advertising decisions. No economist would claim a comprehensive understanding of the impact of Federal government fiscal policy on the economy. At least for any economist who did, one could easily find ten others who considered his conclusions completely erroneous—as is illustrated each time the prime interest rate is changed, the necessity for a tax increase or decrease is proposed, etc. In media advertising, the same lack of understanding exists. No one would claim to understand the precise relationship between the expenditure of dollars on television commercials and the benefit obtained in terms of additional sales of the advertised product.

Yet in both cases—fiscal policy and advertising—the fact that we do not completely understand the structure and operation of the system *does not* mean that these decision problems cannot be subjected to analysis. What it does mean is that to perform the analysis, it is necessary to make assumptions, to omit some aspects of the problem which we do not understand, and to make other abstractions of the real world.

In doing so, the systems analyst must realize that the problem which has been formulated and constructed on paper is not the real problem. It is a fictitious one which is (hopefully) closely related to the one existing in the real world, and (hopefully again) the solution to the fictitious problem will be helpful to the decision maker in solving the real-world problem. But the differences between the two are of obvious importance, and the decision maker or analyst who seeks to apply "paper solutions" directly to real problems is likely to be in for a rude shock.

In fact, often the abstraction process which has just been described may not even be feasible. The analyst may find that his understanding of the system's structure is so limited that any formalization he might make would bear little resemblance to the real problem. Caught in such a quandry, he may be unsure as to the best course. However, when one realizes that the alternative to an attempt at explicit analysis is a completely subjective approach, his apprehensions concerning the *relative value* of formal analysis—properly applied—begin to disappear.

Human beings are not known for their ability to comprehend complex problems involving many interacting factors. Any formal analysis—or attempt at formal analysis—is usually valuable since it serves at least to make the decision maker think about the right things. Although systems analysis may not, in the final analysis, be able to unerringly tell the decision maker the "right" thing to do, it does require him to enumerate the alternatives, to ask himself what it is that he is trying to achieve, etc. Moreover, the decision maker is presented with a precise statement of what he should know in order to make a rational decision. Even if he does not know all that he should or have all the necessary information, a knowledge of just what he should have will usually provide him with a better basis for making a decision, such as to be wary and to choose conservatively or to err on the positive rather than the negative side of an issue. And, of course, if the necessary information is not available, the recognition of its significance can lead him to obtaining it—if not for use in the problem at hand, at least for use in future, similar problems.

G. H. Fisher, of the RAND Corporation, expressed this very well when he said: [14]

> The conclusion itself may not be the most useful thing to the decision-maker. . . . most high-level decision-makers are very busy men, with the result that they do not have time to structure a particular problem, think up the relevant alternatives (especially the *subtle* ones), trace out the key interactions among the variables of the problem, and the like. This, the analyst, if he is competent, can do and should do. And it is precisely this sort of contribution which is most useful to the decision-maker. The fact that the analysis reaches a firm conclusion about a preferred alternative may in some instances be of secondary importance.

The role of judgment in systems analysis

We have already discussed the importance of human judgment in decision making—even in those decision problems which are analytically solved. The role of judgment is not confined to the complementary function which has

[14] G. H. Fisher, "The Analytical Bases of Systems Analysis," address before a symposium on systems analysis in decision making sponsored by the Electronics Industries Association, Washington, D.C., June 23, 1966.

been described, however. The conceptual framework for analysis, which is known as *decision theory* and is discussed in Chapter 3, directly incorporates human judgment into the formal analysis of the decision problem.

Human judgment is incorporated into formal analysis in two ways—in the context of *likelihood judgments* and in the context of *value judgments*. Thus, in most decision problems involving the uncertain future, it is necessary to assess the likelihood of future events—"It will rain tomorrow," "Our product's sales will be over a million," etc. Such assessments are often best made on the basis of experienced judgment. So, too, it is necessary to evaluate outcomes as a part of the formal analysis of decision problems. If, for example, it is predicted that one level of marketing effort will lead to a profit of $100,000 coupled with a market share of 25 percent, while another level will lead to a profit of $110,000 and 23 percent of the market share, the question of the relative worth of the two outcomes can be answered only through human judgment. In one case involving, say, a newly introduced product where great concern is given to penetrating the market, the larger market share might predominate over a few thousand dollars of immediate profit, while in the case of a mature product, immediate profit might be of primary concern. Such a problem of relative worth can be resolved only through the judgment of the decision maker.

One of the values of systems analysis is that these two varieties of judgment are treated separately and distinctly from each other, whereas in the mind of a decision maker they may often become confused. In the next chapter, we shall discuss the conceptual framework for systems analysis and demonstrate this point further.

Summary

An understanding of systems analysis and the role which it can play in strategic decision making revolves around the concepts of a decision problem, the important elements of a decision problem, and the idea of a problem solution.

Systems analysis is a methodology for analyzing and solving decision problems through a systematic examination and comparison of alternatives on the basis of the resource cost and the benefit associated with each. As a part of this examination, explicit consideration is given to the uncertainties involved in decisions which will be implemented in the future.

While systems analysts often make use of logic and mathematics in solving problems, there is no necessary connection between systems analysis and sophisticated mathematics. Complex problems are often analyzed and solved without resort to anything more complex than high school math.

The role of human judgment in systems analysis is often misunderstood. Systems analyses are complementary to the experienced judgment and intuition of the decision maker. Moreover, in some ways, systems analysts can make use of judgments more effectively than can the individual decision maker. In the next chapter, we shall discuss the conceptual basis of systems analysis and develop the complementary role of analysis and judgment further.

Recommended readings

Brown, Harold: "Planning Our Military Forces," *Foreign Affairs,* January, 1967, pp. 277–290.

Churchman, C. W., R. L. Ackoff, and E. L. Arnoff: *Introduction to Operations Research,* John Wiley & Sons, Inc., New York, 1957, especially chaps. 1–5.

Hitch, Charles J.: *An Appreciation of Systems Analysis,* RAND Corporation, DDC AD422837, Santa Monica, Calif., Aug. 18, 1955.

————: "A New Approach to Management in the U.S. Defense Department," *Management Science,* vol. 9, no. 1, pp. 1–8, October, 1962.

Levitt, Theodore: "Marketing Myopia," *Harvard Business Review,* July–August, 1960, pp. 45–56.

Quade, E. S. (ed.): *Analysis for Military Decisions,* RAND Corporation, Report R–387–PR, Santa Monica, Calif., November, 1964.

————: *Cost-Effectiveness: An Introduction and Overview,* RAND Corporation, P–3134, Santa Monica, Calif., May, 1965.

Seligman, Daniel: "McNamara's Management Revolution," *Fortune,* July, 1965.

CHAPTER 3
A Conceptual Framework for Systems Analysis

Jack and Jill went up the hill
   To fetch a pail of water
Jack fell down and broke his crown
   And Jill came tumbling after.

Jack could have avoided that awful lump
   By seeking alternative choices
Like installing some pipe and a great big pump
   And handing Jill the invoices.[1]

The salient aspects of a decision problem, which were discussed in the last chapter, must be considered in the light of a theoretical framework for analysis. This framework provides the basis for thinking about a decision problem in a logical and consistent fashion. It shows the way in which the various elements of a problem relate to one another, and it does so in a manner which permits one to take each individual piece and put it into its proper perspective.

The conceptual framework for analysis which we shall develop here is simple and straightforward. As we shall demonstrate, in addition to its theoretical value it also has a great deal of intuitive appeal. In fact, we shall argue that it is simply a formalization of the way in which everyone knows he should make decisions or, perhaps, the way in which every rational

---

[1] Stacer Holcomb, OSD (SA), as quoted in *The C/E Newsletter*, publication of the Cost-Effectiveness section of the Operations Research Society of America, vol. 2, no. 1, January, 1967.

person believes he *does* make decisions. However, most of us, on contemplating the conceptual framework, will realize that it is virtually impossible for a person to do all that he knows he should do (or thinks that he actually does) in solving a problem. The scope and complexity of real-world problems are simply too great for most human beings to comprehend without the explicit guidance of a framework for decision-problem analysis.

The conceptual framework may be viewed as a way of reminding us what is important and what is not or, better, as a way of reminding us to ask questions about the relative importance of various facets of the problem. Its basic objective is to have the decision maker and analyst *ask the right questions,* for it is axiomatic that a precise answer to the wrong question is undesirable.

The biggest difficulty with a discussion of the conceptual framework for analysis is that it is exactly that—a *conceptual* framework. In some respects, it is unrealistic in that it cannot be rigorously and explicitly applied in detail to all real-world problems, or, at least, it appears at first glance that it is not directly applicable. The astute reader will recognize immediately that many of his real-world problems could not be directly attacked in the fashion to be described. As a result, he may rush to the conclusion that he is again witnessing the gap between the ivory tower of the printed word and the complexities of the real world. To prevent hasty conclusions which may lead to the neglect of useful analytic methods, the authors hasten to point out that the framework for analysis to be developed in this chapter need not always be directly applied in all its detail for it to be a useful analytic tool. The introduction of the framework is accomplished here in terms of overly simple situations which do not reflect the complexity of real-world problems. This is done so that the essential simplicity of the ideas can be demonstrated. After the basic framework has been discussed, we shall look into its values and limitations and attempt to demonstrate the role it can play in managerial planning.

The decision-making process

To gain further insight into decision problems, we shall briefly discuss the process one must go through—either explicitly or implicitly—in solving a decision problem. This process serves as a focal point for the subsequent discussion of the conceptual framework for problem analysis.

Figure 3-1 outlines a series of activities, beginning with the collection and analysis of input data, which describes the general decision-making process. After the basic data have been collected and assembled, the deci-

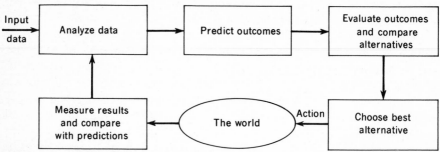

Figure 3-1   The decision-making process.

sion maker predicts the outcomes which may result from each of the various alternatives available to him. Having done this, he evaluates the outcomes in terms of their worth and compares the alternatives on the basis of the outcomes to which each may lead. The best alternative is selected and an action taken which impacts on the "world"—the uncontrollable factors which affect the actual outcome of the decision situation. When the results of the action are known, the decision maker measures the results and compares them with the predicted outcome. The process can then begin anew with new predictions which incorporate the lessons learned in comparing the previous predictions with the actual outcome.

We shall discuss each of the activities which are implicit in the decision-making process in subsequent sections. One of the objectives of the conceptual framework will be the explicit analysis and consideration of those aspects of the decision-making process which are too frequently left implicit in subjective problem solving.

Decision-problem analysis

The alternative which the decision maker comes to select in a decision situation—whether it involves weapon selection, the pricing of a product, or the development of an antipoverty program for the indigent—interacts with the "general state of things." This interaction, together with the actions which may be taken by other rational beings, determines the outcome of the decision situation—the state of affairs which is attained as a result of the chosen alternative, outside influences, and competitive actions. In the pricing of a product, for example, the chosen price interacts with the economic status of consumers and the prices of competitors to result in an outcome which might be described in terms of the number of units sold, the share of market attained, revenue, or any number of other possible *outcome descriptors.*

Outcomes of decision situations represent the states by which success or failure of the chosen actions is gauged. In truth, the aggregate of the outcomes of the many decision situations which face a business enterprise or other organization during a single year determines the success or failure of operations for that year and, in the long run, the success or failure of the organization itself.

The range of outcomes which may result from any particular decision situation is often quite wide. When the Department of Defense sets about to choose a strategic retaliatory force for the nation, it is not inconceivable that the range of outcomes might run from a mix so obviously powerful that it would deter aggression for decades, to one which would be recognized as so unreliable that the nation would be forced to rush in and invest billions to augment it with reliable weapons. Social programs for preschool children illustrate the wide range of possible outcomes even more clearly— at one extreme are those boondoggles which have no noticeable impact, and at the other are projects such as Head Start which has been widely acclaimed as one of the outstanding victories in the war on poverty.

Because of this wide range of possible outcomes, there is great pressure on the decision maker to choose the best, or at least a good, alternative— whether it is a new product, a weapons system, or an antipoverty program. To make such a choice intelligently, the manager must be able to sift the important factors which bear on the problem from the maze of complex trivia with which all significant decision situations abound. This is precisely the role in which the conceptual framework can be most valuable.

The outcome of a decision situation is determined by the interaction of the aspects which are controllable by the decision maker and the factors which are not subject to his control—the uncontrollables. In developing a supersonic transport (SST) airplane, for example, the significant controllables are the design and manufacturer, while the demand for fast, long-range travel, the sonic-boom characteristics of supersonic flight, and the design of competitive airplanes from other countries are all uncontrollable elements which affect the outcome of the United States's SST decision. Both varieties of factors—controllable and uncontrollable—interact to produce the outcome of most meaningful decision situations.

The outcome array

Decision theorists use the terms "strategy" and "state of nature" to describe, respectively, alternatives available to the decision maker and the environmental or competitive factors which bear on the outcome of a decision problem. Thus, in the SST illustration, all the combinations of airframe and engine designs are the strategies in the government's initial decision problem; the state of nature consists of the various uncontrollable environmental factors such as demand for air travel and the various alternative actions which Britain, France, and the Soviet Union could choose in developing their own SSTs.

In the general context, the selected strategy and the existing state of nature interact to produce a single outcome of the decision situation. These interactions may be conceptualized in a two-dimensional outcome array in which each element represents the outcome associated with a particular combination of strategy and state of nature. The entire array displays all possible outcomes which might result from the various combinations of the two interacting elements.

Table 3-1 shows the general form of an outcome array involving three

Table 3-1   Outcome array

	N_1	N_2	N_3	N_4
S_1	O_{11}	O_{12}	O_{13}	O_{14}
S_2	O_{21}	O_{22}	O_{23}	O_{24}
S_3	O_{31}	O_{32}	O_{33}	O_{34}

alternative strategies, four possible states of nature, and hence twelve (3×4) possible outcomes. For convenience, the strategies are labeled S_1, S_2, and S_3; and the states of nature are denoted as N_1, N_2, N_3, and N_4; and the outcomes are symbolized by the letter "O" with two subscripts—the first indicating the corresponding strategy and the second indicating the corresponding state of nature.

We should be careful to recognize in a situation such as that described in Table 3-1 that *only one of the states of nature will occur;* i.e., N_1, N_2, N_3, or N_4 will occur in this case. All four must be considered because we do not know in advance which one will occur. Hence, we must plan for all possible contingencies (states of nature). We do this on the basis of the set of outcomes which are predicted for each strategy–state of nature combination.

Of course, the symbolism in Table 3-1 is for ease of discussion only. In practice, the outcome array would consist of descriptions of each of the possible outcomes.

Let us consider a hypothetical illustration based on the actual SST decision made by the United States government.[2] Two airframe manufacturers (A and B) and two engine producers (C and D) were in contention for the final contract award. There were four possible strategies available to the government:

S_1: (A, C)
S_2: (A, D)
S_3: (B, C)
S_4: (B, D)

Strategy S_1 indicates an award of the airframe contract to A in conjunction with the engine award to C; S_2 involves awards to A and D, etc. Other strategies such as "Do not build an SST" might also be considered in the real problem, but we shall not include them here.

The relevant states of nature in this situation might involve demand levels for supersonic flights and the ability of the SST to operate over land routes (which was undetermined at the time of the contract award because of sonic-boom characteristics). Suppose that demand can be adequately described as "high" or "low" and that a qualitative determination of the aircraft's ability to fly over land can be made ("yes" or "no").[3] The relevant states of nature could then be described as:

N_1: High—yes
N_2: High—no
N_3: Low—yes
N_4: Low—no

State N_1 indicates the possible combination of uncontrollables in which demand is high and the airplane is allowed to operate over land routes, N_2 encompasses high demand together with an exclusion from land routes, etc.

These four strategies and four states of nature could then be arrayed as

[2] The authors emphasize that this illustration is hypothetical. It is an oversimplified reconstruction of the decision analysis which might have been performed and is based on information available from public news media and a good deal of conjecture.

[3] Of course, the determination of the SST's ability to fly over land is really a decision problem itself. Here, we are implying either that uncontrollable physical phenomena (unknown at the time of the decision) uniquely determine whether the aircraft can do so, or that this determination is beyond the scope of the government's decision-making authority.

shown in Table 3-1, and the relevant outcome descriptions entered in the table. These descriptions will normally be stated in terms of measures of the attainment (or degree of attainment) of the decision maker's objectives. The objectives are the decision maker's desire to achieve some state of affairs which is presumably better than that which now exists or that which he can foresee as resulting from his present course. Most decision problems in business and government involve multiple objectives. In the SST illustration, the government's objectives might have been related to providing fast transportation, maintaining the nation's capability in advanced aircraft design, reducing the balance-of-payments deficit by foreign sales, assuring the taxpayer an adequate return on the government's investment and the business enterprises involved a fair profit, etc. Obviously, this is only a partial list. Many other objectives probably were considered, and in the outcome array, it would be necessary to describe the degree of attainment of each objective for each strategy–state of nature combination (each outcome).[4]

Quantitative measures of the degree of attainment of most of these objectives are rather easily developed. The total passenger miles provided and the travel demand going unfulfilled are measures of the "providing transportation" objective. The nation's capability is presumably maintained if any SST is built (but the designs might vary, so that greater technical knowledge would be gained with one design than with another). The effect on the balance-of-payments deficit and both the government's and the contractors' return on investment are also relatively easily measured by costs, revenues, capital requirements, etc.[5]

The outcome array for the SST decision problem might involve the four strategies and four states of nature previously discussed. Each of the elements of the four-by-four array would represent an outcome. For example, the upper left outcome would involve the award of the contracts to company A and company C in conjunction with a high demand level and the plane's being allowed to fly over land routes. The upper left element of the array would contain numerical assessments of the state of affairs resulting from this set of circumstances. The outcome description might take the form:

---

[4] Of course, these outcomes are predictions of the future. Subsequently, we shall discuss how such predictions can be made. Here, we wish only to describe the basic tools and methods of analysis.

[5] The determination of the effect on the balance of payments is not so obvious as it might at first appear. Stephen Enke ("Government-Industry Development of a Commercial Supersonic Transport," *American Economic Review*, vol. 57, no. 2, May, 1967) notes that substitution effects relegate the SST's impact on the balance of payments to an insignificant or negative role.

200,000,000—Passenger miles flown
   500,000—Passenger miles forgone in unfulfilled demand
$1 billion—Balance-of-payments-deficit reduction
       6%—Return on taxpayers' investment
     12%—Return on contractors' investment

Each of the other 15 outcomes would be similarly described in the outcome array.

Although this illustration provides insight into the makeup of the outcome array, it is an easy problem in the sense that good quantitative measures of the degree of attainment of all relevant objectives are available. On the other hand, many other decisions in both government and industry involve situations in which outcomes are not readily measured quantitatively. In choosing among alternative programs in health-depressed areas, for example, the Federal government might decide that reasonable objectives are:

1   To prevent maternal deaths
2   To prevent premature births
3   To prevent infant deaths
4   To prevent mental retardation
5   To prevent physical handicaps
6   To enhance the quality of the environment in which children are raised
7   To provide information about basic rules of sanitation

In practice, of course, the objectives involving prevention would not be feasible in the short run. These goals would be appropriately stated in terms of reducing the incidence of the various occurrences.

When objectives are stated in these terms, quantitative measurement of the degree of attainment of some goals is made possible. The outcome descriptions in the outcome array would be in terms of such measures. From a practical viewpoint, however, it must be recognized that no valid numerical measures can be found for some objectives. In the case of the sixth objective above, for instance, a numerical measure of quality would probably be difficult to develop. Numerical outcome measures appropriate for the first five objectives (stated in terms of reducing rather than preventing) are rather clear—the number of deaths prevented, the number of premature births averted, etc. If no quantitative measures can be determined or developed, or if it is impossible operationally to measure the values which an existing descriptor assumes, the outcome array may include subjective descriptions such as "quality high" or "corporate image maintained." But, of course, quantitative measures or indexes are always more desirable.

Evaluating and comparing outcomes

The solution to a decision problem—or the choice of a best strategy—depends on the outcomes to which each strategy may lead. To compare alternative strategies meaningfully, one must first be able to evaluate and compare the outcomes to which the strategies may lead.

The practical problems arising in the seemingly simple process of comparison of outcomes are immense. Suppose, for instance, that a marketing decision maker has objectives with respect to the market share and profits achieved in a particular decision problem. Two possible outcomes which might evolve are:

Outcome O_1:   Market share $= 10\%$
             Profit $= \$50,000$
Outcome O_2:   Market share $= 15\%$
             Profit $= \$40,000$

There is no clear basis for choice between these two simple outcomes. In O_1, a larger profit is achieved together with a lower market share than in O_2. It is not at all obvious which outcome a particular decision maker or organization might prefer. In fact, it is apparent that two different individuals or organizations might have different preferences regarding these outcomes. The marketing manager associated with a newly introduced product might be very concerned with penetration of the market and might therefore prefer O_2 over O_1, even though less immediate profit is achieved. The manager whose product is mature might prefer O_1.

Economists have long concerned themselves with a concept called *utility,* which may be thought of as the capacity of an event, object, or state of affairs to satisfy human wants. The idea of a basic measure of the degree of human satisfaction which is derived from a state of affairs leads naturally to consideration of using this measure as a way of evaluating and comparing outcomes. If, for example, O_1 is preferred to O_2, O_1 posseses greater utility than O_2. If one had a numerical measure of the utility of each outcome, he could easily select the outcome which had the greatest utility and was therefore to be preferred.

However appealing the concept of utility as indicative of human satisfaction might be, the operational measurement of utility is not well developed.[6] In practice, utility measurements are seldom performed by systems analysts

---

[6] The interested reader may refer to P. C. Fishburn, *Decision and Value Theory,* John Wiley & Sons, Inc., New York, 1964, for a summary of utility measurement techniques and a discussion of the applicability of the concept in problem solving.

if there is any other reasonable alternative. The reasonable alternative to utility measurement which often suggests itself involves the outcome descriptors themselves.

In general, outcome descriptors—or measures of the degree of attainment of objectives—are of two varieties. The *resource costs* associated with a strategy are an intrinsic part of any outcome description. So too are the *benefits* derived from the outcome.

Resource costs are the resources expended in achieving a state of affairs (outcome). Often, it is convenient to think of resource costs as being associated with strategies, e.g., "Spend $1 million on advertising" or "Develop a weapons system at a cost of $1 billion." However, if the strategies are not described in terms of costs, it is often better to think of the costs as being a part of the outcome. Indeed, this sort of thinking is becoming more pervasive as the uncertainties involved in complex systems become greater. For example, in a decision problem involving the selection of a weapons system, various alternative designs and contractors are considered. Attached to each proposal is a cost estimate. If we decide to treat this cost as known, we may consider it to be a part of the strategy. For example, one strategy might be "Proceed with development of XYZ Corp. design at estimated cost of $5 million." However, it is probably better to consider the strategy to be "Proceed with development of XYZ Corp. design" and to realize that the actual cost which will result depends on *both* the design and the environmental factors (states of nature) which may ensue. Thus, the cost of $5 million would be attached to one of a set of possible outcomes which might result from the XYZ design.

Benefits are the returns associated with an outcome, in terms of either the resources gained or the psychological, sociological, or other intangible values derived from the state. Examples of such benefits are the profit earned, the time saved, and the number of maternal deaths prevented, as are the intangibles "greater freedom enjoyed," "freedom from want," "higher quality of life," etc.

Outcome descriptors—whether of the resource-cost or the benefit variety —are measures of the degree of attainment of objectives, and since most complex decision problems involve multiple objectives, it is common to find each outcome in an outcome array described by a number of measures. This is the curse of multidimensionality in systems analysis, for the comparison of outcomes in terms of multiple descriptors is no simple task.

A key method for obviating the problem of multiple outcome descriptors is to reduce them to an overall single measure which reflects their aggregate worth. This is the essence of the utility concept, discussed earlier; however, as we have already pointed out, the problems involved in utility measurement are so great as to impair the usefulness of this approach. The idea of reducing the description of an outcome to a single dimension is still of great importance. A simple illustration will make this point clear. Consider a decision situation involving two strategies and only a single state of nature. Table 3-2 shows the two outcomes described in terms of revenue (benefit) and cost. Note that these outcomes have the same characteristics

Table 3-2

$$N_1$$

S_1	Revenue = \$100,000 Cost = \$40,000
S_2	Revenue = \$110,000 Cost = \$60,000

as those described previously in terms of market share and profit. The outcome for S_2 is better in terms of one measure—revenue—while the outcome for S_1 is better in terms of the other, since it has the lower cost; yet, no one would hesitate to declare that the outcome associated with S_1 is better.[7] Why? Because the *profit* there is \$100,000 minus \$40,000, or \$60,000, while the profit associated with the outcome for S_2 is only \$50,000.

The critical point illustrated by Table 3-2 is that since the resource costs and benefits are expressed in the same terms—dollars—the *difference* between benefits and costs seems to be a valid measure of the aggregate worth of each outcome. Additionally, of course, this difference has an accounting significance which further enhances its intuitive appeal.

Another level of complexity presents itself when we have outcomes such as those discussed previously in terms of market share and profit. Consider the case of Table 3-3, for example. There, we have implicitly superimposed an objective related to market penetration onto those related to dollar costs and revenues.

In Table 3-3, we can make use of the point just demonstrated and make a profit calculation, thus converting the situation to that in Table 3-4. However, after doing so, we have exactly the dilemma discussed earlier, and we cannot readily determine that one or the other of the outcomes is preferable.

[7] This statement implies some assumption about the decision maker's availability of funds, etc. If the alternatives were presented to a large prosperous corporation, the statements made here would invariably be true.

Table 3-3

	N_1
S_1	Market share = 10% Revenue = \$100,000 Cost = \$50,000
S_2	Market share = 15% Revenue = \$110,000 Cost = \$70,000

Table 3-4

	N_1
S_1	Market share = 10% Profit = \$50,000
S_2	Market share = 15% Profit = \$40,000

If we knew the dollar value which the decision maker places on market share, we could arrive at a conclusion, however. Suppose that each 1 percent of market share above 5 percent is regarded as equivalent to \$1,000 in profit. Then, since the outcome for S_1 is 5 percent above 5 percent and that for S_2 is 10 percent above 5 percent, the total worth of the upper outcome is \$55,000, and that of the lower one is \$50,000. Hence, S_1 is best because it leads to the outcome with the greatest total worth. Of course, the determination of the trade-off between dollars of profit and market share would not be easy to determine in any real situation. Even so, the *method* of developing such trade-offs is important to systems analysis.

Decisions under certainty

The two cases just discussed involved simple decision problems under certainty. The word "certainty" is applied because we acted as though we were certain of the uncontrollable environmental factors which would be imposed on us; i.e., we assumed that only one state of nature needed to be considered.

True decision problems under certainty are a rare occurrence in the real world. Almost all meaningful problem situations involve some degree of uncertainty about the outcomes which may result from a given course of action. However, assuming a certainty situation is often a useful way to formulate and analyze a problem.

Since each strategy leads (or is assumed to lead) to a unique outcome in the case of certainty, the decision problem of choosing among strategies is reduced to one of choosing among outcomes. In simple cases, this may be a rather elementary conceptual process. For instance, in the problem of Table 3-2, after we reduced the resource cost and benefits for each outcome to a single aggregate measure—profit—it was a simple matter to choose the best outcome (the one with the highest profit) and hence the best strategy. The best strategy is simply the one which leads with certainty to the best outcome. On the other hand, we showed in Tables 3-3 and 3-4 that the problem of choice under certainty may not be simple if there is no obvious way of reducing the outcome description to a single measure.

Decision problems under certainty may also be more complex than they seem at first glance as a result of the size of the problem, i.e., the number of alternative strategies. Consider, for example, the personnel assignment situation discussed in Chapter 2. In that case, the time required by each person to complete each job was assumed to be known with certainty. The outcome array corresponding to Table 2-2 is shown in Table 3-5. There are two alternative strategies:

S_1:   (Assign person A to job 1 and person B to job 2)
S_2:   (Assign person A to job 2 and person B to job 1).

Table 3-5   Outcome table

	N_1
S_1	Total man-hours $= 5$
S_2	Total man-hours $= 5$

If the only relevant outcome descriptor is "total man-hours to perform both jobs," it is clear from Table 3-5 that there is no basis for preference between the two strategies.

Suppose, however, that the problem involves three people and three jobs rather than two people and two jobs. Such a case is shown in Table 3-6, where each person's performance on each job is still assumed to be known with certainty. The first step in developing an outcome table in such a

Table 3-6   Time required by three people to perform each of three jobs

		Jobs		
		1	2	3
	A	2	2	4
People	B	3	3	2
	C	6	1	5

situation is to enumerate the strategies—the alternative people-job combinations constituting an assignment which will get the three jobs done (one by each person). The reader is asked to develop this table. He will find that there are six alternative strategies. The best of these is "A to job 1, B to job 3, and C to job 2" since it involves a total of five man-hours. The point is, however, that in going from a two-person–two-job situation to a three-person–three-job one, the number of strategies increases from two to six. In general, this sort of progression holds true, so that for 10 people and 10 jobs, the number of strategies is over 3.6 million. From this, it is easy to see how a seemingly simple decision problem under certainty may indeed be difficult to handle. Consider, for example, the military services assignment of people to jobs. Even though it is done on a batch basis—i.e., each group of enlistees out of basic training is assigned to available spaces—the scope of the problem is immense. Typically, several thousand enlisted men must be simultaneously assigned. Hence, the number of alternative strategies is so large as to be incomprehensible.

A revisit to the evaluation and comparison problem

Having described the simplest formulation of a decision problem—certainty —we can return to the question of evaluating and comparing outcomes. For the moment, we can assume that we are dealing with a problem under certainty and that each outcome is described by one measure of each of the two general varieties—a measure of resource cost and a measure of benefit.

There are three general situations with which we may be faced, each of which requires a different approach. First, the most general case is the one in which *both resource cost and benefit are variable*. They are variable in the sense that as we look down the single column of the outcome array, we see various values of both measures. Table 3-7 illustrates this case for some (undefined) measures of resource cost and benefit (where high values of cost are assumed to be bad and high values of benefit are assumed to be good). In such a case, the benefit-cost *difference* or *ratio* may be a mean-

Table 3-7   Outcome array

	N_1
S_1	Cost = 10 Benefit = 20
S_2	Cost = 6 Benefit = 8
S_3	Cost = 8 Benefit = 8

ingful single descriptor of each outcome and, hence, a measure on which to base a choice between outcomes. Profit, for example, is a benefit-cost difference, or a measure of *net* benefit. Return on investment is a ratio measure of benefit to cost which has some accounting significance. Other differences (net benefits) may be appealing as long as the dimensions of benefit and cost are the same, i.e., as long as we are not subtracting apples from oranges. Other ratios may be valid measures even if the dimensions are not the same. For example, "number of infant deaths prevented per dollar spent on health programs" might be a reasonable single aggregate outcome descriptor.

The second general situation which may arise involves *specified benefit levels and variable resource costs*. In this case, outcomes are compared on the basis of the cost required to achieve a given level of benefit. For example, if one's objective is to have a mile run as fast as possible, the best alternative is the runner who expends the least resources (time) in doing so. If NASA's sole objective is to reach the moon, the best strategy for achieving it is the least-cost one.

We should point out here, however, that this general situation—specified benefits and variable costs—is an all-too-easy way of ignoring the significant problems facing an organization. A constant search for cost savings does not necessarily imply good management if benefit levels are ignored. Because of the difficulties in measuring benefits, it is easy to rationalize one's objectives so that benefit levels appear to be fixed, when really both costs and benefits should be treated as variable. When a weapons system is to be selected, it is easy to think of specifying performance levels and then seeking to minimize cost. In practice, however, the small number of alternative designs will vary in performance capability, and variations in both performance (benefit) and cost should be considered in the decision analysis.

The third general situation involves *specified resource costs and variable benefits*. This sort of situation exists in a race in which time is fixed and distance is variable; i.e., all runners will run for, say, two minutes, and the winner will be the one who goes the farthest. The allocation of a fixed budget in an optimal fashion is illustrative of this viewpoint since, presumably, cost is fixed and one wishes to get the greatest total benefit possible.

In the latter two cases, when either resource cost or benefit is fixed and the other is variable, the comparison of outcomes under certainty is rather simple. The single aggregate measure which may be used to describe an outcome is the one which varies. Thus, if cost is variable and benefit fixed, we choose the least-cost outcome and hence, in the case of certainty, the least-cost strategy. If cost is fixed and benefit variable, we choose the benefit-maximizing outcome and (under certainty) the strategy corresponding to it.

However, this does not exhaust the range of difficulties which we may encounter. If we have multiple objectives and multiple benefit or cost measures, we are faced with the dimensional problem discussed previously, and there are no pat answers or formulas which resolve this difficulty. Its resolution depends on the ingenuity of the analyst in using the information at hand to develop benefit measures, cost measures, and aggregate measures which provide meaningful and comprehensive outcome descriptions and at the same time provide a basis for rational choice among alternatives.

Decisions under uncertainty

A more realistic description of real-world problem situations involves uncertainty. Formally, uncertainty differs from certainty in that the latter involves a specified set of environmental conditions—one state of nature—while uncertainty involves a range of possible sets of environmental conditions which may ensue—more than one state of nature.[8] This is the general situation described by the outcome array of Table 3-1.

---

[8] Two problems of semantics arise here. First, a distinction is often made by decision theorists between risk and uncertainty. This distinction is based on a knowledge of the likelihoods associated with the uncontrollable elements. See R. D. Luce and H. Raiffa, *Games and Decisions*, John Wiley & Sons, Inc., New York, 1957. Here, uncertainty is

Most real-world decision problems look more like problems under uncertainty than like problems under certainty. Of course, since the outcome array form is itself an abstraction of the real world, one might argue that the maze which constitutes a real problem looks nothing like the outcome array of Table 3-1, much less looking like that simpler one-column array describing a problem under certainty. This would be a valid comment. The critical point is, however, that it is necessary to think in precise terms such as those of the outcome array in order really to understand most complex problems. Thus, while problems and outcome tables may look quite different, the array is an abstraction which enables us to analyze a problem.

Let us look to the analysis of a well-structured decision problem involving uncertainty as a way of understanding the additional difficulties imposed by this formulation. In doing so, we should remember that the same difficulties inherent in problems involving certainty also occur in those involving uncertainty, so we need not discuss them again here.

Consider the outcome array of Table 3-8, in which the cost and benefit descriptors have already been combined into the aggregate measure profit. With all these simplifying assumptions, we find that it is easy to choose the

Table 3-8   Outcome array in terms of profit

	N_1	N_2
S_1	$50	$100
S_2	$48	$96

best strategy in this table. Why? Because, regardless of whether N_1 or N_2 occurs (and recall that only one of them will), S_1 leads to the better outcome. Since S_1 leads to a better outcome than S_2 for every possible contingency, it is clearly the better strategy.

Of course, all we must do to construct a decision situation in which no such simple answer is possible is to use the same profits in a rearranged outcome array such as that in Table 3-9. There, S_1 is better if N_1 occurs, but S_2 is better if N_2 occurs. Which is better—S_1 or S_2? The answer is: "It depends." It depends on the relative likelihoods associated with N_1 and N_2, for one

used to describe any problem formulation involving more than one state of nature. Hence, it encompasses both risk and uncertainty as the terms are used by decision theorists. The other problem has to do with the kind of uncertainty. Various authors have distinguished between uncertainty due to different sources. For example, see the early paper by C. H. Hitch, "An Appreciation of Systems Analysis," RAND Corporation, P–699, Santa Monica, Calif., Aug. 18, 1955. Here, no such distinction is necessary.

Table 3-9   Profit outcome array

	N₁	N₂
S₁	$50	$96
S₂	$48	$100

thing. For example, if one knew that N_2 was one thousand times as likely to occur as N_1, he would probably choose S_2 because it is best if N_2 occurs, which is extremely likely. On the other hand, if the likelihoods are not so extreme—say, there is a 50:50 chance of N_2 occurring—no clear best alternative is immediately obvious.

The *maximization of expected net benefits* is one way of arriving at a basis for choice in such a situation. The expected net benefit associated with a strategy here is simply the weighted sum of the profit outcomes to which that strategy might lead—the weights being the probabilities for each outcome.[9]

[9] The basic ideas relating to probability are familiar to most of us. Any event whose outcome is at least partially determined by chance, such as the flip of a coin, may be described in probabilistic terms.

The probability of an outcome is most easily thought of as the long-term percentage again and again. In terms of the coin flip, after a long series of flips one might divide of times which the various possible outcomes would occur if the event were repeated the total number of occurrences of the outcome "heads" by the total number of flips and call the resulting decimal the *probability of heads;* in this case, he would be likely to determine the probability of heads to be near one-half. Similarly, the probability of a six on a throw of a single die would be about one-sixth.

The use to which the concept of probability may be put is also based upon sequences of events. *The knowledge that the probability of heads is one-half will in no way help one to predict what the outcome of a particular flip of a coin will be,* for it will be either heads or tails, and one is either right or wrong. This knowledge does permit one to predict that in a long sequence of flips, the relative frequency of heads will be close to 50 percent, however.

To apply probabilities to the analysis of decisions, one must recognize that the basic idea is applicable to the uncertain outcomes of events which can influence these decisions—the states of nature. To conclude that the probability is one-third that June rainfall in Cleveland will exceed 2 inches implies that an investigation of Weather Bureau records for many past Junes has indicated a relative frequency of one-third for such a state. If this is so, and if there is no reason to believe that future weather patterns will be different from those which prevail now or which have existed in the past—i.e., if the process exhibits *stability* over time—one might conclude that the future percentage of occurrence of rainy (over 2 inches) Junes will also be about one-third.

Probability, then, is simply a way of dealing with our uncertainties about the future. In attaching probabilities to states of nature or outcomes, we evaluate the likelihood of their occurring, and we thereby synthesize our information about the future into a single number. The reader who is interested in pursuing basic probability ideas further is referred to William R. King, *Probability for Management Decisions,* John Wiley & Sons, Inc., New York, 1968.

In the illustration of Table 3-9, for example, if it were determined that both states of nature are equally likely to occur, probabilities of one-half would be imputed to them. The expected net benefit (expected profit) associated with strategy S_1 is therefore

$$\tfrac{1}{2}(\$50) + \tfrac{1}{2}(\$96) = \$73$$

and the expected net benefit for S_2 is

$$\tfrac{1}{2}(\$48) + \tfrac{1}{2}(\$100) = \$74$$

Therefore, Strategy S_2 is presumably the better of the two since it has the higher expected net benefit.

We use the word "presumably" here since there are a number of deficiencies associated with the maximization of expected net benefit (profit) which restrict its usefulness in systems analysis. Among these are the presumption that an exhaustive list of environmental conditions—states of nature—can be specified and the undue weight that such a presumption puts on extreme outcomes. In practice, one is seldom able to make a meaningful list of *all* possible contingencies, and if one outcome is either very much better or very much worse than all others, the maximization of expected net benefit leads to results which are counter to one's intuition.[10]

Also, if the states of nature are not simply uncertain environmental factors, but also involve the actions of rational beings whom the decision maker cannot control, the idea of an expected net benefit is only tenuously applicable. Moreover, if one realizes that no simple measure of net benefit, such as profit, is usually available in any but the most straightforward decision situations, the maximization of expected net benefit is relegated to a role of minor importance in terms of analytic usefulness. Like the idea of utility, the maximization of expected net benefit is conceptually interesting and potentially useful,[11] but neither is widely applicable in solving meaningful real-world problems.

Other bases for choice under uncertainty have been proposed. In particu-

[10] Consider the situation which many people face when their alma mater asks for contributions, saying that the average contribution last year was $1,000. The alumnus who is considering giving $50 is awed until he realizes that several people have given very large sums, while most have given $100 or less. The weighted sum of the contributions, called an *average*, is grossly unrepresentative of one's intuitive idea of an average. The expected net benefit discussed here is similar to an average and has the same deficiency.

[11] In particular, the combination of these two ideas—maximization of expected utility—is the theoretical basis for choosing among alternative strategies. However, in practice, it is almost impossible to measure utilities meaningfully. Hence, the concept is not readily implemented.

lar, these bases are applicable in the sort of uncertain situation in which nothing is known concerning the likelihoods associated with the states of nature. Such a situation is probably more descriptive of the real world than the restrictive assumptions of an exhaustive list of the states of nature and a knowledge of the numerical probabilities of each which is inherent in a calculation of expected net benefit. Yet, if one has knowledge of the likelihoods, he should obviously make use of it. We shall discuss this further in the next chapter. Here, we conclude our discussion of uncertainty with a brief summary of some of the other bases for decision making which have been proposed. In doing so, we emphasize that they are ways of thinking about problems rather than hard-and-fast rules about how one should make decisions. In particular, since the several bases to be discussed may well be contradictory in any specific decision problem, it is apparent that none are being put forth as *the* way to solve problems involving uncertainty.

The *maximin* approach to problems under uncertainty is based on the argument that in the face of so large a degree of uncertainty, the decision maker might choose to act pessimistically by deciding that he should maximize his security level. He might reason that if nature is going to be perverse and attempt to give him as small a payoff as possible, he should in turn act to maximize his return consistent with this malevolent intention of nature. In effect, he would identify the worst outcome which could possibly result from each strategy and choose the strategy that will give him the best of these worst outcomes.

In the problem of Table 3-10, in which we have assumed a single (undefined) measure of net benefit, the decision maker finds that if he chooses S_1, the worst which can happen is a net benefit of 5. Similarly, under S_2 it is 10, and under S_3 it is 0. These worst outcomes are security levels for each of the strategies in that the decision maker can be confident that no worse can happen under that strategy.

To make the best of the solution, the decision maker may act to ensure himself of the best of this set of worst outcomes. He can do this by choosing S_2.

Table 3-10 Payoff table

| | States of nature | | | |
	N_1	N_2	N_3	N_4
S_1	50	30	30	5
S_2	80	40	10	15
S_3	120	50	5	0

The worst which can happen under S_2 is a net benefit of 10, while lower net benefits could result under both S_1 and S_3. These 10 net-benefit units represent the *maximum security level* which he can obtain. By choosing S_2, he can be certain of getting no less than 10 units, and he cannot be certain of as much as 10 under any other strategy.

This idea of a best strategy in such a case of uncertainty, the one which maximizes the minimum net benefit which can be achieved, is appropriately termed a *maximin strategy*. To select a maximin strategy, one determines the worst outcome for each strategy and then selects the strategy which has the largest value of this minimum. The decision maker is guaranteed at least the maximin payoff, since whatever state of nature is actually realized, no lesser payoffs can be obtained using the maximin strategy.

Operationally, one determines the maximin strategy simply by finding the lowest payoff for each strategy (the smallest entry in each row of the payoff table) and then choosing the largest of these lowest payoffs. The strategy associated with this "largest of the smallests" is the maximin strategy.[12]

If the decision maker chooses to be completely optimistic rather than pessimistic, he might use a *maximax* criterion, i.e., choose the strategy which makes the best of the best which can occur. In this case, he would choose the largest net benefit for each strategy and then choose the strategy which is associated with the largest of these—in effect, he would simply determine the greatest payoff in the table and select the strategy which *may* result in this greatest payoff. The optimistic decision maker in this case decides to "go for broke."

In the example of Table 3-10, the largest payoff is the 120 units associated with O_{31} (involving strategy S_3 and state of nature N_1); hence, the maximax strategy is S_3.

It should be noted that this criterion completely ignores the relative sizes of the payoffs for each strategy. The choice of S_3 would still be dictated by the maximax criterion if the least of the other payoffs under S_3 were 119, 0, or minus 1 billion. The maximin criterion has the same failing since it completely ignores the larger payoffs associated with a strategy.

Savage [13] has proposed an alternative criterion for decision making under uncertainty which is based upon a common psychological quirk. Most of us,

---

[12] If one is dealing with the minimization of resource costs for a given benefit level, the equivalent to maximum is minimax, i.e., the maximization of minimum loss. This is so because the worst outcomes have the smallest numerical values in such cases.

To determine a minimax strategy, one simply chooses the largest number in each row and then the smallest of the largests. The associated strategy is a minimax strategy. All other arguments are the same as for the maximin criterion. One must remember only that to ensure the best security level, he plays *maximin when dealing with gains* and *minimax when dealing with losses*.

[13] L. J. Savage, *The Foundations of Statistics*, John Wiley & Sons, Inc., New York, 1954.

when confronted with the outcome of a choice situation, apply our 20/20 hindsight vision and view the outcome which we *could* have obtained had we known in advance that the realized state of nature would occur. Savage used the term "regret" to describe the dissatisfaction associated with not having fared as well as one would have if the state of nature had been known. In effect, the decision maker views the past and regrets having chosen the alternative he did.

A measure of this regret for any outcome might be the difference between the payoff for the outcome and the largest payoff which could have been obtained under the corresponding state of nature. In the situation of Table 3-10, the regret associated with outcome O_{11} is 70—the difference between the 50 net-benefit units realized and the 120 which could have been realized had one known in advance that N_1 would occur. The remaining regrets are given in the regret table 3-11. It should be noted that there is at least one outcome

Table 3-11   Regret table

	States of nature			
	N_1	N_2	N_3	N_4
S_1	70	20	0	10
S_2	40	10	20	0
S_3	0	0	25	15

which has no regret for each state of nature—the outcome which has the highest payoff for that state of nature. If one chooses the strategy which leads to the highest payoff for the state of nature which is actually realized, he experiences no regret at not having chosen a better strategy.

To utilize Table 3-11 in a decision criterion, one must recognize that the regrets are of the nature of losses. Hence, the pessimistic decision maker might decide to use a strategy that would minimize his maximum regret— a *minimax regret* criterion. In this case, the maximum regret for each strategy would be 70, 40, and 25, respectively. The strategy which minimizes maximum regret is S_3, with a security level of regret of 25.

The appeal of this criterion is diminished for many by a logical flaw which appears to be inherent in it. If we add a fourth strategy (S_4) which has net benefits of 60, 40, 30, and 60, respectively, for the four states of nature, the regret table becomes that shown in Table 3-12. The minimax regret payoff here is 45, and the minimax regret strategy is S_2.

Consider now what has resulted from the introduction of S_4 into the decision problem. Although S_4 is not chosen as best, its consideration has

Table 3-12   Revised regret table

	States of nature			
	N_1	N_2	N_3	N_4
S_1	70	20	0	55
S_2	40	10	20	45
S_3	0	0	25	60
S_4	60	10	0	0

shifted the preference from S_3 to S_2 *within the set of previously considered strategies.* That this is illogical is perhaps best illustrated by a simple example. If one is offered a choice of an apple or an orange and he chooses the apple, it is assumed that in a choice among an apple, an orange, and a peach, he will choose either the apple or the peach—but not the orange, since he has already expressed a preference for the apple over the orange. The introduction of a new alternative—the peach—should not cause a shift in preference between the apple and the orange. This is exactly what has occurred here. The introduction of S_4 has caused a shift in preference from S_3 to S_2. Logically, if S_3 were the best strategy from the set consisting of S_1, S_2, and S_3, the introduction of S_4 should not result in a switch in preference from S_3 to S_2.

This logical deficiency—termed the *independence of irrelevant alternatives* —forms the basis for much of the criticism of the regret idea. To some, however, the cases in which the invalidity of the criterion can be demonstrated on these grounds seem to be pathological. To them, the criterion is a good one for most practical purposes.

Summary

The conceptual framework for systems analysis discussed in this chapter is not a panacea which will solve all strategic planning problems. On the contrary, it sometimes raises more questions than it solves; yet we shall argue that these questions are more apt to be the right ones than those which might be raised without the approach.

The basic tool of the conceptual framework is the outcome array. Conceptually, it represents the array of all possible circumstances which might ensue after any of the specified actions are taken and environmental conditions are realized. In any real problem, one may not actually construct an outcome array. Indeed, the problem may be too large to permit one to do so. The value of the outcome array is that it requires the decision analyst to think in terms of the wide scope of consequences (outcomes) which can result from an action. In doing so, the decision maker is precluded from focusing undue attention on what he thinks is most likely to occur. Of course, he should give attention to this, but he should also carefully consider the other possible outcomes.

This simple table has many other values aside from its formal use as an enumeration device. In attempting to describe outcomes meaningfully, one is forced to consider resource costs, benefits, and their relationship. More importantly, this often leads to a reconsideration and questioning of objectives, which produce valuable insight into the problem.

Decision problems in the real world do not exist in terms of outcome arrays. Even if they can be formulated as such, they do not normally fall neatly into the certainty-uncertainty dichotomy which we have discussed here. Indeed, the majority of problems are most naturally formulated in terms of uncertainty, since the very nature of meaningful problems is such that the potential consequences are uncertain. However, as we shall see in the next chapter, the certainty-uncertainty taxonomy is useful for purposes of analysis. For example, sometimes the analyst can analyze a complex problem as though the outcomes were certain and learn enough in doing so to reformulate the problem in a more meaningful way under uncertainty.

The essential appeal of the conceptual framework is that it is descriptive of the way in which everyone knows he should, or thinks that he does, make decisions. Its value is that it forces him to give proper attention to enumerating the alternative strategies, the entire range of contingencies, and the scope of possible outcomes in a fashion which would be impractical if the problem were approached at an intuitive or informal level. Moreover, the outcome descriptions force the decision maker to spell out clearly just what it is that he is trying to do—his objectives—and to develop reasonably precise measures of the degree of attainment of the objectives. In most instances, this process leads to a degree of comprehension of the salient features of the decision maker's responsibilities which is superior to any insights and understanding that he might otherwise gain. Frequently, this is itself sufficient justification for a formal problem analysis, and the better strategy which is selected as a result of analysis is something of a by-product.

Recommended readings

Archer, S. H.: "The Structure of Management Decision Theory," in W. A. Hill and D. Egan (eds.), *Readings in Organizational Theory: A Behavioral Approach*, Allyn and Bacon, Inc., Englewood Cliffs, N.J., 1966, chap. 28.

Churchman, C. W., R. L. Ackoff, and E. L. Arnoff: *Introduction to Operations Research,* John Wiley & Sons, Inc., New York, 1957.

Enthoven, A.: "Decision Theory and Systems Analysis," lecture sponsored by Metropolitan Washington Board of Trade Science Bureau, Washington, D.C., Dec. 5, 1963. Available from OSD (SA), The Pentagon, Washington, D.C.

Hill, W. A., and D. Egan (eds.): *Readings in Organizational Theory: A Behavioral Approach,* Allyn and Bacon, Inc., Englewood Cliffs, N.J., 1966.

King, William R.: *Quantitative Analysis for Marketing Management,* McGraw-Hill Book Company, New York, 1967, chaps. 1–4.

Luce, R. D., and H. Raiffa: *Games and Decisions,* John Wiley & Sons, Inc., New York, 1957, chaps. 1 and 2.

Miller, D. W., and M. K. Starr: *Executive Decisions and Operations Research,* Prentice-Hall, Inc., Englewood Cliffs, N.J., 1960.

Simon, H. A.: "On the Concept of Organizational Goal," in W. A. Hill and D. Egan (eds.), *Readings in Organizational Theory: A Behavioral Approach,* Allyn and Bacon, Inc., Englewood Cliffs, N.J., 1966, chap. 4.

CHAPTER 4
Methods of Systems Analysis

Systems analysis as it exists today is
an imperfect instrument, an advisory
art with many limitations.[1]

The difficulties of systems analysis
are rooted in the nature of . . .
problems. Other methods . . . do
not escape them and have limitations
of their own. . . . Systems analysis
provides a framework for combining
the knowledge of experts in many
fields to reach solutions which
transcend any individual expert's
judgment.[2]

The conceptual framework for systems analysis which was spelled out in the
previous chapter does not represent a practical operating procedure. There,
we illustrated the way in which the analysis *should* be done and enumerated
some of the related problems. In this chapter we shall discuss how it *is* done,
and as we shall see, although there are real problems involved in applying
the framework, the two are not very different.

Models in systems analysis

The basic operating device used by systems analysts is a model. The layman's understanding of models is simultaneously helpful and injurious to
one's understanding of the scientific use of the term. Discounting the female

---

[1] Charles Hitch, *An Appreciation of Systems Analysis*, RAND Corporation, P-699,
Santa Monica, Calif., Aug. 18, 1955, p. 15.
[2] *Ibid.*, preface.

fashion variety, if the proverbial man in the street were asked to react to the word "model," he would be likely to respond with some familiar example such as a child's model airplane. Indeed, this kind of model is familiar to all of us.

Such a model is simply a scaled-down *representation* of a real-world system—the full-size airplane. Each exterior dimension of the real airplane is accurately represented in miniature on the model. In addition, many features of the real airplane are completely excluded from the model; e.g., the model is often of solid construction, while the airplane's interior is a maze of electronic gears and cables. This feature of the child's model is an intrinsic part of the scientific model; that is, in both kinds of models, some aspects of the real system are included (such as exterior dimensions, color, markings, etc.), and some are excluded (interior configuration, materials, etc.). This is consistent with the scientist's idea of a model as an *abstraction of reality*.

Other models of the same system might abstract different elements of the system. For example, the ground training devices used for pilots are little more than movable enclosures which incorporate all the interior makeup of the cockpit, but little else. The pilot seats himself in an exact representation of a portion of an airplane's interior and is closed off from his surroundings. By reference to the instruments in the cockpit, he proceeds to "fly" the training device while sitting in a room with other such devices. The device responds to the pilot's actions in a manner which is quite similar to that in which the real airplane would respond in actual flight.

Such training devices are also models of airplanes. The elements of the real system which they incorporate are very different from those included in the child's model, however. In a training device, no attention is paid to exterior detail and dimensions since the pilot cannot see outside. The interior instruments and dimensions are faithful duplicates of those of the real system, however, because the pilot is expected to carry over what he has learned in the training device to the operation of the real airplane.

These two kinds of airplane models illustrate, in their similarity, the applicability of the layman's view of a model as a "representation of something else" to the scientific concept of a model. Although they are different models of the same system, their similarity lies in their inclusion of important aspects of the real system and exclusion of unimportant aspects of the real system. The determination of which factors are important and which are unimportant clearly depends on the use to which the model is put. In the case of the model to be used to decorate a child's room, the exterior configuration, color, and markings are important, and the portions which are not visible are unimportant. In the case of the training device, the aesthetic value is insignificant, and the interior design is of utmost importance.

However, since both of these models involve changes in physical structure, their applicability to the more abstract scientific use of the term "model" is limited.

A model, in the scientific sense, is a representation of a system which is used to predict the effect of changes in certain aspects of the system on the performance of the system.

The applicability of the first part of this definition—"a representation of a system"—to the layman's use of the term "model" has already been illustrated. The essential distinction lies in the next part—"used to predict the effect of changes in certain aspects of the system on the performance of the system." Clearly, most commonly known models are not used in this particular way.

In terms of the conceptual framework, a model is a set of relations between the objectives, strategies, and states of nature. Looking back to the outcome arrays of Chapter 3, we see that this is precisely what an outcome array represents—a relationship among strategies, states of nature, and objectives (since it will be recalled that each outcome is described in terms related to objectives). Thus, the outcome array may be thought of as a model, although it is better to think of it as presenting the *results* of a model. In this case, the model is the set of calculational *predictive* relationships used to determine the array for a particular decision problem. This conceptualization reflects the time dimension which is inherent in most decision problems. In general, the point in time at which a strategy is selected by the decision maker precedes that at which the outcome is realized. This implies that at the time the alternatives are being evaluated, the outcome descriptors in the outcome array are predictions of future states which will result from the various strategy–state of nature interactions.

We have defined scientific models as representations of systems which may be used in predicting performance. If we recognize that the outcome descriptors which we must choose are of the system-performance variety, one possible use for models becomes apparent. We need to have outcome (performance) predictions in order to apply the conceptual framework, and models may be used as devices to predict performance. Hence, models may be used to generate the predicted states of affairs associated with each strategy–state of nature combination in the outcome array. This is one simple way of viewing the role of models in the conceptual framework—as devices for predicting the performance level associated with each outcome. These performance levels will normally involve both resource cost and benefit dimensions, and perhaps a number of each.

Models are widely varied in form. A profit and loss statement is a calculational model of a system which can be used for predictive purposes. A model may also be graphical in nature; for example, Weimer [3] uses the model shown in Figure 4-1 to depict the flow of cash through a business firm. Of course, such a model is limited in the predictions which can be made from it.[4]

However, gross qualitative predictions can be made from the model more easily than they could be made without it. Moreover, such a model contributes to the ease with which one can comprehend the intricacies of cash flows through an organization.

The models used to represent systems for purposes of decision analysis are

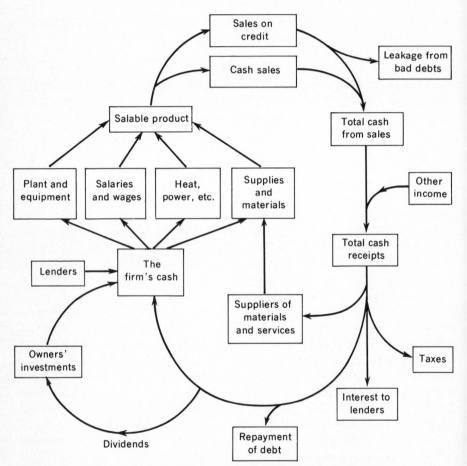

Figure 4-1 Pictorial model of flow of cash through a business firm.

[3] A. M. Weimer, *Business Administration: An Introductory Management Approach,* Richard D. Irwin, Inc., Homewood, Ill., 1966, p. 426. Chart developed by Robert R. Milroy and Donald H. Soner. Reproduced with permission.
[4] Most such models are used in textbooks for pedagogic purposes.

often symbolic in nature. Such models may take the form of mathematical equations, inequations, or other logical relations. Even in the simplest such instance, there is usually no single equation which constitutes the model; rather, it is usually made up of a number of components. For example, systems analysts frequently use *cost models*—devices for predicting costs—in conjunction with similar mathematical devices for predicting benefits—*benefit models*. Alternatively, a decision model might well be in the form of a flow diagram, a graph, or a physical model (such as the "toy" models used by industrial engineers to try out various locations for machines in industrial plants).

Basically, the value of a model lies in its substitutibility for the real system. The physical scientist might proceed toward the solution of a decision problem by experimentation; i.e., he would try various combinations of controllables in a planned fashion and observe the results. In most problems of business and government, this procedure is either impossible or impractical. Who, for example, would propose that we simply "try" a number of different weapons systems? To do so, even on a restricted pilot-study basis, would obviously be too costly. Thus, the need in decision-problem analysis is for a representation of the system which can be used in place of the real system. A model is such a device. In using a model, the analyst makes assertions which express the relationship of various elements of the system with one another and, in turn, their effect on the performance of the system. In doing so, he creates an entity—the model—which he can use in lieu of the actual system. He can then experiment on the model and on this basis make his predictions of the effects which changes in the system will have on its performance.

A model airplane might be used in the same way. If we were to place the model in a wind tunnel and vary the angle of sweep of the wings in order to predict the effect of various angles on the performance of the airplane, we would have a representation of the airplane which was being experimented on. Hence, the model airplane would be a model in the scientific sense. The key distinction between the common, garden-variety model and a scientific model is *the use to which the model is put*.

Let us consider the kind of model which might be used in the organizational decision problems which we discussed in the last chapter. In the SST illustration, a cost model might be determined statistically from past experience with other aircraft. The form of this model might be

$$TC = a\mathrm{W} + b\mathrm{N} + c$$

where TC is total cost, W is the weight of the aircraft, N is the passenger capacity, and a, b, and c are numbers which are estimated from past data.

Of course, this is an overly simple illustration, but it shows the basic form of a statistically developed cost model.[5]

In the illustration involving programs in health-depressed areas, one of the objectives was related to a reduction in the incidence of infant mortality. A bit of research reveals that there is a high correlation between the weight of a newborn baby and its chances of survival. This suggests that a program to provide expectant mothers with proper nutrition would result in their giving birth to larger babies, and hence would further the objective of reducing the incidence of infant mortality. This is a verbal model which is gross but useful. It is predictive in the sense that it spells out observable (and probably causal) relationships between alternatives and objectives.

To perform an analysis, one would need to quantify some of these relationships, but even this qualitative set of relations is useful. Such a gross model is deficient, of course, in some obvious ways. Yet, even with its deficiencies, it may be a useful predictive device, which would probably be supplemented by a pilot study before large-scale expenditures were recommended.

General cost-benefit models

The models which are most frequently used in systems analysis are those general economic models involving mixes of resources. This is the case partly because systems analysis was first instituted in government in the Department of Defense by economists who were asked to analyze military force composition problems. There are also more logically appealing reasons for this, since the nature of most strategic decisions is economic. However, we should point out that these models are not representations of all strategic planning problems. Rather, they represent approaches to particular classes of subproblems which are frequently important parts of overall strategic planning. In a subsequent section, we shall deal with the question of putting these pieces together to form a unified whole.

If we think back to an earlier discussion of strategies which may be composed of combinations of other strategies, we get the flavor of resource-mix situations. For example, one resource to use in support of ground troops is artillery; another is missiles. However, some combination of both may be

---

[5] In fact, because of the paucity of experience with titanium aircraft, it is unlikely that it was possible to obtain cost estimates in this fashion in the actual problem. These estimates were probably made primarily by engineers on the basis of their knowledge of the materials, the technological problems which would be encountered, and their experience with the costs of overcoming such difficulties in the past.

superior to either under some circumstances. In fact, some combination is likely to be best to achieve an overall capability for a wide variety of possible circumstances.

Generally, there are a number of submodels used in any analysis involving costs and benefits. Here, we shall illustrate a general economic model and method of approach which itself involves the use of a number of submodels. The context for the illustration will be a resource mix in a manufacturing enterprise.[6] An industrial firm can utilize various combinations of manpower and machinery to produce goods, just as the military can use either artillery or missiles in support of ground troops. If we use "quantity of goods produced" (simply a physical count) as our measure of benefit, we can think of a number of strategies, ranging from virtually complete automation (with few human workers) to an Asian-like situation involving much hand labor. In general, some combination of manpower and machinery might be best, and it is the industrial manager's problem to determine which.

The two resources—men and machines—interact with each other to produce benefits. Often they reinforce each other's effectiveness, and sometimes they detract from each other. To begin, let us think of a certainty situation in which each strategy (combination of men and machines) is represented by a point on a set of axes. Figure 4-2 shows that the axes are scaled in terms of number of men and number of machines. The point in the upper right involves the strategy "100 men and 10 machines," and the assumed benefit is 1,100 output units of the product. This is indicated by the number attached to the point. If the number of machines is held constant at 10 and less manpower is used—say, 75, 50, or 25 men—output would be less. This is indicated by the series of points showing outputs (benefit) of 1,000, 900, and 500 units, respectively, across the top of Figure 4-2. Thus, 10 machines in conjunction with 75 men can produce 1,000 units of output, but 10 machines and 50 men can produce only 900. And if 10 machines are used but the number of men is reduced to 25, only 500 units of output will result (since presumably this few men will not be able to operate the machines efficiently).

If we were to determine the output associated with each of the feasible points on the graph in Figure 4-2, we would be generating the benefit portion of the outcome description for each of the feasible strategies.[7] To do so would require a *benefit model*—a way of representing the production

---

[6] Parts of the following illustration are adapted from an excellent paper by R. N. Grosse, *An Introduction to Cost-Effectiveness Analysis,* Research Analysis Corporation, McLean, Va., RAC Paper RAC–P–5, July, 1965.

[7] Note that the delineation of feasible strategies is rather simple in such cases. All those strategies involving a requirement for more men or machines than it would be possible to add to the existing organization during the planning period might well serve to define the infeasible ones, for example.

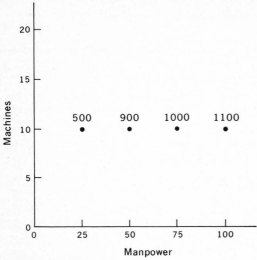

Figure 4-2   Benefit levels for four manpower-machine levels.

system which permits us to express benefit in terms of resources (men and machines) and to predict the benefit levels that will result from various combinations of resources.[8] In this case, the resource mixes are the controllables which make up the strategies.

One way of concisely depicting many benefit levels is through the use of equal-benefit lines.[9] Hypothetical lines of equal benefit are shown in Figure 4-3. There, benefit (output) of 900 units is shown to be attained for various combinations of labor and machinery. The line connecting all points for which the benefit level is 900 units is the 900-unit equal-benefit line. Other equal-benefit lines can be similarly interpreted. The four strategies shown in Figure 4-2 would be represented as points on their appropriate benefit lines in Figure 4-3.

To arrive at a mix decision, we need a *cost model* to complement this simple benefit model. In this case, we shall assume that the unit costs of the manpower and machinery resources are known, so that lines of equal cost may be drawn on the manpower-machinery graph as shown in Figure 4-4. These lines assume that each unit of manpower costs $200 and that each machine costs $1,000. Thus, an expenditure of $10,000 on machines alone

[8] The economist refers to this particular submodel as the *production function*.

[9] In economics jargon, these are called "isoquants." In reality, the production function relating output to the two resource inputs could be plotted in a third dimension "above" Fig. 4-2. The isoquants would then be projections onto the manpower-machinery plane of the lines of intersection of equal-output planes with the output surface.

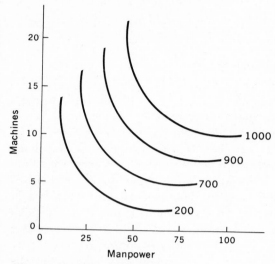

Figure 4-3   Equal-benefit lines.

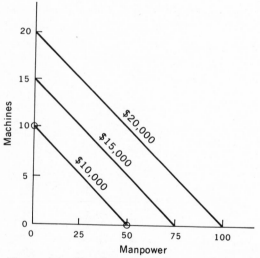

Figure 4-4   Equal-cost lines.

would result in 10 machines being used. This is indicated by the circled point at the upper left. A similar expenditure on manpower alone would result in 50 men being used, as represented by the circled point at the lower right. All other combinations of men and machines which would result in a total expenditure of $10,000 lie on the $10,000 equal-cost line, all mixes involving a $15,000 total expenditure lie on the $15,000 equal-cost line, etc. In effect, these equal-cost lines are *budget lines*. A given budget level fixes the line, and the points on the line represent all possible mixes of resources at that level of total expenditures.

If we superimpose the benefit model's lines of equal benefit and the equal-cost lines, we obtain Figure 4-5. This information is useful for analysis since it enables us to answer such questions as: "What is the *best* mix of manpower and machinery for a budget level of $15,000?" Referring to Figure 4-5, we can see that the 700-unit equal-benefit line just barely touches (is tangent to) the $15,000 equal-cost line. No equal-benefit line involving more than 700 output units touches this equal-cost line, but many such lines involving *less* than 700 output units do so. For example, the 200-unit equal-benefit line intersects the $15,000 equal-cost line, as do all those equal-benefit lines between 200 and 700 which are not shown on the graph. Thus, the point at which the 700-unit equal-benefit line touches the $15,000 equal-cost line gives the answer to our question. This point is shown on the graph of Figure 4-5. The dashed lines to the manpower and machinery axes indicate that the strategy which results in the greatest benefit at a $15,000 expenditure level is the one involving about 8 machines and 35 men.

So, too, will the information provided by Figure 4-5 provide the answer to questions like: "What is the least-cost resource mix which will enable us to

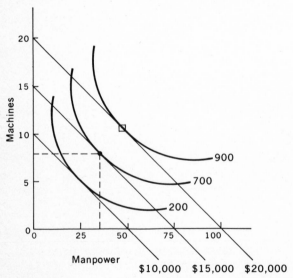

Figure 4-5

achieve an output of 700 units?" The answer is the same. At the resource mix indicated by the point of tangency of the 700-unit equal-benefit line and the $15,000 equal-cost line, 700 units of benefit are achieved at a cost of $15,000. This level of benefit cannot be achieved with any other mix at a lesser cost. This is so because the 700-unit equal-benefit line crosses only other equal-cost lines involving a greater expenditure than $15,000.

If we are not attempting either to maximize the benefit achieved for a fixed expenditure or to minimize the cost associated with achieving a required benefit level, we need further information to determine the best resource-mix strategy. The cost model provides one of the necessary elements of information. From Figure 4-5, we can determine the lowest-cost mix to achieve each benefit level, or the greatest benefit from a given expenditure level. The curve which connects these series of points is plotted (on a cost-benefit set of axes) as Figure 4-6. The point determined above (representing a strategy consisting of 8 machines and 35 men) is the one which achieves the lowest cost for a fixed benefit level of 700 units. Hence, it appears on the curve of Figure 4-6 as shown.

This curve is a *total-cost curve* in the sense that it represents the cost-benefit combinations which the rational person would use, i.e., the least cost for each specified benefit level.

The other necessary element of information to determine the best overall resource mix is the revenue which will be derived from each level of output. If the output is priced at $300 per unit and the firm's sole objective is to maximize profit, the best benefit level can be determined from Figure 4-7. There, the revenue function is plotted along with the total-cost curve. The

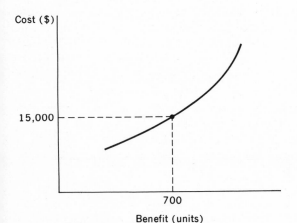

Figure 4-6   Total-cost curve.

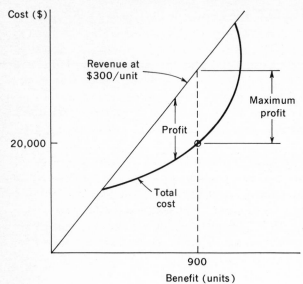

Figure 4-7   Total-cost and revenue curves.

revenue curve is simply $300 times the number of units of output (benefit)—
a straight line. The vertical distance between the revenue and total-cost
curves represents the organization's profit.

Profit is maximized at a point where this vertical distance is greatest. The
dashed line in Figure 4-7 shows the approximate position of the optimal
benefit—the output level which maximizes profit.

The circled point represents the cost-benefit combination which is associated with the maximum profit. It involves 900 units of benefit and a cost of
$20,000. Since this is a point on the total-cost curve, it is also one of the
points of tangency between an equal-cost ($20,000) and equal-benefit (900)
line in Figure 4-5. By referring back to Figure 4-5, where this point is indicated by a small square, we can determine the resource mix associated with
this point. This is the strategy involving about 11 machines and 45 men.
Thus, this is the resource mix which maximizes profit. The associated benefit
level is 900 units of output at a cost of $20,000.

We can also determine the optimal profit by recognizing that the product
sells for $300 per unit. Hence, 900 units will produce $27,000 in revenue.
Since the total cost is $20,000, the gross profit is $7,000.

If such a model were available, the profit-maximizing firm would have no
difficulty in determining the best mix of resources to use. Of course, if
the revenue curve of Figure 4-7 were unavailable, as it is in most governmental decision contexts, this would not be the case. Since many meaningful

problems in a variety of contexts—both governmental and industrial—have this characteristic, we shall wish to discuss it extensively. However, first we should place the general cost-benefit model into the context of the conceptual framework which we developed in the preceding chapter.

Interpreting the model in terms of the conceptual framework

The conceptual framework for systems analysis which was developed in Chapter 3 may appear to be quite different from the general cost-benefit model just described. In fact, however, the model is simply an implementation of the conceptual framework in terms of graphs rather than in tabular form.

Let us consider first the salient elements of the conceptual framework—strategies, states of nature, and outcomes. Each strategy is a particular combination of manpower and machines. Thus, an infinity of available strategies might be enumerated as:

S_1: (50 men, 15 machines)
S_2: (35 men, 8 machines)
S_3: (45 men, 11 machines)
.
.
.
etc.

Only one state of nature is involved in the model since, in effect, it presumes that each strategy leads with certainty to a single known outcome. This is made more clear when one considers the form of the outcome array as shown in Table 4-1. There, the state of nature N_0 is not explicitly defined, but the form of the table shows that the outcome array is equivalent to the graph of Figure 4-5; i.e., each point on the graph represents a particular outcome described in terms of cost (dollars) and benefit (units of output). The equal-cost and equal-benefit lines in Figure 4-5 have no significance other than the obvious one of facilitating interpretation of the general relationship between the strategies (resource mixes) and outcomes (described in terms of costs and benefits) which they permit. Also, of course, these lines enable one easily to recognize the strategies which lead to minimum cost for a fixed benefit level and to maximum benefit level for a fixed cost. In effect, by drawing equal-cost lines, we are defining a subset of all the possible outcomes which can be compared on the basis of the benefit outcome descriptor. In doing so, we are thinking in the terms described in Chapter 3

**Table 4-1   Outcome array corresponding
to Figure 4-5**

	N_0
S_1 (50 men, 15 machines)	Cost = \$25,000 Benefit = 1,000 units
S_2 (35 men, 8 machines)	Cost = \$15,000 Benefit = 700 units
S_3 (45 men, 11 machines)	Cost = \$20,000 Benefit = 900 units
.	.
.	.
.	.

as "specified resource costs and variable benefits." Of course, we are applying this concept only to a subset of the possible outcomes rather than to all possible outcomes. This would be descriptive of a real-world situation if a fixed budget were to be spent, for example. In such a case, the best strategy (of the subset involving exactly the budgeted expenditure level) is the one which achieves maximum benefit for a fixed cost level.

The equal-benefit lines of Figure 4-5 have a similar significance. Each of these lines defines a subset of outcomes having specified benefit levels and variable costs. To choose the best strategy from among the subset, one merely chooses that which leads to an outcome having minimum cost for the fixed benefit level.

Of course, since a revenue curve of the form of that shown in Figure 4-7 is presumed to be known in this case, the array of outcomes—which in its entirety involves, in the language of the previous chapter, outcomes described in terms of variable resource costs and variable benefits—can be described using the benefit minus cost aggregate measure (profit), and the strategy can be chosen (from the entire range of possible outcomes) which maximizes profit. So, the selection of the profit-maximizing strategy in Figure 4-7 is conceptually equivalent to the choice of a strategy from an outcome array involving an aggregate cost-benefit measure as described in Chapter 3. Table 4-2 shows such an outcome array. Thus, the conceptual framework and the general cost-benefit model are indeed equivalent. The graphical form of the model as outlined in this chapter is merely a clear and efficient way of *implementing* the conceptual framework. Indeed, since there are an

Table 4-2   Profit outcome array corresponding to Figure 4-6

	N_0
S_1	Profit = \$5,000
S_2	Profit = \$6,000
S_3	Profit = \$7,000
.	.
.	.
.	.

infinity of available strategies here, it would not be possible to apply the conceptual framework without some variety of graphical or mathematical simplification.[10]

Operational systems-analysis models

Models such as the general cost-benefit models are sometimes directly applied to decision problems in business and government. Frequently, however, theory and practice are somewhat different because of the difficulties encountered in the real world. In this section we shall discuss some of these practical difficulties and their implications for systems analysis. In doing so, we shall be contrasting the real world with two things simultaneously—the conceptual framework of Chapter 3 and models such as the general cost-benefit model just discussed. In effect, these form the theory, and it is the practice on which we shall focus attention here. The difficulties in applying the conceptual framework, and the way in which analysts have surmounted them, form the practice of systems analysis.

Measuring costs and benefits

The first difficulty which arises in the application of a cost-benefit model involves measurement. In the general cost-benefit model, it was assumed

[10] In fact, this is the role which is played by many of the sophisticated mathematical techniques and algorithms which are commonly associated with systems analysis, and it is the explanation for the disclaimer which systems analysts frequently make that although the use of mathematics often provides a useful and efficient way of solving problems, there is no intrinsic connection between sophisticated mathematics and systems analysis. If the reader has doubts about this, he should note that little or no mathematics has been introduced in this text.

that the unit costs of the resource inputs were known and fixed. Of course, this is not normally the case. Most frequently, the unit cost of the resource inputs must be estimated in advance—frequently in the absence of much "hard" information. For example, how is one to predict the costs of future military weapons systems that exist only in the minds of men? Such costs incorporate costs of research and development, initial investment, operating costs, and service and maintenance costs; thus, they are not simple entities that are easy to predict.

However, it is the measurement of benefit which causes the most practical difficulty. In determining costs, the measure is clearly defined in terms of dollars; in measuring benefit, this is frequently not the case. The benefit concept is directly related to the objectives—to what we are trying to achieve. Often it is difficult to determine measures of the degree of attainment of objectives. For example, what if the morale of our troops is an important concept related to the outcomes of a decision problem—i.e., what if one of our objectives in a military decision problem has to do with morale? As Charles J. Hitch has put it: [11]

> How do you quantitatively distinguish between men who are highly motivated, and those who are demoralized? In fact, how do you quantitatively predict what it is that motivates or discourages a man? And which man? The fact that we simply cannot quantitize such things (and there are many other similar examples) does not mean that they have no effect on the outcome of a military endeavor—it simply means that our analytical techniques cannot answer every question.

In making this evaluation, Hitch is restating the idea which was put forth in Chapter 2 concerning the role of systems analysis. There, we argued that objective analysis cannot treat all aspects of a problem and that it is complementary to, and not duplicative of, qualitative analysis. Here, in the context of measuring the benefits to be associated with the outcomes of a military decision problem, we find a good illustration of an aspect of a problem which cannot be easily handled quantitatively—morale. Hitch recognized this when he said, in the same speech, that this difficulty is

> . . . widely recognized, particularly by those in the military profession who have had to live with these realities. But does that mean that all analysis becomes meaningless? I think not. Every bit of the total problem which can be confidently analyzed removes one more bit of uncertainty from our process of making a choice.

[11] Charles J. Hitch, Assistant Secretary of Defense (Comptroller), address before the U.S. Army Operations Research Symposium, Duke University, Durham, N.C., Mar. 26, 1962.

The second aspect of benefit measurement which causes difficulty is the *comprehensiveness* of the measure. Often, it is possible to define a benefit concept and a measurable quantity which is related to this concept but is not a comprehensive indicator of it. Consider the concept of marketing performance, for example. If we wish to measure this, we might choose the rather comprehensive measure "profit" (which obviously encompasses both costs and benefits), as we did in the general model in the previous section. If the sole objective of the firm is to maximize profit, this may be adequate. However, suppose we are engaged in introductory sales of a new product. Is profit a comprehensive measure of the degree of attainment of corporate sales-performance objectives? The answer is probably "No" because marketing performance, in this context, means something more. One of the additional things that it means has to do with expectations; i.e., how well was the product expected to do during its introductory period? Most frequently, new products are not expected to be immediately profitable, and a small loss might well have positive implications. Also, there is the market-penetration aspect of performance. What share of the market has been attained? What proportion of the total consuming public has tried the product at least once? What proportion has purchased it more than once? Then, there is the trend aspect of performance which is particularly important with new products and which is not measured by profit. A market in which the trend of sales is highly positive is better than one in which trends are stable or negative, even though the total profit may be the same. Another aspect is the time dimension. Is the profit to be maximized in the short run or the long run; e.g., would present profits be sacrificed in the hope of reaping future profit rewards? Thus, while profit is presumably a good cost-benefit measure for the short-run-profit-maximizing firm, few firms have such simple objectives. Most have objectives related to overall marketing performance, but for most, there is no simple numerical measure which comprehensively describes the degree of attainment of this concept.

A similar difficulty in benefit measurement involves both the comprehensiveness of the measure and the validity of a predictive model involving the measure. Consider, for example, that we are using a resource-mix model of the kind described previously to determine the best mix of fixed-wing aircraft and helicopters, both of which are to be used for observational support of ground troops. What benefit measure can be used? The basic question is: "What are our objectives?" To answer this requires a definition of "observational support of ground troops" and a further question: "What is the objective of the military operation?"

In these days of limited war, this question is difficult enough to answer. Is our objective to win the war or to gain territory from the enemy?

Let us suppose that the objective is the latter—to gain ground—since it is easily measurable. Now, if we wish to support ground troops, this should be our objective in the observational aircraft problem too. But how is it possible to relate the number of helicopters and airplanes to ground gained, i.e., to develop a model which will enable us to predict the ground gained as a result of various mixes of the two varieties of observational aircraft? Of course, it is very difficult to do so, and because of our lack of understanding of the relationships involved, we would probably choose a less comprehensive but more easily predicted benefit measure, say, the number of satisfactory missions flown. This could be used as the benefit measure on a graph such as that in Figure 4-3, and we could perform an analysis such as was described for the general cost-benefit model.

In such instances, the benefit measures used are usually directionally related to the benefit concept in the objectives; e.g., we believe that more missions are directly related to more ground gained, or at least that more missions do not cause less ground to be gained.

As another example, suppose we wish to develop a military establishment which provides maximum deterrence. What is deterrence? In fact, it is something that exists only in the minds of our potential adversaries, so the systems analyst will choose a benefit measure which is measurable, predictable, and directionally related to deterrence, such as the number of mortalities inflicted or the number of buildings destroyed.[12] In doing so, he is optimizing with respect to a *proxy* benefit measure—one which is used as a substitute for the benefit concept which defines our objectives.

Predictive accuracy

In the military illustrations involving observational aircraft and strategic deterrence, we have touched on aspects of predictive accuracy which are of great significance in systems analysis. In deciding that "ground gained" would not be used as a measure of benefit, we were making the assessment that we could not predict this measure accurately enough because we did not understand the structure of the causal relationships involved. Even in simpler cases, where the benefit measure is not so comprehensive, it still may be difficult to predict accurately. Consider the case involving the use

[12] Deterrence is such a complex concept that it may well be argued that these benefit measures are not even directionally related to it, i.e., that an ability to inflict more damage does not necessarily involve increased deterrence. Also, even if a casualty-producing capability is directionally related to deterrence, it is not our assessment to which it is related but, rather, our enemy's; i.e., how many casualties does *he* think we can produce?

of "number of casualties" as a proxy benefit measure for deterrence, for instance. E. S. Quade, of the RAND Corporation, has said: [13]

> It is the opinion of one analyst who is studying the problem of estimating casualties that if a pre-World War II estimator had worked analogously to his brother of today, had known his trade exceptionally well, had been knowledgeable about the means by which World War II military actions produced casualties, and known the probabilities associated with each weapon, and could have estimated the number of people subject to each weapon—then such an estimator would have underestimated the total cost in human lives of the war to the Soviets by a factor of between three and four.

The implications of low predictive accuracy may be significant to the results of systems analysis, or they may not, depending on the alternatives which are being considered. Quade continued, in the same talk, to say:

> Such an error in the measurement of effectiveness may not be too important if we are comparing two systems that are not radically unlike one another—two ground attack aircraft, say. But at higher levels of optimization—tanks versus aircraft or missiles—gross differences in system effectiveness may be obscured by gross differences in the quality of damage assessment.

Incommensurate benefit measures

In the last comment, Quade touches on the single greatest difficulty involved in applying the conceptual framework to *strategic* decision problems—the problem of incommensurate benefit measures. This problem exists at both the measurement and the predictive level. (Quade's comment has to do with predictive accuracy.)

Incommensurate benefit measures are measures which have different dimensions. Thus, if we are setting the Federal budget and we must compare a program involving aid to health-depressed areas with a military expenditure for helicopters, how do we compare the benefits? Suppose we have thoroughly analyzed both problems independently and have used "number of deaths averted" as a benefit measure in the one case and "number of successful missions flown" in the other? How do we compare the two?

Of course, the reader may question the need to make the comparison at this level. However, the same problem exists at much lower levels. In the military case, suppose one analyst applied the general cost-benefit model

[13] E. S. Quade, "Cost-Effectiveness: An Introduction and Overview," address before the Symposium on Cost-Effectiveness Analysis of the Washington Operations Research Council, June 14–15, 1965.

to the mix of helicopters and fixed-wing aircraft and used "number of successful missions flown" as his benefit measure, while another analyst modeled the mix of artillery versus missiles using another benefit measure. How could these two be compared in trying to analyze strategic problems of force composition? As the reader might surmise, there is no simple answer to such a question. The answer revolves about our knowledge of a trade-off between the two benefit measures; i.e., how much is one unit of one measure worth in terms of the other? As we have illustrated in Chapter 3, such trade-offs are difficult to determine in most real problem situations.

However, such difficulties do not prevent us from performing a systems analysis or even from arriving at a definite conclusion from the analysis. To illustrate another of the many ways in which one may use common sense and judgment to complement formal analysis, consider a situation similar to that which may have faced the U.S. Department of Defense in the early 1960s. Prior to that time, military emphasis had been placed on strategic weapons. General cost-benefit curves could be developed for strategic weapons and tactical weapons, but the benefit (military effectiveness) measures were incommensurate. Suppose that these curves were those shown in Figure 4-8a and b. Although the analyst is unable to compare the benefit units symbolized as B_1 for strategic weapons with those symbolized as B_2 for tactical weapons, he can obtain other useful information to help the decision maker. For instance, he could try to determine the *current operating level* on both graphs.

Suppose that the current operating levels are those described by the circled points and dashed lines in Figure 4-8a and b. What would this tell the decision maker? Rigorously, it would tell him little, since the benefit measures are incommensurate and he does not rigorously know how to com-

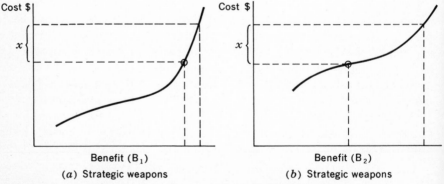

(a) Strategic weapons   (b) Strategic weapons

Figure 4-8   Cost-benefit curves for strategic and tactical weapons.

pare units of B_1 with units of B_2, but practically speaking, the decision maker's intuitive grasp of the relative worth of these two varieties of weapons might lead him to reason that (1) the current operating point in strategic weapons indicates that additional expenditures would buy little additional benefit B_1 and (2) the current operating point in tactical weapons indicates that additional expenditures would buy relatively large increments of B_2. This is so because as more money is spent for strategic weapons, we move up the curve of Figure 4-8a. Since we are currently operating on a steep portion of that curve, little additional benefit is gained. Consider, for example, the point marked with a cross in the figure. It involves only slightly more than benefit B_1 at x dollars greater cost than the current operating situation does—as indicated by the circled point. Similarly, a small move down the strategic-weapons curve involves only slightly less benefit at significantly less cost.

On the tactical-weapons curve of Figure 4-8b, the situation is quite different. An expenditure of x dollars more above the current operating level will involve a move up the curve to the point indicated by a cross. Significantly greater benefit B_2 is obtained at that point than at the current operating level.

Thus, although such an analysis would not provide a decision maker with a rigorously determined best solution, it would give him a sound basis for using his "feel" for the situation, and he might well choose to spend additional moneys for tactical weapons.

Suboptimization

Suboptimization is both a difficulty associated with systems analysis and a method of attacking real-world problems in a way which integrates the conceptual framework with the practicalities of the real world. Suboptimization means, in simple terms, choosing the best alternative for a subsystem of the total decision system.

In business and government, the natural tendency of the manager to focus attention on a particular specialized function, rather than on the complex system composed of the business organization and its environment, has often led to an avoidance of true managerial decision problems. Even though problems which involve complex systems are usually difficult to solve and, in fact, often difficult to formulate in understandable form, they are nonetheless the truly important problems which organizations face. The enterprise will not progress if actions are constantly taken which enhance the performance of one department at the expense of another. Such actions are called *suboptimum*. It is the desire of the systems-analysis approach to develop optimum solutions to problems—those which are best, or at least good, for the organization as a whole, rather than for a single portion of it. The systems approach to management is therefore incompatible with the idea of operating a functional unit just as you would operate the family grocery store, for there may be occasions when a small decrease in the apparent performance of one functional unit results in a large increase in the performance of the total organization.

In the production-marketing context, for example, the production of a wide variety of products with high machine teardown and setup costs between each product may result in increased total sales, since no customers who desire quick delivery will be turned away because of low inventories of the product they desire. These increased sales may more than offset the increased production setup costs, resulting in a higher profit for the enterprise. In this case, the apparent high costs incurred by the production department are not at all indicative of poor performance, but rather are indicative of the systems approach to the solution of decision problems.

In government decisions, when one chooses, for example, the highway-safety program which is predicted to save the greatest number of lives at a given cost, he is suboptimizing in the sense that other ways to save lives (such as by providing nutrition to pregnant women) are not considered and compared. If the objective is simply the saving of lives, government expenditures in all programs and all departments are presumably aimed at the same end, and the Federal government decision system involves both highway-safety and health programs.

So too, when a military planner determines the best mix of helicopters and fixed-wing aircraft and another independently determines the best mix of artillery and missiles, neither has answered the question of whether it would be best to forgo some artillery pieces in order to buy additional helicopters. Thus, suboptimization is first an analytic error to be avoided by the systems analyst, for indeed the word "systems" implies an overall, and not a piecemeal, approach to decision problems.

To develop optimum solutions to managerial problems, it is necessary to view the organization in as large a context as possible. In solving a marketing problem, for example, one must consider the effect on production, finance, quality control, and other relevant organizational entities, while simultaneously weighing the relative influence of competitors, the government, suppliers, and other elements of the system. To do this in its entirety, of course, might require infinite analytic resources. In practice, one accounts for limited analytic capability by abstracting out much of the real-world complexity of the problem and considering systems which may involve less than the total organization. At all times, however, *the effect of making these approximations should be evaluated.* In effect, the scope and complexity of many problems, the limited analytic resources which are usually available, and the demand for results and not just studies often force the systems analyst to begin his analysis at a low level and to build toward the solution of the strategic problem. In doing so, he finds that the answers to all the strategic questions are not simply the aggregate of the answers to smaller questions. What is best for the production department, the sales department, and the accounting department do not necessarily combine to constitute what is best for the organization as a whole. In fact, these suboptimum answers are frequently incompatible with one another.

Thus, a prudent systems analyst utilizes suboptimization because many real systems are too complex to be viewed in the whole. Yet, when he puts together suboptimum solutions, he recognizes that the best alternative for the organization as a whole may not be simply the sum of the alternatives chosen at each stage. He recognizes that while it may not be possible to assess these interactions with perfect accuracy, it is necessary at least to consider their implications. The difficulties involved in doing this should not be discounted. Quade illustrates these difficulties as follows: [14]

> Suppose a family has decided to buy a television set. Not only is their objective fairly clear, but, if they have paid due attention to the advertisements, their alternatives are well-defined. The situation is then one for cost-effectiveness analysis, narrowly defined. The only significant questions the family need answer concern the differences among the available sets in both performance and cost. With a little care, making proper allowance for financing, depreciation, and maintenance, they can estimate, say, the five year procurement and operating cost of any particular set and do so with a feeling that they are well inside the ball park. They will discover, of course, that finding a standard for measuring the performance of the various sets is somewhat more difficult. For one thing, the problem is multidimensional—they must consider color quality, the option for remote control, portability, screen size, and so forth. But, ordinarily, one consideration—perhaps color— dominates. On this basis, they can go look at some color sets, compare costs against color quality, and finally determine a best buy.
>
> Now suppose the family finds they have more money to spend and thus decide to increase their standard of living—a decision similar to one to strengthen the U.S. defense posture by increasing the military budget. This is a situation for a broader analysis. They first need to investigate their goals or objectives and look into the full range of alternatives—a third car, a piano, a country club membership. They

[14] E. S. Quade, *Cost-Effectiveness: An Introduction and Overview*, RAND Corporation, P–3134, Santa Monica, Calif., May, 1965, pp. 2–3.

then need to find ways to measure the effectiveness of these alternatives and establish criteria for choice among them. Here, because the
alternatives are so dissimilar, determining what they want to do is
the major problem; how to do it and how to determine what it costs
may become a comparatively minor one.

However, the analyst who is able to determine these interactions by
specifying overall objectives, determining satisfactory ways of measuring joint
performance, etc., is better able to develop an optimal solution. Of course,
he is seldom certain that he can do so, but he does know that a bad solution
has not been used because of a failure to consider the effect of trade-offs and
interdependencies between various subproblems.

Certainty versus uncertainty

In each of the illustrations of this chapter, we have dwelled on decision
problems formulated as involving certainty—one state of nature or set of
environmental conditions. In practice, most real-world problems involve
great uncertainty as to the state of nature which will occur. By analyzing
a decision problem under certainty, one is again reducing the scope of the
problem so that it can be managed in the time and with the resources allocated to analysis. In studying the certainty case, the analyst learns about
the problem to a degree which is usually impractical without the searching
questioning of objectives, alternatives, costs, and benefits that is an intrinsic
part of system analysis. Having done so, he is better prepared to analyze a
more realistic problem model involving more than one state of nature.

Thus, in this context we view the problem-solving process as sequential
in nature. First, the problem is formulated as though a specified state of
nature were certain to occur. Then, after the system is better understood
and some tentative results are achieved in the certainty case, the analysis is
expanded to include other states of nature which may occur. In military
planning in the Department of Defense, analysts might assume a given state
of nature: "Our enemy will be country X; the war will be of the guerrilla
variety; it will be fought in the desert of North Africa; only conventional
weapons will be used by our enemy; etc." A force structure would then be
developed which would best meet this contingency. In answering this restricted question, the analyst will have asked the right questions; e.g., "What
controllables significantly affect the battle's outcome?" and "How are they
related to one another?" Then, when he has answered these questions and
determined the best force structure for this contingency, he is better able
to ask the right questions about another enemy fighting in another part of
the world with different weapons, etc.

Of course, as was illustrated in the discussion of uncertainty in the previous chapter, the determination of a best overall strategy is not a direct extension of one's knowledge concerning the best strategy for each state of nature. In general, the strategy which leads to the best outcome for one state of nature will not necessarily lead to the best outcome for another. Hence, problems under uncertainty, as we discussed in the previous chapter, are complex.

This is particularly true in the context of military force-structure decisions. It is relatively easy to design a force structure which would be best to fight a particular enemy in a particular location, but it is much more difficult to design a force structure to meet a wide variety of possible contingencies, say, war in the jungles of Asia, the deserts of North Africa, the polar region, etc. Similarly, it is relatively easy to determine the best structure if our potential enemies proceed with a given course of action, but it is rather difficult to determine a structure which is good for a wide range of competitive actions.[15]

Values and limitations

In discussing operational systems-analysis models, we have emphasized the discrepancies between theory and practice. We would be less than fair to systems analysis if we did not point out, as Charles Hitch has put it, that ". . . the difficulties are in the problems—not in the analysis." [16] If one looks at each of the areas in which some practical limitations need to be placed on the conceptual framework and general economic cost-benefit models, he quickly realizes that the same difficulties are inherent in any other approach to solving problems. Indeed, these difficulties are characteristic of the problem rather than of the analysis, and *any* other approach, whether analytic or not, either encounters the same difficulties or unknowingly avoids them altogether.

One of the great virtues of the systems-analysis approach has to do with the question of avoidance. Most, if not all, alternative problem-solving approaches "assume away" or ignore the difficulties with which systems analysis explicitly grapples, however unsuccessfully. It is a matter of reasoned faith to the scientist that it is better to have considered an insurmountable problem than to have completely neglected it. This is exactly what systems analysis does—grapple with the imponderables—rather than

[15] We do not mean to imply that such situations cannot be handled; some of the ways in which they can be approached are discussed in Chap. 3 under "Decisions under Uncertainty."
[16] See the quotation which introduces this chapter.

providing answers which either are not really answers at all or are answers to the wrong questions. If, by using a systems-analysis approach, the decision maker is led to ask the right questions about the salient features of the problem, he has gotten the greatest benefit from analysis, even though it has provided him with no quick answers. If at the same time he has obtained some insight into the determination of the strategy which is best in the real world, he is doubly blessed.

Summary

In this chapter, we have tried to emphasize that the practice of systems analysis is neither the dogmatic application of a set of rules to a situation which may not be susceptible to rules nor the ceding of decision-making authority to a mystical set of mathematical equations or to a computer.

At this stage of development, the practice of systems analysis is largely an art. Indeed, the foundations of the art evolve from basic scientific and logical precepts, and the conceptual framework is a rigorous basis for analysis, but in practice, human judgment and intuition play an overwhelmingly significant role in the decision itself, in the analysis which is made of the decision problem, and in the decisions involved in "deciding how to decide," i.e., in constructing the analysis, the measures to be used, etc.

Here, we have focused attention on the role of models in systems analysis and on the practicalities of the real-world application of models. As we have shown, explicit systems-analysis models—whether they are mathematical, graphical, or physical—are not really much different from the mental models which everyone constructs in solving any problem. The primary difference is that systems-analysis models are explicit, and thus they can be manipulated more easily and constructed to be a more comprehensive description of the real world than the subjective models which most people use to solve problems.

Recommended readings

Bross, Irwin D. J.: "Models," chap. 33 in Irwin D. J. Bross (ed.), *Design for Decision*, The Macmillan Company, New York, 1953.

Churchman, C. W., R. L. Ackoff, and E. L. Arnoff: *Introduction to Operations Research*, John Wiley & Sons, Inc., New York, 1957.

Enke, Stephen (ed.): *Defense Management*, Prentice-Hall, Inc., Englewood Cliffs, N.J., 1967.

Ernst, M. L.: "Operations Research and the Large Strategic Problems," *Operations Research,* vol. 9, no. 4, pp. 437–445, July–August, 1961.

Grosse, R. N.: *An Introduction to Cost-Effectiveness Analysis,* Research Analysis Corporation, RAC–P–5, July, 1965.

King W. R.: "Human Judgment and Management Decision Analysis," *Journal of Industrial Engineering,* December, 1967.

Prest, A. R., and R. Turvey: "Cost-Benefit Analysis: A Survey," *The Economic Journal,* December, 1965.

"Putting a Dollar Sign on Life," *Business Week,* Jan. 21, 1967, pp. 86–88.

Quade, E. S.: *The Limitations of a Cost-Effectiveness Approach to Military Decision-making,* RAND Corporation, P–2798, Santa Monica, Calif., September, 1963.

———: *Cost-Effectiveness: An Introduction and Overview,* RAND Corporation, P–3134, Santa Monica, Calif., May, 1965.

Rainey, R. B., Jr.: "Mobility: Airlift, Sealift, and Prepositioning," in Stephen Enke (ed.), *Defense Management,* Prentice-Hall, Inc., Englewood Cliffs, N.J., 1967, chap. 9.

Schlesinger, J. R.: "The Changing Environment for Systems Analysis," in Stephen Enke (ed.), *Defense Management,* Prentice-Hall, Inc., Englewood Cliffs, N.J., 1967, chap. 6.

CHAPTER 5
Planning

There is nothing about an
organization more important than
its future.[1]

In this chapter we shall discuss basic ideas of planning and develop a planning system for the enterprise. This system will cover long-range and short-range planning and is intended to embody a planning philosophy aimed at achieving better organizational performance. It is our belief that an organization must not tacitly accept its fate in the environment of the future; it can favorably influence its performance by studying and thinking about the future.

This, of course, is a rather generally accepted view in modern management, but it is interesting to note that this was not always the case. Successful entrepreneurs of the past relied primarily on their ability to *adapt* to a changing environment, rather than taking the initiative and trying to predict the future, with its opportunities and its pitfalls.

[1] Paul E. Holden, Launsbury S. Fish, and Hubert L. Smith, *Top Management Organization and Control,* Stanford University Press, Stanford, Calif., 1941, p. 4.

Planning: an organic function

Planning today in American business is recognized by most managers as an organic function which precedes the complementary functions of organizing, motivating, and controlling. Planning is concerned with the development of a plan; it involves mental activity and specifies what should be done, how it should be done, when action is to be effected, who is responsible, and why such action is necessary. Planning is the selection of suitable alternatives from a myriad of choices; the degree of futurity in planning usually becomes greater as higher organizational levels participate.

Planning can be defined as the process of deciding where an organization is headed and what methods and means should be used to get it there. As expressed by one pair of authors: [2]

> Planning is the function of selecting the enterprise objectives and the policies, programs, and procedures for achieving them. Planning is, of course, decision-making, since it involves choosing among alternatives.

Planning involves making a prediction about the conditions of a future environment—and deciding where and how an organization should proceed. It does not necessarily follow that all decision making is planning; e.g., those decisions concerned primarily with efficient ways of achieving predetermined goals are best thought of as a part of the execution functions of the manager. In the planning process, today's decisions invariably have future implications, particularly regarding the commitment of resources and organizational strategy. For example, a decision to begin development of a new product has resulting effects throughout the business in the determination of production and marketing techniques, financing arrangements, and other related matters. This is so because of the desirability of sustaining an *overall organizational effort* over some future time period. There is an inescapable interdependence between the product-development activities and all other company efforts necessary to support that product in a competitive future environment. A product-development decision constitutes an aspect of the essence of a total corporate strategy. Planning must therefore encompass all aspects of the business and provide for the correlation of development, marketing, financial, production, and other realities of the future environment.

It is generally agreed that planning is a salient function of all managers, regardless of their position within the organization. While the head of a company may be concerned with long-range plans for the company as a

[2] Harold Koontz and Cyril J. O'Donnell, *Principles of Management*, 2d ed., McGraw-Hill Book Company, New York, 1959, p. 35.

whole, even the lowest-level manager should be concerned with plans for his organizational unit. One might very well ask why there should be all this emphasis on planning at all levels in view of the fact that any approach to the future is always fraught with risk, change, and uncertainty. Of course, it is rarely possible to predict the future precisely, and even though it may be necessary to deviate from the most carefully developed plan because of unforeseen events, planning is beneficial because it does reduce the likelihood of unforeseen contingencies which can seriously affect the organization's future.

Types of plans

There is a wide variation in the planning processes used in various organizations and by managers at various levels within organizations. One useful way of gaining an appreciation of the magnitude and variety of the planning actions is to review the various types of plans that may be a product of the planning process.

OBJECTIVES   Objectives are the end results to which the organizational activity is directed. The decision problem involved in setting necessary objectives is a fundamental responsibility of top-level management. Often, objectives arise from preliminary planning studies. Objectives are hierarchical in nature in the sense that the general overall objectives are formulated by top management after economic, social, and political forces affecting the company have been appraised. These overall objectives provide guidelines for subobjectives throughout the organization and become the standard against which progress can be measured.

POLICIES   Policies are general statements of intended behavior of the organization; they provide guidance for thinking and decision making within the framework of existing or anticipated resources. Policies tend to limit the scope within which decisions must be made and to assure that necessary decisions will contribute to the accomplishment of overall objectives.

PROCEDURES   Procedures are much like policies except that they are more specific and provide for a definitive response in the handling of future activities. Their essence is the delineation of a chronological sequence of actions to be taken.

BUDGETS   Budgeting is the process of defining anticipated circumstances involving the funds of an organization. A business budget is a plan covering the funding implications for all phases of operations for a definitive period in the future.

PROJECT PLANS   Project plans are a combination of objectives, policies, procedures, budgets, and other elements necessary to carry out a predetermined specific objective. Project plans are the basic building elements of the organization's system of plans.

FUNCTIONAL PLANS   Functional plans are those which outline intended action in a functional area such as marketing, production, finance, etc. They are a compilation of actions necessary to provide functional support to the accomplishment of overall corporate planning goals.

The time dimensions of planning

Long-range and short-range planning are similar in technique and application; one obvious difference is in their respective time dimensions. Contemporary literature often refers to long-range planning as that planning which extends one or more years into the future, and to short-range planning as that which concerns periods of less than one year.

Complex factors determine both the functional and the overall corporate planning period; some of the important determinants are the industry peculiarities, the market demand, the availability of resources, the lead time involved in the product life cycle, and the strategic objectives of the organization. In speaking of "how far ahead organizations plan," caution must be exercised to clarify whether one is speaking of the overall organizational long-range planning period, of the planning period for a specific functional area of effort, or of a particular element of long-range planning such as that directed toward the availability of resources.

The length of the future period for which long-term plans should be made is an important technical factor. As a rule, the planning period should be based on an economic projection which follows trends without regard to cyclical fluctuations of the economy. An organization should plan as far ahead as is useful, but only as far as can be done with some reasonable degree of accuracy. It is axiomatic that the farther one extends his planning horizon into the future, the less certain his predictions become. Also, his perception of the impact of his predictions becomes less sharp as his planning period is extended.

Most literature cites three to five years as the most common long-range planning term. However, consider the problem of determining a corporate long-range planning period. The span of an overall planning period could be determined as any of the following:

1   The average planning period for the conglomerate functional areas of effort
2   The longest single period of functional-area long-range planning
3   The time period required to provide for the amassing of necessary resources
4   An arbitrary period which in the judgment of the executive group best fits the long-range objectives of the firm
5   A period which encompasses the most critical areas of long-range planning within the corporation
6   A period which provides for the best market advantage in terms of economic cycles and long-term growth

The above list suggests a multiple horizon of planning. The precise period of time is less important than the determination of *the ability of the organization to realize a return on the resources that have been committed in the planning process.* According to Koontz and O'Donnell: [3]

> There should be some logic in selecting the right time range for company planning. In general, since planning and forecasting that underlie it are costly, a company should probably not plan for a longer period than is economically justifiable; yet it is risky to plan for a shorter period. The logical answer as to the right planning period seems to lie in the "commitment principle," that planning should encompass the period of time necessary to foresee (through a series of actions) the fulfillment of commitments involved in a decision.

For example, pulp, paper, and lumber companies are reported to plan in terms of a forty-year horizon, whereas a cosmetics manufacturer would have no need for such a long time frame.

Abundant literature exists with respect to short-range planning, i.e., planning that is less than one year in duration. Both theory and practice have progressed further in this area than in the long-range planning sphere, and there is a large body of knowledge about short-range planning containing sound generalizations and excellent insights. But American industry and business are becoming more and more concerned with long-range objectives; current attention to long-range comparative rates of the national economic growth of the United States and Russia, for example, appears to indicate this. In industry, evidence exists to support the idea that management is giving greater attention to time horizons well beyond those to which they were previously accustomed. In addition, long-range planning has grown

[3] Harold Koontz and Cyril J. O'Donnell, *Principles of Management*, 3d ed., McGraw-Hill Book Company, New York, 1964, p. 87.

into a more or less formalized process covering a wider range of corporate interests than it did in the past. As a result, the developing concept of long-range planning raises many issues and dimensions which are not answerable in terms of existing empirical and theoretical bases.

Long-range planning

Long-range planning is conceived by the authors as planning that extends in excess of one or two years into the future, encompasses all functional areas of the business, and is effected within the existing and long-term future framework of economic, social, and technological factors. Long-range planning is more than a time dimension; it is a continuous planning process of broad scope which reflects a new way of thinking about the future, a new pattern of business and industrial life. As a force making for the coordination of all the people, functions, effects, and external factors of the organization, long-range planning is developed on a scientific and objective basis and a philosophy of management. Long-range planning is more than business forecasting using trends and projections; it goes further by helping management to determine how to take advantage of the trends, how to minimize the effects of unfavorable trends, and how to attain full realization of the organization's objectives.

The basic elements of long-range planning

As the first step in planning, the organization asks itself: "What business are we really in?" The answer to this question imputes goals to the enterprise and serves to define the scope of its activities. This is another one of those obvious points which are often overlooked. Levitt [4] has pointed out, for example, that many of the difficulties of the United States railroads could have been avoided had their business been defined as that of ground transportation rather than railroad activities, as it implicitly was.

Although such an indictment of an entire industry may be viewed as a frivolous exercise of the 20/20 hindsight vision of which even the least perceptive of us are abundantly possessed, *it is precisely the preclusion of the opportunity for such retrospective judgments which is the purpose of long-range planning.*

In this vein, we see today that many businesses are indeed broadening their horizons and opportunities by asking this vital question. Thus, oil

[4] Theodore Levitt, "Marketing Myopia," *Harvard Business Review*, July–August, 1960, p. 45.

companies have begun to view themselves as being in the travel business rather than the oil business. The manifestations of this are already being seen, e.g., in the marketing of travel insurance via correspondence with credit-card holders. Similarly, insurance companies are beginning to view their role as one of providing financial services rather than just insurance. In government, the delineation of output-oriented programs involving governmental goals such as defense, the promotion of health, etc., is a response to the basic planning question.[5]

Values of long-range planning

E. Kirby Warren [6] has delineated four "realistic expectations" for long-range planning which, in effect, represent the values of a long-range planning system:

1   Clearer understanding of likely future impact of present decisions
2   Anticipating areas requiring future decisions
3   Increasing the speed of the flow of relevant information
4   Providing for faster and less disruptive implementation of future decisions

The values of long-range planning, then, have to do with better current decisions and better and more efficient future decisions. Hence, strategic decisions, long-range planning, and the systems-analysis approach, which in previous chapters we have argued is the best basis for good decisions, are intrinsically intertwined. In effect, long-range planning is the overall objective of systems analysis, for one can apply analysis to a particular decision and "solve" a problem without effectively integrating that solution into an overall plan for the future. Thus, while strategic decisions and the analysis of those decisions are a necessary part of long-range planning, they are not synonymous with it.

Environmental influences

Successful planning involves more than effective reactions to a changing environment. An organization cannot rely on chance to provide a demand for its product or service. Attention must be given to, and advantage taken of, the economic and political systems which surround the organization, for

---

[5] We shall illustrate in the next chapter that in many ways related to decision making, the Federal government has traditionally been uncertain as to what "business" it is really in. In that chapter, we shall also go into the program concept mentioned here.

[6] E. Kirby Warren, *Long-range Planning: The Executive Viewpoint*, Prentice-Hall, Inc., Englewood Cliffs, N.J., 1966, pp. 29–31.

it does not exist in a vacuum, free to draw on its environment when and if needed. Rather, the organization exists interdependently with other systems in the society, and its destiny is inescapably interwoven with the destiny of the larger system of which it is a part. Seymour Tilles has put it this way: [7]

> While it is convenient to introduce the concept of a system as an entity in itself, any attempt to deal with actual systems, whether atoms, people, or companies, immediately reveals that such things do not exist in themselves. They are intimately concerned with a wider variety of other units which cannot really be ignored if meaningful statements about system behavior are to be made.

The business executive must constantly be concerned with how the parts of the business system relate to the environmental system. Concern over the systems relationships extends to the interrelated parts that constitute the parent system and to a wide variety of extraorganizational agencies that exert a profound influence on the actions of the planning team—for example, the wide variety of external entities such as competitors, customers, government, financial institutions, and so on which influence the planning activity. A long-term corporate plan which requires substantial financing through the issue of securities must consider the attitude of, and acceptability of the plan to, investment bankers and potential investors who may put forth the funds required for the successful accomplishment of the plan. Should an insurance company desire to extend a long-term loan in support of a corporate plan, that company will have a direct and continuing involvement in the long-range endeavor. The basic notion here is that just as the business is a system of related parts, so too is the business entity a subsystem existing in a larger system comprised of the entire economic society. Implicit in this concept is a degree of wholeness which makes the whole different from the individual units considered separately. The planner must develop procedures and policies which define the company as a system and long-range planning as the process by which the system adapts its resources to dynamic external and internal conditions. The individual activities involved in long-range planning constitute an indissoluble whole, no part of which can be affected without influencing all the other parts.

Forecasting and long-range planning

The importance of the environment to the future of the enterprise must be quantitatively assessed if effective plans are to be made. In terms of the

[7] Seymour Tilles, "The Manager's Job: A Systems Approach," *Harvard Business Review*, January–February, 1963, p. 74.

conceptual framework outlined in Chapter 3, this means that various states of nature must be considered and outcomes must be predicted.

A basic predictive method for uncontrollables is *forecasting*. Forecasts of the future are inherently uncertain, and yet so too are the guesses, conjectures, or hunches which so often are a part of any other alternative to formal forecasting. Although there are many risks involved in forecasting, their implications, as far as long-range plans are concerned, can be minimized by (1) tempering the corporate long-term planning to the basic secular trends in the economy rather than to forecasts which reflect yearly fluctuations in the business cycle and (2) planning for fluctuations in the economy and long-term changes in the political, technological, social, and legislative climate.

The role of forecasting in long-range planning is to project future business conditions and company performance as related to the future environment. Forecasting per se does not include the function of altering company policies and strategy to take advantage of, or protect against, projected business conditions; however, important management decisions are expected to result from the forecast. Forecasting does not have the innate function of acting to affect the course of company progress. The function of forecasting is clear: given the present position of the firm, it seeks to determine what the effect of future economic, legislative, technological, and other factors of the environment on the long-term objectives of the firm will be.[8] Specific forecast information includes a broad base of economic, political, and social phenomena derived from the environment in which the business is functioning and from records and individuals within the firm itself. Collectively, this intelligence provides the knowledge required to make assumptions and decisions about the organization's future posture. Application of these economic, political, and social data depends on the answer to the basic planning question: "What is it that we are trying to do?" The information used in the forecasting process may include, but is not necessarily limited to:

1   External information (qualitative and quantitative)
    Government statistics (employment, housing, etc.)
    Trade association data
    Social mores (fashion and styles)
    Legislative actions
    Political environment
    Market potential
    International affairs
    Capital availability
    Government expenditures and controls

[8] As Abraham Lincoln said, "If we could first know where we are and whither we are tending, we could better judge what to do and how to do it."

Gross national product changes
Demographic changes
Technological progress
Industry trends [growth and (or) decline]
Competitors' actions
Business-cycle behavior
Government fiscal policy

2   Internal information (qualitative and quantitative)
Organizational posture
Corporate objectives
Present competitive position
Availability of human and nonhuman resources (quality and quantity)
Organizational history
Executive expectations

Three kinds of forecasts are implied by the above input elements: time-series forecasts, forecasts using statistical economic indicators, and technological forecasts.

TIME-SERIES FORECASTS   A time series is a sequence of values of some quantity corresponding to particular points or intervals of time. For example, production or price data arranged chronologically represent a time series.

Time-series forecasts seek to extend a historical series into the future as a prediction of future values of the quantity in question. The methods used to do so range from simple extrapolations done "by eye" on a graph of the series to sophisticated statistical techniques which seek to measure long-term trends and seasonal and cyclical effects. As noted earlier, long-range planning must be based primarily on secular trends—the long-run growth or decline pattern of the series. However, it is usually necessary to evaluate seasonal and cyclical factors in order to measure the trend.

The basic models used in statistical forecasting relates to these salient elements. For example, an additive model might be used:

$$O = T + S + C + R$$

where T is trend, S is the seasonal effect, C is the cyclical effect, and R represents random (or unexplained) variation. The symbol O represents the basic time-series historical data. Thus, the assumption of the model is that each point in the series occurs as a result of four factors (T, S, C, and R) combining in additive fashion.[9] By using the known quantities in the series (the

---

[9] Of course, there is nothing sacred about an additive model. Many other forms have been used to relate these four basic factors. See *Forecasting in Industry*, National Industrial Conference Board, Studies in Business Policy, no. 77; and *Forecasting Sales*, National Industrial Conference Board, Studies in Business Policy, no. 106. A basic reference is Julius Shiskin, *Electronic Computers and Business Indicators*, National Bureau of Economic Research Occasional Paper 57, 1957.

Os), we can estimate the other quantities. Then, having estimated them, we can forecast future values of O.

STATISTICAL ECONOMIC INDICATORS   Whereas the time-series forecasts assume that the past can be projected into the future, the use of economic indicators in forecasting assures that combinations of things happening today can be used to predict things which will happen in the future. For example, a number of "leading indicators" are used by economists in the belief that they consistently precede changes in business activity. Thus, they serve as a basis for predicting such changes. In reality, most often a number of indicators are viewed simultaneously in making such forecasts. For example, such indicators as constant-dollar GNP, an index of industrial production, and sales of retail stores may be viewed (in the context of their historical time series) as indicative of the level of future business activity.

The relationships used may be either qualitative or quantitative. Statistical techniques are often used to estimate the numerical relationships involved, or frequenly the directional changes in indicators, taken as a group, are used to predict qualitative directional changes in business activity. Business periodicals often report such happenings as "all but two of the leading indicators turned down last month" as foretelling of dire consequences for the future of the economy, for instance.

TECHNOLOGICAL FORECASTS   Opinion-based forecasting techniques are similar to some techniques of technological forecasting.[10] Technological forecasts aim at setting timetables for the meshing of the need for products and services and the technological feasibility of producing them. Such forecasts are of obvious importance to long-range planning since the development of new products is a result of a myriad of decisions involving capital investments, research expenditures, market analyses, etc., which must be made sequentially over a long period of time.

A method developed by the RAND Corporation, called "Delphi," is employed in seeking opinions relevent to technological forecasts.[11] It involves querying and requerying a wide range of experts on their expectations for future technological events.

One of the essentials of technological forecasting has to do with the interdependence of scientific breakthroughs. For example, three-dimensional movies and photographs are a rather obvious extension of current technology;

[10] Many other opinion polls are also used for forecasting. For example, McGraw-Hill surveys of businessmen's plans for making expenditures on plant and equipment are published regularly in *Business Week* and are widely used as forecasting bases.
[11] *Business Week* reports on Delphi and derivations of it used by TRW, Inc., in "New Products: Setting a Timetable," May 27, 1967, pp. 52–56.

yet their development depended on that of the laser. So too did the development of advanced weapons depend on that of microelectronic circuits. The available technology in one area—say, rocket propulsion—often must wait on developments in other fields—e.g., electronic circuits—before a product involving both (a long-range missile) can be produced.

TRW, Inc., is reported [12] to be forecasting 401 probable technological developments of the future and the time they should occur. This is done in terms of a categorization based on company interest. Networks designed to show the interrelated steps necessary to achieve these developments [13] permit the company to plan toward developing the product itself or to participate in its development through the production of components.

Of course, not all technological forecasting is done entirely on subjective bases. Quantitative statistical estimates of technological factors are also feasible. The best illustrations of this are the statistical forecasts of aircraft speed which have been made by aerospace companies. These companies have accurately forecast speed capabilities of new designs, including the supersonic transport, on the basis of past increases in speed of sequential aircraft designs.

A system of plans

The output desired from the long-range planning system is a hierachy of plans which describe what the business system will do under forecast conditions. These plans should have three essential characteristics:

1 An element of futurity, the degree thereof depending on the organizational level at which the plan is conceived and the functional area involved
2 Specific tasking of organizational elements in terms of roles and missions in the plan
3 Personal involvement of key individuals

The plans are documentary manifestations of the planning activity that is being carried on in the organization; the tangible and intangible results that these plans eventually bring forth provide a common denominator of understanding. The long-range planning system manager eventually sees organizational and product changes as the *real* output of the planning system. More specifically, these changes would include such things as:

1 New product lines (or research and development directed toward new product lines)

[12] *Ibid.*
[13] We shall discuss the use of networks for planning and control in a later chapter.

2   Product diversification
3   Company acquisitions
4   Executive development programs
5   Company reorganizations
6   Divestments and liquidations
7   Changes in management philosophy
8   New facilities
9   Change in corporate strategy

The information about, and the approach to, business planning may be structured in a system framework to provide a conceptual model for an overall planning system. In this system, project plans are the building blocks and are arranged in successive elements as portrayed in Figure 5-1.[14]

Each echelon of a plan receives guidance from a prior plan and further defines it by focusing on groups of activities having a common purpose. The system of plans covers all time periods and allows for planning on all levels of the organization and in terms of all the major functions, from research to administration.

The strategic plan

The strategic plan of the organization is at the summit of all the plans; it outlines the broad objectives and strategies that the firm wants to achieve presently and at some future period of time. It includes the answers to such questions as:

> What are the broad missions and roles of the organization?
>
> What strategy is required to move from today's position to a competitive position desired in the future?
>
> When compared with the other plans that are developed in the organization, how realistic is the overall organizational strategy?
>
> What image does the organization want to portray in the greater system (social, economic, political) of which it is a part?

The strategic plan is important because it becomes a standard for deciding what direction the subsidiary plans in the organization should take. It is the overall document used to determine the organizational compatibility of the project plans with the other plans. The strategic plan guides the organization in decisions involving the current product (or service) and the future generation of products and markets.

[14] This system of planning has been adapted from *A Framework for Business Planning* Stanford Research Institute, Report no. 162, Menlo Park, Calif., February, 1963. Used by permission.

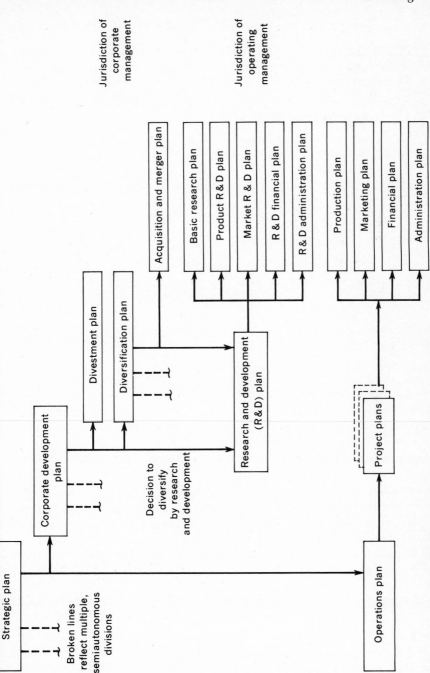

Figure 5-1   The system of plans.

The corporate development plan

The next echelon is the *corporate development plan,* which determines the activities necessary for a new generation of products or services. At the same time, the corporate development plan maps in greater detail the route toward the future position of the organization that has been specified by the strategic plan. The corporate development plan answers such questions as:

> What will the future environment consist of in terms of demand for our goods or services? What will be expected of our organization in that future time period?
>
> What favorable conditions must be created within the organization in order that new products and new markets can be conceived and defined?
>
> What techniques will be used to screen out poor investments and products and high-risk ventures?
>
> What are the expected resource requirements for the new products or services?

The corporate development plan provides the guidance for three succeeding plans:

THE DIVESTMENT PLAN   This plan deals with the divestiture of major elements of the organization. These elements can consist of products, services, property, or organizational entities.

THE DIVERSIFICATION PLAN   This plan describes the development of new products, services, and markets to join or replace the current generation of products. It selects new product areas and determines when entry should be made by merging with another organization or by conducting in-house research and development which builds on existing competence.

THE RESEARCH AND DEVELOPMENT PLAN   This plan specifies action and creates new products or processes for existing demand or a new market for existing products or processes. It is where the organization does basic and applied research to advance the state of the art of what it has to offer. This plan cuts across all elements of the organization to include products, markets, finance, and administration.

The operations plan

This plan, one of the two plans supporting the strategic plan, is the blueprint for current business action. It guides activity by which the current generation of products and services is distributed to the existing markets. The operations plan exists within each functional area of effort—production, marketing, finance, and administration—and as a composite of the project plans involved in the effort.

The operations plan specifies the total work to be accomplished in the functional area of jurisdiction. It subdivides the work into logical work units, defines work flow, allocates resources, and establishes authority and responsibility patterns between the principals in the effort. And, of course, it sets gross schedules and budgets. Part of this planning is cyclical, such as plant layout, organization, and routine procedures.

The project plan

Project plans are reflected as the plans covering a specific project within the other plans. For example, the corporate development plan will be supported by a series of *ad hoc* plans covering the details of a singular undertaking related to the implementation of the corporate development plan. Project plans are the basic building blocks of a planning system. Thus, the project plans can have short-, intermediate-, and long-range implications. What makes the project plan unique is its concern with an identifiable effort having cost, schedule, and technical parameters. Project plans are found at all levels in the organization. They should deal in sufficient specifics so as to be useful as a standard for control.

The project plan should go into considerable detail in outlining how the project will be developed and produced. In the management of a project which cuts across different functional lines, specificity of the plan is a critical requirement since the participating individuals and organizations may have competing and conflicting objectives.

Appendix 1 includes an illustrative specification for a project plan. This specification is designed to answer the following questions about the project:

1   Why is the action required?
2   What action is to be taken?
3   What resources will be required to support the action?
4   What will the action accomplish?
5   When are the results of the action expected?
6   What objectives and conditions must be met?

Planning and analysis in the planning process

In most large organizations, planning must take place over a long time period at various organizational levels. Indeed, planning is probably best accomplished as a continual, year-round process which becomes vocal at periodic reviews. No organization plans effectively if the planning process is compacted into a few days or weeks before a planning review. Moreover, effective planning must involve organizational elements of various levels in both line and staff capacities.

A typical planning process will serve to illustrate the salient features and the interactions of the various organization elements:[15]

1 Promulgation of corporate objectives, planning guidelines, tentative goals and strategies, key assumptions, etc.

2 Preparation of one- and five-year plans at project and(or) levels within major divisions

3 Review, analysis, and consolidation by corporate budget and analysis group

4 Financial review, analysis, and consolidation by corporate budget and analysis group

5 Review by corporate staff

6 Final review by corporate management committee

The first phase of this process involves a flow from the corporate level of various guidelines and assumptions to be used at lower levels. This ensures some consistency and comparability among plans developed by different units at different levels. Although each subunit should not be compelled to adhere rigidly to each forecast made at the corporate level, deviations should be justified in the plan submitted.

The plans themselves, at all levels, typically involve two key parts. The first is the budget, which summarizes in financial terms what the unit expects to do and what resources will be required to do it. The second portion of the plan is verbal in nature, involving statements of economic, environmental, and operating assumptions (either those taken from corporate-level guidelines or others developed independently,[16] basic objectives of the unit (stated in terms of organizational outputs), and programs designed to accomplish those objectives.

At the major divisional level, each unit's plans are reviewed, consolidated, and summarized. If divisional management has participated in the preparation of plans on a continuing basis, this can be a meaningful review which leads to insights into the goals of the division and how they should be sought, If not, this stage may involve only the shuffling and forwarding of documents.

---

[15] In this section, we shall discuss the planning process in terms which are descriptive of the business enterprise. In the next chapter, planning processes in nonbusiness organizations will be taken up.

[16] If all guidelines, assumptions, and forecasts passed down from the corporate level are used in the plans, the verbal portion would probably simply summarize these to indicate that they form a part of the plan.

If an analytic capability—in terms of either professional analysts or analytically oriented managers—is available, a continuing dialogue between divisional unit planners should produce better plans. Thus, while alternative ways of achieving goals should be compared at the lowest possible level, it is usually most practical to have plans made at one level and to have staff analysts, who may advise and participate in the analysis, review the conclusions at the divisional level. Of course, the level at which formal analysis is done depends heavily on the size of the organization.

If there is time to do so (and the process should be structured so that corporate goals do not become submerged in planning review deadlines), the key objectives, assumptions, and forecasts should be circulated among the divisions of the company. This will permit one division to challenge another and to provide information to others. Moreover, it increases the likelihood of joint actions among divisions.

The budget and analysis group of the controller's function consolidates financial data and depicts their impact on the overall corporate budget. If the plans are based on analysis and the objective comparison of alternative ways of achieving goals, it is possible for the budget and analysis group to challenge assumptions and forecasts and to "analyze the analysis." This is the most meaningful contribution which can be made at this level. The verbal portion of the plan may be reviewed by relevant corporate staff groups in parallel with the financial analysis. The marketing staff would focus on marketing issues in the assumptions, objectives, and programs, just as the production staff would give attention to issues within their domain.

Ideally, corporate-level analysis of both the financial and the verbal aspects of plans should be conducted by objective analysts who have no vested interests in the divisions. This ensures that challenges to overly realistic assumptions and forecasts will be made. Such objectivity can be acquired by having corporate planning analysts rewarded in terms of measures related to planning rather than corporate or divisional results. Thus, while operating managers naturally tend to focus on achieving short-run results (often at the expense of the future), the corporate analyst's personal advancement should depend on his taking exactly the opposite view. If the future is sacrificed for today's results by a division, the corporate planning analyst should bear a portion of the blame. Similarly, if the future is well cared for at the expense of the present, the corporate analyst should be rewarded.[17]

[17] Here, we are discussing a corporation which is well prepared for today. Our comments would be inappropriate in the case of a company experiencing current financial problems. Indeed, in such a case, long-range planning should probably be forsaken, or at least reduced, until current problems are attended to and solved.

In the subsequent phase of the planning process, corporate management is called on to review the plans in the light of their previously determined objectives, assumptions, and guidelines. Their function is to check the plans and ensure broad compatibility with corporate goals and resources. Of course, at this level, judgment is supreme. The executive committee may ask that some plans be revised as a result of the insights gained concerning the lack of validity of the guidelines laid down, the need for greater inter-action among divisional plans, the desire to see a wider range of alternatives considered, etc.

One important aspect of corporate review is a *comparison of present plans with past plans and with actual results.* No one would expect results and past plans to be in perfect agreement, or even past plans and present plans for the same time period to agree. However, these deviations should be ex-plained. If goals are changed, top management should be told the reason, or if forecasts have been radically changed on the basis of newly available information, this fact should be brought out into the open and its impact discussed.

The greatest benefit of a review of new plans, old plans, and actual results may well be in the implied accountability for planning. Too frequently the "ideal" planning system deteriorates into a valueless exercise when man-agers find that their payoff is solely on the basis of short-run performance. If some accountability for planning is applied to managers as well as to analysts, the likely result is better planning.

Summary

Planning is viewed as an organic function of management, the critical dimension of which is time. Short-range planning is better developed than long-range planning. The reasons for this are its greater apparent criticality and the greater degree of certainty (and hence understanding) involved.

Long-range planning involves a questioning attitude on the part of man-agement: "What business are we in?" "What business should we be in?" "What opportunities are likely to become available to us?" "How can we take advantage of them?"

Environmental influences play a large role in long-range planning. The organization must make assumptions and forecasts concerning the future and plan for these circumstances. The output of planning is a system of plans which serves to guide the organization's thinking and actions into desirable channels.

In the next chapter, we shall discuss the salient aspects of the planning-programming-budgeting system which has been instituted in the Federal government. There, we shall show that it represents an application in a huge organization of many of the planning concepts developed in this chapter.

Recommended readings

Ansoff, H. Igor: *Corporate Strategy: An Analytic Approach to Business Policy for Growth and Expansion*, McGraw-Hill Book Company, New York, 1965.

Baumgartner, J. S.: *Project Management*, Richard D. Irwin, Inc., Homewood, Ill., 1963.

Berg, Norman: "Strategic Planning for Conglomerate Companies," *Harvard Business Review*, May–June, 1965, pp. 79–92.

Brown, Harold: "Planning Our Military Forces," *Foreign Affairs*, January, 1967, pp. 277–290.

Ewing, David W. (ed.): *Long-range Planning for Management*, Harper & Row, Publishers, Incorporated, New York, 1964.

Kaprielyan, S. Peter: "NASA Management at the Crossroads," *Aerospace Management*, vol. 1, no. 2, Summer, 1966.

Kopkind, Andrew: "The Future Planners," *New Republic*, Feb. 25, 1967, pp. 19–23.

Levitt, Theodore: "Marketing Myopia," *Harvard Business Review*, July–August, 1960, pp. 45–56.

Mace, Myles T.: "The President and Corporate Planning," *Harvard Business Review*, January–February, 1965, pp. 49–62.

Optner, Stanford L.: *Systems Analysis for Business and Industrial Problem Solving*, Prentice-Hall, Inc., Englewood Cliffs, N.J., 1965.

Smalter, Donald J.: "Influence of Department of Defense on Corporate Planning," *Management Technology*, vol. 4, no. 2, pp. 115–138, December, 1964.

Smiddy, Harold F.: "Planning, Anticipating and Managing," *Management Technology*, vol. 4, no. 2, pp. 83–91, December, 1964.

Steiner, George A.: "How to Assure Poor Long-range Planning for Your Company," *California Management Review*, vol. 7, no. 4, pp. 93–94, Summer, 1965.

——— and William G. Ryan: *Managerial Methods of Successful Project Managers*, NASA Research Project, NASA Research Paper no. 1, University of California at Los Angeles, Graduate School of Business Administration, Division of Research, Los Angeles, Calif.

Total Package Procurement Concept, Department of the Air Force, May 10, 1966.

Warren, E. Kirby: *Long-range Planning: The Executive Viewpoint,* Prentice-Hall, Inc., Englewood Cliffs, N.J., 1966.

CHAPTER 6
Planning-Programming-Budgeting and Systems Analysis

A very new and very revolutionary
system of planning and budgeting
[should] be instituted through the
vast Federal Government.[1]

President Johnson's directive containing the above passage represented the start of a new era in government management since it denoted the formal recognition by our nation's leaders that formal long-range planning and objective analysis were reasonable and necessary complements to subjective analysis and informal short-run planning in determining the actions and future course of a huge organization whose actions affect the daily life of virtually every human being.

Before that time, formal planning and analysis were already playing a large and successful part in the tactical decisions of both government and industry. Formal analytic techniques were widely used in determining the best truck routes for the Post Office Department, the best number of toll houses to have open on a turnpike, etc. In the U.S. Department of Defense, systems analyses had been successfully conducted for over five years on complex strategic problems where objectives were rather obscure and the

---

[1] President Lyndon B. Johnson, as quoted in *Time*, Sept. 3, 1965, p. 20.

notion of systems efficiency was not clear-cut. Similarly, the analytic approaches of systems analysis, management science, and operations research had by this time become an important part of the strategic decisions in many large corporations. Only the governments—Federal, state, and local— had not (aside from the Department of Defense) used systems analysis to great advantage in arriving at better decisions.

Although there is no theoretical connection between the planning-programming-budgeting system (PPBS) which has been instituted in the Federal government in recent years and any individual's narrowly defined field of inquiry called "systems analysis," there is a definite link between analysis and PPBS. In practice, the basic ideas of systems analysis and the approaches which lead to successful planning, programming, and budgeting are the same.

Because many people have the mistaken idea that systems analysis *is* mathematics, we should again emphasize here that mathematics is not even an integral part of systems analysis. Systems analysis is a way of thinking or a way of viewing problems. Often, mathematics plays a useful role in analysis, but just as sophisticated mathematics is not a necessary part of systems analysis, neither is it a necessary part of PPBS.

We should also emphasize that although the best-known and most publicized PPBS is that which has been instituted in the executive branch of the Federal government, similar systems are operating in business, industry, and state and local governments. In fact, many of the basic ideas of PPBS were developed in the business world and borrowed by government planners.[2]

The need for PPBS

The need for PPBS in the Federal government arises simply from the scarcity of resources which is at the root of most organizational decisions. Every government has the same broad objectives, as stated in the preamble to the United States Constitution—to "provide for the common defense" and to "promote the general welfare." In modern terms, this is interpreted to mean defense; the maintenance of order; the promotion of health, education, and welfare; economic development; and the conduct of essential services such as the Post Office. Each modern government does all these things to one degree or another, but no one attains each of these objectives to the ultimate. No one would claim, for instance, that the United States' defenses are per-

[2] For example, see George Steiner, "Program Budgeting: Business Contribution to Government Management," *Business Horizons,* Spring, 1965, pp. 43–52.

fect, or perhaps even as good as those of some other nations of the world. On the other hand, the educational level of the United States population is higher than that of most other countries. Thus, the attainment of government objectives is a process involving the *allocation of resources*—of compromises between money spent in one way to better achieve one objective and that spent in another way to achieve another objective. Once this basic concept of resource allocation is recognized as equally applicable to the activities of Federal, state, and local governments and to those of the military or business, the necessity for formal planning and analysis to achieve "best" allocations becomes clear. Such planning and analysis is the goal of PPBS.

Programs

Essential to PPBS is the concept of a program. However, this concept is not precisely defined, because it must be given a somewhat different interpretation in different organizations. Programs are closely related to the objectives of the organization. In fact, it is in part because the objectives of large organizations are often difficult to define that no single definition of a program is satisfactory. In practice, a number of criteria may be applied in the definition of a program.

One essential feature of a program is clear; it is *output oriented.* In other words, programs are defined first in terms of what the organization is trying to achieve, rather than in terms of the resources which the organization can bring to bear (inputs). The Bureau of the Budget uses the following principles to guide the development of appropriate output categories: [3]

1   *Program categories* are groupings of agency programs (or activities or operations) which serve the same broad objective (or mission) or which have generally similar objectives. Succinct captions or headings describing the objective should be applied to each such grouping. Obviously, each program category will contain programs which are complementary or are close substitutes in relation to the objectives to be attained. For example, a broad program objective is improvement of higher education. This could be a *program category,* and as such would contain Federal programs aiding undergraduate, graduate and vocational education, including construction of facilities, as well as such auxiliary Federal activities as library support and relevant research programs. . . .

2   *Program subcategories* are subdivisions which should be established

[3] U.S. Bureau of the Budget Bulletin 66-3, Oct. 12, 1965, p. 4.

within each program category, combining agency programs (or activities or operations) on the basis of narrower objectives contributing directly to the broad objectives for the program category as a whole. Thus, in the example given above, improvement of engineering and science and of language training could be two program subcategories within the program category of improvement of higher education.

3 *Program elements* are usually subdivisions of program subcategories and comprise the specific products (i.e., the goods and services) that contribute to the agency's objectives. Each program element is an integrated activity which combines personnel, other services, equipment and facilities. An example of a program element expressed in terms of the objectives served would be the number of teachers to be trained in using new mathematics.

For instance, a program structure for the United States Forest Service might be made up of such categories as timber production, outdoor recreation, and natural beauty. The Coast Guard's structure might include search and rescue, aids to navigation, law enforcement, etc. A university might use science and humanities categories, involving teaching and research subcategories. In business, natural programs are products or product lines. The obvious differences in these program structures imply that the designation of appropriate program structures is not subject to any inviolable rules.

Objectives and programs

The basic difficulty involved in defining appropriate programs has to do with the nebulous objectives of most large organizations. Even businesses, where profit maximization may seem to be the sole objective, in reality have much more complex objectives. This is evidenced by their charitable contributions and the periodic objections of some stockholders at annual meetings to their non-profit-oriented activities. In government and educational organizations, the objectives are not usually operationally defined, i.e., defined in a way in which attainment can be readily measured. For instance, the typical educational institution's objectives are, at best, vaguely stated as "preparing students to be good citizens" or "advancing our understanding of our environment."

Because objectives are often vaguely stated, the relationships between the organization's activities and its objectives are seldom precisely understood. However, most frequently the organization knows, or believes that it knows, those areas in which achievement will lead to the attainment of its goals. Such a nonrigorous relationship between outputs and goals is often an adequate basis for the definition of a meaningful program structure for an organization. The examples of potential program structures for the Forest

Service, the Coast Guard, and a university which were discussed above show this to be true, even though comprehensive goals for those organizations on which all branches of the Federal government would agree might not be easy to determine.

Determining a program structure

Since there are no hard-and-fast rules involved, the determination of a program structure is a pragmatic undertaking, involving alternative structures and a recognition that the structure chosen can itself have an important impact on the decisions which are to be made.

An important criterion to be used in this determination is that *the program structure should permit comparison of alternative methods of achieving objectives*, however vaguely defined these objectives may be. However, programs may also consist of a number of interactive components—the effectiveness of each of which depends on the others. Thus, in the Defense Department, Strategic Retaliatory Forces is a program because it relates to a national defense objective and can be broken down into elements—manned bombers, ICBMs, submarine-launched missiles, etc.—which are to some extent substitutes for one another and which involve questions of resource mix such as were treated in the previous chapter. On the other hand, the elements of a program may be complementary to one another, as in the case of the research and teaching elements of a university program.

Programs should emphasize extended planning horizons, say, five or ten years. This enhances the value of programs as bases for long-range planning.

Other practicalities and peculiarities of particular organizations enter into the definition of programs. Frequently, for instance, the time period over which the goal will be pursued is a natural criterion. Pure research is the best illustration of an activity which is not easily related to organizational outputs. Thus, its long-range nature naturally defines it as a distinct program of many organizations. However, applied research and development is most often related with specific organizational objectives, and thus it should be included in the same program category as the other activities related to the same objective.

It is sometimes necessary to have programs defined in terms of intermediate outputs rather than final outputs. Thus, while Strategic Retaliatory Forces, Continental Defense, and General Purpose Forces are Defense Department programs related to final outputs (national objectives), Airlift and Sealift is a program which is clearly related only to an intermediate output. However, since it lends itself nicely to the comparison of alternatives (mixes of airlift and sealift, for example), it is considered a program.

There is also a General Support program in the Department of Defense's program structure. This includes items which cannot be identified with another specific program but for which an accounting must obviously be made. In most organizations, it will be necessary to have some sort of catchall program as this. It is axiomatic to say that such catchalls are potential devices for hiding activities which are in fact closely identifiable with objectives and for which alternatives are conceivably available for consideration. Care should be taken at all levels to avoid having this happen, either purposefully or accidentally, since such a perversion of the program structure can easily negate the greatest value of the concept—that of comparing alternatives.

The program structure of an organization should not be allowed to become either (1) a reflection of the organization's administrative structure or (2) a way of putting new labels on old budget activities. The program structure need not reflect the organization's structure. It is often desirable to have basic program categories which cut across organizational lines to facilitate the comparison of alternative elements which are potential substitutes for one another. So too should a relabeling of old budget activities be avoided. As we shall see, there is nothing incompatible about a traditional budgeting process such as that which has been used by the Federal government and the program budget. The former can be developed from the latter. However, to do this meaningfully requires that planning and programming be done in the light of objectives and not in terms of inflexible budget categories.

Program budgeting

A *program budget* is a financial expression of a program plan, just as any budget is a plan for future expenditures. Usually the time period involved in such a plan is a year or two. However, every organization must orient its thinking toward a planning horizon which is much beyond one year. In industry, for example, the development and testing of a new product often require several years, and consumer-product life cycles—which often extend over many years, but seldom over many decades—require that business organizations look toward the distant as well as the short-term future. In government, the same need for advanced planning arises; e.g., a weapons system requires years for development, and a welfare program must be instituted, changed, and evaluated over a long period of time.

Traditionally, the budget of the Federal government has had two important characteristics which its critics regard as limiting the effectiveness of government expenditures. First, it is an annual budget, and thus it has limited usefulness as a basis for comprehensive long-range planning. Second, it is broken down into functional or object-class categories such as pay and allowances, construction, etc., rather than into categories which are related to governmental objectives.

In the context of defense planning, it became apparent that a budget of this variety was inadequate. The short-range nature of the annual budget precluded its use as a long-range planning document. Using the budget information, it was extremely difficult to gather together all the costs which would eventually result from a decision to undertake a program or to purchase a weapons system. Since the costs involved were scattered among a variety of appropriations and the budget projected requirements for only a year, the United States government found itself in the position of having purchased and operated many weapons systems and programs with little regard to, or knowledge of, the total cost. For example, operating costs, which may often be more significant than development and procurement costs, were not made apparent in the budgeting process.

Clearly, this confusion concerning the amount and timing of costs did not discourage various governmental units from proposing projects that could not be funded to completion. The visible evidence of this was the large number of weapons-system development projects which were canceled, at least partly because adequate advance planning was not required by the budgeting process.

Some important weapons systems had been specially "costed" under the traditional Federal government budgeting process for purposes of decision making, but such a procedure was not a natural product of the budget. The institution of a program budget, as a complement to the traditional budget, provided a basis for costing weapons systems and output-oriented programs of the government. Such costings are essential to the comparison and evaluation of alternatives, which is, in turn, a vital part of the conceptual framework for analysis of decision problems. Thus, the concept of a program and the program budget provide the basis for utilizing objective scientific analysis in strategic decision making.

The interaction of the programs, operating units, and staff functions of an organization in program budgeting is illustrated in Figure 6–1, which gives a hypothetical description of the U.S. Department of Defense. Each of the Armed Forces and each staff function conceivably cuts across each major program. Thus, by budgeting on a program basis, duplications can be eliminated and valid requirements for the accomplishment of objectives can be determined. For example, both the Navy and the Air Force contribute toward the strategic retaliatory mission via submarine-based missiles and long-range bombers. Also, all staff functions must exert efforts toward accomplishing these objectives.

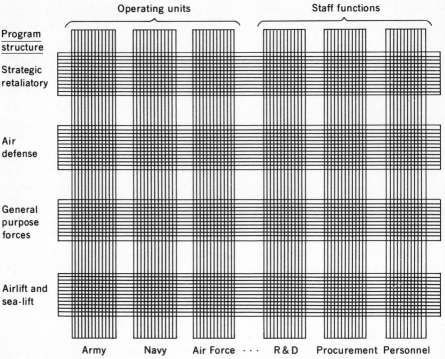

Figure 6-1   Programs and functions in the Department of Defense.

In the civilian sector, we may construct a hypothetical corporation to illustrate a similar interaction. Figure 6-2 depicts the interaction of operating units, staff functions, and programs for a corporation in the same fashion that Figure 6-1 does for the U.S. Department of Defense. One major program of the fictitious organization is plant nutrition. The corporation's chemical-products division is obviously involved, as is the agricultural-marketing division (which may sell bulk fertilizers to farmers) and the consumer-products division (which may sell both lawn-care chemicals and equipment to individual consumers). Similarly, in the animal-nutrition program, the chemical-products and agricultural-marketing divisions have interests in farm animal foods, just as the chemical- and consumer-products divisions might be concerned with pet-food products.

These statements succinctly summarize the important underpinnings of any PPBS. Moreover, they go beyond this to suggest both the procedures to be used and the analytic and staff resources which are necessary to accomplish the PPBS objectives.

There are three key elements in these basic concepts which should be ex-

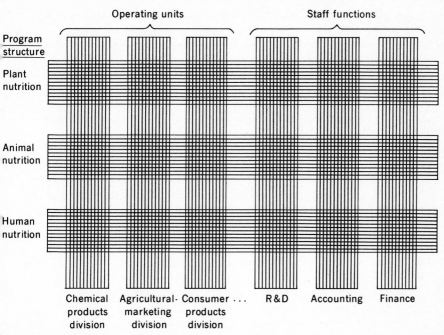

Figure 6-2   **Program and functions in a corporation.**

panded upon: analytic capability, the planning-programming-budgeting process, and information systems.[4]

Analytic capability

As we pointed out earlier, there is no necessary connection between a narrowly defined field called "systems analysis" and PPBS. There is, however, a necessity for analysis and the comparison of alternative ways of achieving objectives. Indeed, one of the primary purposes of instituting PPBS is to enable government decisions to be made on the basis of best choices from a considered range of alternatives.

Secretary of Defense Robert S. McNamara argued this cogently in an appearance before Congress.[5]

[4] Gene H. Fisher has discussed three essential considerations in program budgeting which are similar to those used here. See Gene H. Fisher, "The Role of Cost-Utility Analysis in Program Budgeting," in David Novick (ed.), *Program-Budgeting: Program Analysis and the Federal Budget*, RAND Corporation, Santa Monica, Calif., 1965, chap. 2.

[5] Secretary of Defense Robert S. McNamara, statement before the Committee on Armed Services on the Fiscal Year 1965–1969 Defense Program and the 1965 Defense Budget, Jan. 27, 1964.

As I have pointed out in previous appearances before this Committee, in adding to a Defense program as large as the one we now have, we soon encounter the law of diminishing returns, where each additional increment of resources used produces a proportionately smaller increment of overall defense capability. While the benefits to be gained from each additional increment cannot be measured with precision, careful cost/effectiveness analyses can greatly assist in eliminating those program proposals which clearly contribute little to our military strength in terms of the costs involved.

This principle is just as applicable to qualitative improvements in weapons systems as it is to quantitative increases in our forces. The relevant questions not only "Do we want the very best for our military force?", but also, "Is the additional capability truly required, and, if so, is this the least costly way of attaining it?"

Let me give you one hypothetical example to illustrate the point. Suppose we have two tactical figher aircraft which are identical in every important measure of performance, except one—Aircraft A can fly ten miles per hour faster than Aircraft B. However, Aircraft A costs $10,000 more per unit than Aircraft B. Thus, if we need about 1,000 aircraft, the total additional cost would be $10 million.

If we approach this problem from the viewpoint of a given amount of resources, the additional combat effectiveness represented by the greater speed of Aircraft A would have to be weighed against the additional combat effectiveness which the same $10 million could produce if applied to other defense purposes—more Aircraft B, more or better aircraft munitions, or more ships, or even more military family housing. And if we approach the problem from the point of view of a given amount of combat capability, we would have to determine whether that given amount could be achieved at less cost by buying, for example, more of Aircraft B or more aircraft munitions or better munitions, or perhaps surface-to-surface missiles. Thus, the fact that Aircarft A flies ten miles per hour faster than Aircraft B is not conclusive. We still have to determine whether the greater speed is worth the greater cost. This kind of determination is the heart of the planning-programming-budgeting or resources allocation problem within the Defense Department.

This statement makes it clear that analysis and the comparison of alternatives play an important role in the program budgeting of the Department of Defense. They also play just as significant a role in other parts of the government and in business. The reader should recall that systems analysis, as we have viewed its conceptual framework and its practice in the preceding two chapters, is a way of thinking which facilitates the comparison of alternatives in the light of objectives. As such, it represents today's best version of the analytic support which is essential to any successful PPBS.

The planning-programming-budgeting process

In Chapter 5, we described the long-range planning process in an industrial context. Our discussion of planning here is oriented toward the Federal government's system, but it is easy to see that the two are identical. *The Federal government's PPBS is a long-range planning system.* The reader will recall that in the last chapter, programs and budgets were treated as an intrinsic part of the planning process. Thus, the only difference is one of semantics. In the industrial environment, we call the entire process, beginning with the delineation of objectives and the definition of programs to fulfill those objectives, a *planning process.* In the Federal government, the process is called a *planning-programming-budgeting* system.

In the Federal government, plans are generated using guidelines laid down by the President, the Bureau of the Budget, and agency heads. Analyses are performed within agencies, and alternatives are compared for the agency head's consideration. The Bureau of the Budget performs much the same role that was described for the corporate budget and analysis staff in the civilian context of the previous chapter. Then, programs and budgets go to the President for review and final decision, culminating a planning process which is completely analogous to that described in Chapter 5.

Information systems

Just as analysis is basic to the support of good planning, programming, and budgeting, so too is information, in turn, essential to good analysis.

The primary tool of systems analysis is a model: an abstraction of the real world which is used to predict the effect of changes in a system on the performance of the system. As was illustrated in the previous chapter, we may need several levels and kinds of models in attacking strategic organizational decisions. *The rudiments of models, at all levels, are informational inputs.* In order to predict costs, one must have information concerning either historical costs or the relationship between cost and technology. In order to predict benefits, analogous data bases are necessary.

Thus, not only does the institution of PPBS require the development of an analytic capability, but it also requires that this capability be supported with an information system which provides both analysts and managers with *information appropriate to decision making.* This last phrase should be emphasized, since an accounting or budgeting system does not necessarily provide such information. Indeed, the Federal government budgeting system has not traditionally done so. Also, traditional accounting procedures, particularly those of the Federal government, have focused on the need to maintain checks on the honesty of officials and to limit their discretionary power.

Modern organizational accounting is of the *cost-accounting* variety, which is designed to fulfill some informational requirements necessary to the analysis of alternative programs. However, it is unlikely that any accounting system which is set up with the provisions of information for decision making and analysis as merely a convenient by-product will be a sufficient source of decision-oriented information.

In the past few years, great emphasis has been placed on the development of *management information systems* in government and industry. Management information systems are those which are developed on the basis of information requirements for decision making, as opposed to those traditional accounting systems which are oriented primarily toward information uses in terms of reports, information flow, concurrences, etc.[6]

Thus, the development of management information systems is essential to the support of analysis for the implementation of PPBS. In fact, it may well be that the greatest benefit to be derived from PPBS is precisely the information system which must be set up. The reason for this is the artistic nature of systems analysis and decision making. It is not inconceivable, for example, that the combination of the judgment and intuition necessary to all strategic decision making and the information required for rational decision making will result in less, and not more, emphasis on formal analysis. It may well be that the quality of decisions is more sensitive to the quality of information inputs than to the amount of formal systems analysis which is performed. Thus, while it is conceivable that an individual's subjective analysis could substitute for objective systems analysis, it is not possible that subjective analysis could obviate the need for high-quality relevant information as an input to decision making.

Of course, it is not likely that better relevant information will actually result in less emphasis on explicit systems analysis in the near future. Ample evidence is available to support the thesis that subjective analysis and objective analysis are complements rather than substitutes. Also, at the current state of our knowledge, it is usually the conceptual framework and models of systems analysis which are used to define the best informational inputs for decision making. Thus, when we speak of "relevant" information, we recognize that, in practice, the relevance of information is usually determined by its necessity as a part of, or as a complement to, objective systems analysis.

[6] See Thomas R. Prince, *Information Systems for Management Planning and Control*, Richard D. Irwin, Inc., Homewood, Ill., 1966.

PPBS in planning and execution

In discussing analysis and information systems as basic to PPBS, we have emphasized the need for information in support of the analysis of strategic decisions. There is no less need for high-quality analysis and relevant information in the execution phase of management.

Once decisions have been made and programs have been embarked on, the reporting of progress is an essential element of project control. Information concerning progress is thereby the primary ingredient necessary to ensure that goals are attained, or at least that progress is being made toward the attainment of desired goals. PPBS provides a standard against which progress toward organizational goals can be tracked and evaluated. For example, a comparison of actual versus budgeted financial and schedule data in a program can answer the question: "How well are we doing in the particular program?" Such information can then be used to redirect the organizational resources being applied to that program.

So too are there many decisions involved in the execution phase of management which require analysis. Although these decisions are of the tactical rather than the strategic variety, they are as important to project goals as strategic decisions are to overall goals.

Thus, the analytic capability and the management information system which support PPBS are important in both the planning and the execution phases of management. Since this part of the text is devoted to planning, we shall defer consideration of the execution function and the information-system implications until Part 3.

The Federal government's PPBS

The objectives of the Federal government's PPBS are stated in the basic Bureau of the Budget bulletin as follows: [7]

> The overall system is designed to enable each agency to:
>   1 Make available to top management more concrete and specific data relevant to broad decisions;
>   2 Spell out more concretely the objectives of Government programs;
>   3 Analyze systematically and present for agency head and Presidential review and decision possible alternative objectives and alternative programs to meet those objectives;
>   4 Evaluate thoroughly and compare the benefits and cost of programs;

[7] U.S. Bureau of the Budget Bulletin 66-3, Oct. 12, 1965, p. 3.

5   Produce total rather than partial cost estimates of programs;
6   Present on a multi-year basis the prospective costs and accomplishments of programs;
7   Review objectives and conduct program analyses on a continuing, year-round basis, instead of on a crowded schedule to meet budget deadlines.

The accomplishment of these objectives in the Federal government is based on a recognition of the three-dimensional nature of planning, programming, and budgeting. The first of these dimensions is universally recognized—resource inputs. These are the people, equipment, and organizational units to be allocated to various activities. The second dimension involves the variety of missions and goals to which the organization is directed—the output. Third is the time dimension, since few complex organizations pursue programs which are entirely short-range in nature.

These three dimensions are illustrated in Figure 6-3. Each element of that figure represents an expenditure of a given resource on a specific program during a given year. For example, the darkened element represents R&D allocations to program P_4 during the current year, and the row of elements behind the darkened one represents future R&D allocations to P_4.

In previous sections of this chapter, we discussed the salient features of the PPBS. To understand its operation in terms of these three dimensions, it is useful to consider the basic outputs of the Federal government's PPBS.

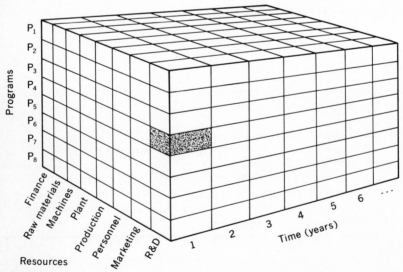

Figure 6-3

The two basic output documents are the *multiyear program and financial plan* (PFP) and the *program memorandum* (PM). Special studies constitute the third output element which plays an important role in decision making and budgeting.

The program and financial plan

A multiyear program and financial plan is a translation of concretely specified organizational objectives into combinations of activities and operations designed to achieve objectives within specified time periods.

The PFP is stated in terms of the program structure and covers, on a year-by-year basis, a period of years as determined by the nature of the organization's objectives and operations. In the Federal government, this period is frequently of five years' duration, but for many projects, longer durations may well be appropriate; e.g., for timber production, the appropriate time period may be much longer than five years.

The PFP should reflect a plan for the future. It is not constrained because authorizations for programs are expiring or because appropriate approvals have not been obtained. Rather, it should show programs at the levels which are deemed best for the duration of the multiyear plan.

The form of the PFP is essentially that of an outcome array under certainty. The multiyear nature of the plan implies that costs and benefits are to be broken down on a year-by-year basis. Table 6-1 summarizes the

Table 6-1   Benefit portion of outcome array for PFP

	LAST YEAR	THIS YEAR	NEXT YEAR	TWO YRS HENCE	THREE YRS HENCE	FOUR YRS HENCE	FIVE YRS HENCE
I. Manpower development assistance							
A.							
B. Manpower training							
1.							
2. On-the-job training (No. of workers trained—000)	xx	xx	xx	xx	xx	xx	xx

benefit portion of the plan for a government program category, "manpower development assistance"; a subcategory, "manpower training"; and an element, "on-the-job training." The appropriate benefit descriptor might be the number of workers trained. Other similar tables can also be presented as part of the PFP for other important benefit measures. The reason for determining these outcome descriptors of benefit is to permit the assessment of the degree of accomplishment of organizational objectives in quantitative terms. Doing so permits comparisons to be made on an objective basis. Of course, it will not always be possible to do this. As we have pointed out in discussing the practice of systems analysis, the development of comprehensive benefit measures is one of the greatest difficulties in applying the conceptual framework in the real world.

Two bases for comparison often prove useful in illustrating program benefits. One of these is historical. Note that Table 6-1 includes columns headed "last year" and "this year." Since this is a planning document for subsequent years (beginning with "next year"), historical benefit data on continuing programs are provided as a point of reference. Also, relative measures should be included wherever possible. By "relative measures," we mean those which relate the benefits to a standard such as the total possible benefit which could potentially be achieved. In using a benefit measure involving the number of workers trained, for example, one could relate the absolute number to the entire population of workers desiring or requiring training.

Other comparative bases are often included in PFPs as "special tabulations." For example, Federal agencies might tabulate the known programs of state and local governments or private companies which are directed toward similar objectives.

To complement these tabular presentations of the benefit portions of outcomes the cost portion should be presented in a form similar to that of Table 6-1. In doing so, the systems costs should be used, i.e., capital outlay, research, development, operating, maintenance, etc.

Thus, the basic elements of the PFP are simply a sequence of tables which present the benefits and costs associated with various program categories, subcategories, and elements of an organization. It represents, in concise summary form, a plan of recommended levels and mixes of programs for an organization. The word "recommended" should be emphasized since the PFP represents the results of analyses involving choice among alternatives and the assessment of priorities.

The PFP is reviewed, reappraised, and updated by the organization annually. Of course, the column headings in the tables are indexed by one year in doing so. In the Federal government, these reviewed PFP's after approval and modification by the agency head, the Bureau of the

Budget, and the President, form the basis for the agency's annual budget request.[8]

Program memorandums

A program memorandum (PM) for each of the program categories in the PFP should be prepared on a regular basis. *The PM supports the conclusions and recommendations presented in the PFP.* The PM should present the results and a summary of methodology used in analyzing and comparing alternative programs.

As outlined in the basic Bureau of the Budget bulletin on PPBS, the PM should: [9]

1 Spell out the specific programs recommended by the agency head for the multi-year time period being considered, show how these programs meet the needs of the American people in this area, show the total costs of recommended programs, and show the specific ways in which they differ from current programs and those of the past several years.

2 Describe program objectives and expected concrete accomplishments and costs for several years into the future.

3 Describe program objectives insofar as possible in quantitative physical terms.

4 Compare the effectiveness and the cost of alternative objectives, of alternative *types* of programs designed to meet the same or comparable objectives, and of different *levels* within any given program category. This comparison should identify past experience, the alternatives which are believed worthy of consideration, earlier differing recommendations, earlier cost and performance estimates, and the reasons for change in these estimates.

5 Make explicit the assumptions and criteria which support recommended programs.

6 Identify and analyze the main uncertainties in the assumptions and in estimated program effectiveness or costs, and show the sensitivity of recommendations to these uncertainties.

In effect, the PM objectively summarizes the systems analyses which have been performed and presents the results in the form of recommendations. The PM serves as a basic planning document throughout the organization, since it represents in summary form the analytic statement of, and justification for, the organization's current objectives and programs.

[8] Since the Federal government's budget is of the object-class variety rather than the program variety, program costs must currently be translated into the financial terms used in budget preparation, presentation, and reporting.

[9] U.S. Bureau of the Budget Bulletin 66-3, Oct. 12, 1965, p. 8.

One of the basic virtues of objective analysis is made clear by the PM. This feature—the reproducibility of analysis—means that a succinct statement of assumptions, objectives, and methodology should be an adequate basis for a check on the analysis performed. If, for example, other alternatives are brought to light after the PM is made up, it should be possible to reproduce the analysis and thereby compare the new alternative with those which had previously been considered.

Special studies

The Federal government's PPBS also specifically incorporates a provision for special studies which may be carried out at the request of top management or on the initiative of analysts. These studies are envisioned to be complementary to the program studies carried out for incorporation into the PMs. In general, their purpose is to cast light on areas in which knowledge would be helpful to decision making, even though specific programs may not be anticipated in the area.

The budget process

The PMs and special studies form the basic inputs to the budget process in the Federal government's PPBS. All annual budget requests are based on the "next year" portion of the PFP as adjusted by top management.

An illustrative annual cycle for a Federal agency has been given by the Bureau of the Budget. It envisions a year-round process of reevaluating and updating objectives, programs, and predicted outcomes (benefits and costs): [10]

> *January.* Changes are made by the agency to the prior multi-year program plan to conform to Presidential decisions as reflected in the budget sent to Congress.
>
> *March.* By March bureaus or similar major organizational units within the agency will submit to the agency head their current appraisals of approved program objectives and multi-year plans and their proposals for (a) needed modifications, including measures to meet new needs and to take account of changing and expiring needs, and (b) extension of plans to cover an added year. . . . The Director of the Bureau of the Budget will advise the agency head of any change in the overall policies and objectives upon which the currently approved plan is based.
>
> *April.* On the basis of instructions from the agency head following his review of bureau submissions, bureaus develop *specific* program plans.

[10] *Ibid.*, pp. 10–11.

May. Analytic staffs complete Program Memoranda. Agency head reviews program plans and approves Program Memoranda for submission to the Bureau of the Budget. He may want to assign additional studies on the basis of this review.

May–June. The budget preview is conducted by the Bureau of the Budget. The basic documents for this preview are the Program of Memoranda prepared by agencies which are to be submitted to the Bureau of the Budget . . . and Special Studies to be submitted. . . . Presidential guidance will be obtained, where necessary, on major policy issues and on the fiscal outlook.

July–August. Appropriate changes to program plans are made on the basis of the guidance received and of congressional legislation and appropriations. Budget estimates, including those for new legislative proposals, are developed on the basis of the first year of the currently approved program plans. . . .

September. Budget estimates and agency legislative programs are submitted to the Bureau of the Budget.

October–December. Budget Bureau reviews budget estimates, consults with agencies, and makes its recommendation to the President. Presidential decisions are transmitted to agencies, the budget is prepared for submission to Congress, and the legislative program is prepared.

January. Changes are again made by the agency to the multi-year program plan to conform to Presidential decisions as reflected in the budget sent to the Congress.

Summary

The institution of PPBS in any large organization calls for the development of an analytic capability and a management information system. These two facets are important in their own right and also in terms of their implications for the other portions of the organization.

For example, the development of a program structure requires that the organization subjectively analyze its goals and relate them to overall objectives. Therefore, the organization which has accomplished this initial phase of instituting a PPBS has invariably come to understand itself better than it did previously.

Thus, *analysis* and *information* are key elements of PPBS—both in terms of hiring analysts and purchasing data-processing equipment and in terms of the insights which analysis and information gathering provide to the people who make up the organization.

The relationship between PPBS and analysis is an intrinsic one. Analysis provides the basis on which alternatives are compared and choices are made. Therefore, the conceptual framework and the practice of systems analysis, as described in previous chapters, are closely related to the implementation of an effective PPBS.

Recommended readings

Enke, Stephen (ed): *Defense Management,* Prentice-Hall, Inc., Englewood Cliffs, N.J., 1967.

Grosse, Robert N., and Arnold Proschan: "The Annual Cycle: Planning-Programming-Budgeting," in Stephen Enke (ed.), *Defense Management,* Prentice-Hall, Inc., Englewood Cliffs, N.J., 1967, chap. 2.

Hitch, Charles J.: "A Planning-Programming-Budgeting System," in Fremont E. Kast and James E. Rosenzweig (eds.), *Science, Technology, and Management,* McGraw-Hill Book Company, New York, 1963, chap. 6.

————: "Plans, Programs and Budgets in the Department of Defense," *Operations Research,* vol. 11, no. 1, pp. 1–17, January–February, 1963.

Kast, Fremont E., and James E. Rosenzweig (eds.): *Science, Technology, and Management,* McGraw-Hill, Book Company, New York, 1963.

Kopkind, Andrew: "The Future Planners," *New Republic,* Feb. 25, 1967, pp. 19–23.

McKean, Roland N.: *Efficiency in Government through Systems Analysis,* John Wiley & Sons, Inc., New York, 1958.

————: "Remaining Difficulties in Program Budgeting," in Stephen Enke (ed.), *Defense Management,* Prentice-Hall, Inc., Englewood Cliffs, N.J., 1967, chap. 4.

Niskanen, William A.: "The Defense Resource Allocation Process," in Stephen Enke (ed.), *Defense Management,* Prentice-Hall, Inc., Englewood Cliffs, N.J., 1967, chap. 1.

Quade, E. S.: *Systems Analysis Techniques for Planning-Programming-Budgeting,* RAND Corporation, P–3322, Santa Monica, Calif., March, 1966.

Smalter, Donald J.: "Influence of Department of Defense on Corporate Planning," *Management Technology,* vol. 4, no. 2 pp. 115–138, December, 1964.

Steiner, George: "Program Budgeting: Business Contribution to Government Management," *Business Horizons,* Spring, 1965, pp. 43–52.

PART 3

PROJECT MANAGEMENT IN EXECUTING DECISIONS

CHAPTER 7
The Project Environment

Adoption of the program [project]
management concept has been
influenced by rapid technological
advancements, changing industrial
complexes, the rise of an adverse
world power, and critical lead times.[1]

More and more during the last decade, contractors doing work for government agencies have established special offices, each of which is concerned with the management of a single project. Project managers and project-management techniques have become so well accepted that many authorities now believe that a company organized along functional lines only cannot successfully handle more than one large project at a time. Where multiple projects are being conducted, some reorientation of the functional organization is required. This modification of the industrial structure to form temporary task forces creates unique relationships. People from several different functions—both *line* and *staff*—are thrown together to attain a common objective. This changing organizational posture is a product of our dynamic technological environment.

Project management has been used in government agencies and in industries involved with government, particularly the Department of Defense,

[1] Fremont E. Kast and James E. Rosenzweig, *Science, Technology, and Management: An Overview*, McGraw-Hill Book Company, New York, 1963, p. 30.

for some time. Government is widespread and has become an important part of our national economy. The maintenance of an effective defense force, the research that is being conducted in the area of space travel, and the growing involvement of the Federal government in other economic affairs of the country indicate that government-related activities will continue to expand and that project-management techniques will also expand.

Weapons-system management

The Department of Defense is the largest single customer of the American industrial complex; the government depends almost exclusively on private industry for the development and acquisition of weaponry.[2] Unlike the situation in the civilian consumer market, the magnitude and scale of the military market are determined by advance planning in the government.[3] The Federal budget plays a primary role in determining the direction for defense buying. Military expenditures are authorized as the result of continual interaction of many demands and requirements—not only of the defense sector of the economy, but of nondefense programs and policies as well.

Recent experience in military preparedness suggests that a requirement will continue to exist for a high level of military technology. The Office of the Secretary of Defense has received greater authority in the management of the military, economic, and social aspects of national defense. Traditional roles and missions of the military departments have changed drastically. Some functions of the Armed Forces have been merged and unified, and a single national system of defense may evolve. Technical breakthroughs, protracted weapon development cycles, and increasing attention to the cost-effectiveness relationship of weaponry have stimulated the need for innovation in existing management philosophies.

It is in this environment that the weaponry of today is developed and produced; the process is a dynamic one, carried out in an environment of risk and uncertainty. Peck and Scherer have divided uncertainty factors into two broad classes: [4]

[2] "Weaponry" is a general term connoting the varied instruments designed to inflict damage on an enemy through the destruction of physical or mental capabilities. The term "weapons system" refers to a highly sophisticated weapon composed of a combination of equipment, skills, and managerial know-how, which as an integrated entity is capable of effectively destroying an enemy.

[3] For our purposes, a *market* is defined as a place where buyers and sellers exchange a commodity or a service.

[4] Merton J. Peck and Frederick M. Scherer, *The Weapons Acquisition Process: An Economic Analysis*, Harvard University, Division of Research, Graduate School of Business Administration, Boston, 1962, p. 24.

Internal (or technological) uncertainties relate to the possible incidence of unforeseen technical difficulties in the development of a
specific weapon system. External uncertainties relate to factors external
to an individual project and yet affecting the course and outcome of
the project. They originate in the pace of technological change in
weaponry, changes in strategic requirements, and shifts in government
policy.

Comparing the consumer-goods, and the defense markets

The risk and uncertainty factors that characterize the defense market create
market conditions for defense products that are different from those found in
the consumer market. Other markets, while not as singular as the defense
market, do have many of the characteristics of the defense market. For
example, the market for industrial goods (goods, such as machine tools,
which are used in producing consumer goods) and the construction market
have some of the problems of defense buying and selling. One such aspect
is that the purchasing process is consummated with a formal contract after
bids have been submitted and terms have been negotiated.

However, in the defense market, the financial and managerial risks of the
contractor center around a small number of ventures. It is this environment
in which project-management techniques had their genesis and where these
techniques have become well accepted.[5]

In the defense market, the actual exchange of the product (e.g., the
weapons system) takes place long after the contract for it has been consummated. But there is something more complex in the producer-consumer
relationship in this particular market than just a contractual agreement.
A defense producer begins the study and development phase of the work
well in advance of the government's request for a contractual bid. Companies in the defense industry are constantly studying and evaluating the
military market, hoping to determine the direction military technology will
take. Frequently, unsolicited proposals are submitted to the government,
and hence a dependent relationship exists between government and the
defense industry long before (and after) a defense contract is signed. The
involvement between the Department of Defense and a defense contractor
develops into a bilateral monopoly market, and the government's dependence on a given contractor to fulfill the commitment increases the risk and
uncertainty factors.[6]

[5] See David I. Cleland, "The Project Manager: Manager Extraordinary," *Defense
Industry Bulletin*, May, 1965.
[6] A bilateral monopoly, in economic terms, is a one-buyer–one-seller relationship,
whereas the relationship in the consumer-goods market is more typically one involving

The salient characteristics of the defense and the consumer-goods markets in the United States are summarized in the following table.

CONSUMER-GOODS MARKET	DEFENSE MARKET
Seller provides initiative for producing products. The basis for his decision is an analysis of the potential market, but he has no certain knowledge of the product's salability.	Buyer establishes the requirement for the product, after which the producer formally begins development and production.
Production for inventory is made necessary by differences in economies of aggregation at producer and retail levels.*	Production is for immediate use.
Many homogeneous products; buyer has a wide range of choice. There is some real or imagined product differentiation.	Relatively few heterogeneous products are produced. The buyer has a choice but because of the time and cost involved in bringing the substitute into fruition, there is no real substitutability.
Price is a dominant factor in choice because adequate and competing substitutes are often available.	Price is only one of many factors, including quality, availability, and technology, necessary to support a specific military requirement.
The operation of the market is somewhat impersonal; it is the aggregate of the wants and needs of many buyers and sellers acting independently.	Market system is personal; the buyer's agent becomes deeply involved with the seller's organization. The marketplace centers around a few buying agencies operating under executive control of the Department of Defense.
Producer finances the development-production effort himself.	In the main, the buyer finances most of the development and may provide equipment and facilities for the producer to use.

a few sellers (or many sellers) and many buyers. A bilateral monopoly arises when a single seller deals with a single buyer. There is a high degree of interdependency; one cannot survive without the other.

* These differences in the economies of aggregation mean simply that producers find it economical to manufacture in large quantities, while retailers desire small quantities of wider varieties of products.

CONSUMER-GOODS MARKET	DEFENSE MARKET
Market is characterized by monopolistic competition.	Market is essentially one-customer. Although different agents are involved, they all function under uniform policies and procedures of the Department of Defense.
Prices for the most part are determined by competition in the usual economic sense.	Price is determined by an evaluation of expected and actual costs. Significant competition may occur between a few producers before the final producer is chosen.
Relatively insensitive to domestic and international politics.	Highly sensitive to domestic and international politics and intrigue.
Demand is either relatively constant (e.g., for staples) or tends to be a function of income (e.g., for nonessentials).	Demand is a function of the technology offered by the seller or our nation's estimate of that possessed by the potential enemy. Scientific achievement may be a major requirement.
Requirements for a given model are relatively stable. Model changes affect demand, but the basic utility of the product changes slowly.	International tension can cause requirements to fluctuate rapidly and violently. The product may be obsolete in terms of military technology as soon as the prototype is produced.
Little or no price negotiation is carried on; the product is offered at a price that is met or not, depending on individual consumer motivation. With a wide range of alternatives, the consumer elects an alternative source rather than haggle over prices.	Price is negotiated, in the main, with selected suppliers chosen by the buyer. The defense customer of a large weapons system normally requests proposals from the producers capable of developing and producing one.

The consumer-goods market operates on the basis of supply and demand, which involves some risks and uncertainties. However, even though a vast proportion of new consumer products become marketing failures,[7]

[7] It has been estimated that 80 to 90 percent of newly introduced packaged grocery products are marketing failures, for example. See Peter J. Hilton, *New Product Introduction for Small Business Owners,* Small Business Management Series, no. 17, Government Printing Office, Washington, D.C.

the risks and uncertainty involved do not compare with those to be found in the defense industry. The financial outlay required for research, capital equipment, and unique test facilities to develop a weapons system is frequently of such magnitude that a private company alone cannot afford it. The government has recognized this and often supports these efforts by providing industrial facilities, advance and progress payments, and assistance in acquiring strategic materials.

The nature of the uncertainties is also different in the two markets. Even though consumer acceptance is better defined in the defense market, rapid product obsolescence, changes in military demand and Department of Defense management philosophies, high technological risk (a continual widening of the state of the art), and the vagaries of potential enemy behavior all contribute to great uncertainty. These risk factors, when combined with changes in managerial and organizational relationships, create an environment substantially different from that found in the consumer-goods market.

Perhaps the greatest difference between the consumer-goods market and the defense market is the buyer-seller interdependency and the organizational involvement this entails. Although there are many "agents" representing the government, they operate under standard policies of the Department of Defense. The result is a one-buyer–one-seller relationship in a joint venture extending throughout the life cycle of the system or project.

Thus, one cannot today look at the defense industry environment and assume transferability of characteristics, policies, and *modus operandi* from the consumer-goods industry. There are different forces and motivations in the two markets which serve to differentiate them in ways which are both obvious and subtle.

Traditional management thought [8]

To make a meaningful comparison of project management and traditional management, one must begin with the ideas behind traditional management theory. It should be recalled, however, that these ideas were developed for organizations that were smaller and environments that were simpler than those of today.

---

[8] Some of the thoughts in this section have been paraphrased from William H. Read, "The Decline of Hierarchy in Industrial Organizations," *Business Horizons,* Fall, 1965. Used by permission.

The mainstream of traditional thought

The traditional theory of management evolved slowly over a period of time from the charismatic leader-follower arrangement. Some of the basic assumptions of traditional theory are those of bygone times.[9]

PYRAMIDAL STRUCTURE   The organization is viewed as a vertical pyramidal structure functioning as an integrated entity on a scalar basis. Implicit in this thought is the gradation of value placed on the different levels in the organization. The vertical levels approximate the gradations of competency. Therefore, the decisive and salient business is conducted up and down the hierarchy. Goals are established by assigning them as the responsibility of an official in the hierarchy; this official exercises specific authority derived from the level of his organizational position. The more crucial and important decisions are made at higher levels in the organization. Strategic decisions are combined with strategic policies and planning; routine decision making is delegated downward to a lower echelon in the hierarchy. Authority to execute decisions is passed down the hierarchy; information and responsibility are exacted upward through the intervening layers of executives.

SUPERIORS AND SUBORDINATES   Since the enterprise functions vertically, it relies almost entirely on superior-subordinate relationships.[10] Therefore, a strong superior-subordinate relationship is required to perserve unity of command and ensure unanimity of objective. If healthy relationships exist in the recurring chain of superiors and subordinates in the organization, the objective will be attained and the participants in the organization will gain economic, psychological, and sociological satisfaction in their jobs. The superior located higher in the structure presumably has more authority. Peer, associate, and informal relationships are present, but do not interfere with the legal distribution of power and influence in the organization.

DEPARTMENTATION   The alignment of an organization is based on some technique of departmentation, such as functional homogeneity, similarity of product, territorial location, etc. In organization by functional homogeneity, certain functions are organic; that is, they are basic functions

[9] There have been many attacks on the traditional school, whose origin can be traced to Frederick W. Taylor, Henri Fayol, and Max Weber. For example, see Waino W. Suojanen, *The Dynamics of Management*, Holt, Rinehart and Winston, Inc., New York, 1966. The authors do not propose to continue this attack. What is desired is a comparison of the *functional* and the *project* approaches.

[10] Frank J. Jasinski, "Adapting Organization to New Technology," *Harvard Business Review*, January–February, 1959, p. 80.

whose performance is vital to the perpetuation of the activity.[11] Separation of the business into organic functions encourages parochialism; each manager will be more concerned with his area of effort than with the overall coordinated effort. However, the functional manager will be able to maintain integrated staff action through lateral staff coordination.

LINE AND STAFF   Organizational groups have a basic dichotomy, i.e., the *line* and the *staff*. Line makes the salient decisions by exercising command prerogatives. Staff does the thinking and planning. The staff official advises and counsels; his authority to command is limited by his ability (based primarily on technical competence) to influence the line official. The staff member does not issue orders to a line official, but facilitates and prescribes methods and procedures. Those in line positions plan and decide. Specialized activities apart from the line organization are staff functions. The nature of the line-staff relationships depends on a command-counsel parity. The staff is expected to influence the judgment of the line official; therefore, the staff exercises its authority by providing counsel to the line official.

THE SCALAR CHAIN   The authority patterns in the traditional model of management follow the scalar chain of command. Authority flows from the highest to the lowest level, following every link in the chain. Subordinates receive orders from one superior only. Work is accomplished by relatively autonomous functional units of the organization. Individual authority is more or less constrained by the boundaries of the unit and by explicit delegation extended in the documentation. Everyday activities are set by the alignment reflected in the organizational chart. Horizontal relationships exist through informal organizations, committees, staff meetings, or formal coordination processes.

GOALS   Goals are established only by making them the responsibility of some official and some office. When a new task is evolved, it must be assigned to an appropriate unit in the hierarchical chain. Higher-level individuals exercise authority and do most, if not all, of the directing and guiding of important matters. Authority patterns between managers and technicians in different independent organizations are ignored.

DECISION MAKING   Qualitative management theory has, in the main, approached decision making from the basis of several distinct phases:

---

[11] See Ralph C. Davis, *The Fundamentals of Top Management*, Harper & Row, Publishers, Incorporated, New York, 1951, for a full discussion of the organic business functions.

Defining the problem
Analyzing the problem
Developing alternative solutions
Selecting the best solution
Converting the solution into effective action

Each of these phases has several steps and provides a framework for analyzing decision making in management. In the traditional approach, heavy reliance is placed on developing executive judgment for decision making through careful selection, education, and training of the individual. The role played by experience in the decision process has been stressed; i.e., experience in various management positions sharpens one's ability to select the most favorable alternative from among the choices available.

COMMITTEE ACTION   Meetings, outside organizations, and committees are the means for the horizontal and external relationships needed to maintain the integrity of the organization. Here, the traditional and time-consuming formal channels of communication are bypassed, and the organizational activities, both within the parent unit and beween the parent unit and other organizations, are coordinated in the total managerial environment.

ORGANIZATIONAL POSITION   Each position within the organization has a fixed and official area of jurisdiction, and this area is delineated in authority patterns and evidenced in job descriptions, policy manuals, etc. The specific description of a position within the hierarchy includes the facilities necessary to perform a task or group of tasks except for an element of supervision held in the superior position. To each position, except the lowest, a degree of authority is given, and a reciprocal degree of responsibility is exacted. A clear distinction must be drawn between the duty assignments for different jobs. Responsibilities for each job should be clearly defined, thereby encouraging everyone to conform to his job specification. No one should be responsible for many different activities except as those activities relate to the achievement of a common objective.

REWARDS AND PUNISHMENT   The system of rewards and punishment in organizations is copied from that of the church, the state, and the military establishments. This system relies on the assumptions stated by Shull: [12]

[12] Fremont A. Shull, *Matrix Structure and Project Authority for Optimizing Organizational Capacity,* Southern Illinois University, Business Research Bureau, Carbondale, Ill., October, 1965, p. 100.

. . . motives and attitudes of people are the same without regard to the collectivity in which they perform or the nature of the external environment in which the organization exists;
    . . . leadership, communication, and participation needs of organizations are alike without regard to the nature of, and emphasis upon, specific survival and growth needs; and thus . . . the nature and type of the coordination and inducement systems in different organizations should be more similar than dissimilar.

MANAGEMENT PRINCIPLES   Proponents of the traditional form of organization tend to explain and justify their organizational forms and their *modus operandi* in terms of principles of the organization.[13] The principles relating to the management function apply to the management of any kind of enterprise. They provide the conceptual framework for the theory and are used as fundamental truths, applicable to any given environment and valuable in predicting results. The body of related principles is referred to as the "theory." A bureaucracy is guided by general goals or objectives in a framework of a management theory and by a set of rules and principles which determine all conduct. The individual and the bureaucratic position are separated, with an impersonal, routine, rational result.

SPAN OF CONTROL   Since areas of responsibility in the organization are limited and fixed, and since each area of responsibility has its limits of authority, the number of subordinates that a supervisor controls must be correspondingly limited. Each organizational position (except, of course, the last one in the chain of echelons) has responsibilities that cannot be delegated; thus, the responsibilities of a position increase with the number of subordinate units it controls. In traditional theory, this "span of control" has received much attention, directed toward showing how restricting the span of control can improve executive effectiveness.[14] Several writers have attacked the validity of the span of control in terms of its theoretical soundness. Herbert Simon finds fault with the principle in that it produces excessive red tape.[15] Each contact between organizational members must be carried upward to a common superior—a needless waste of time and effort.

---

[13] For example, see the principles of organization listed by James D. Mooney in his essay in L. H. Gulich and L. Urwick (eds.), *Papers on the Science of Administration*, New York Institute of Public Administration, New York, 1937. For a current discussion of management principles, see Harold D. Koontz and Cyril J. O'Donnell, *Principles of Management*, 3d ed., McGraw-Hill Book Company, New York, 1964.

[14] See, for example, A. V. Graicunas, "Relationship in Organization," in Gulick and Urwick, *op. cit.;* and Lyndall F. Urwick, "The Manager's Span of Control," *Harvard Business Review*, (May-June, 1956).

[15] Herbert A. Simon, *Administrative Behavior*, The Macmillan Company, New York, 1947, pp. 26–28.

Davis discusses the problem of "layering" in large organizations,[16] due to the inactive role of intervening layers of executives in the hierarchy. The search for an optimum span of control has, in the authors' opinion, created intervening levels and increased the distance between the top-level executives and the front-line supervisors directly concerned with organizational objectives. Recent literature on the span of management (span of control) reflects a growing disenchantment with the concept and recognizes that many variables in the management environment affect the number of subordinates one can supervise effectively.

Bureaucracy

The principal proponent of traditional theory is *bureaucracy*. The bureaucratic organization is an easy object of ridicule, but this is somewhat ironic since bureaucratic organizations provide a significant proportion of today's employment. Bureaucratic organizations run our government and manage our military forces. Some religious organizations contain vestiges of a bureaucracy, and heads of bureaucratic organizations shape our economic, social, and industrial worlds.

CHARACTERISTICS   An organization can be considered bureaucratic when it exhibits characteristics such as the following:

1 It is so large that the individuals cannot know all the other members.

2 Its members pursue a career in the organization and depend on it for most of their income. Individuals have a serious commitment to the organization and its provincial viewpoint. They feel restricted in voicing personal views, particularly if these views run counter to the prevailing modes of thought.

3 It includes many levels of management in the hierarchy, and promotions are based on how well the individual performs the organizational role. The individual's personal objectives are subordinated to the organizational goal. Efficiency, integrity, loyalty, and individual motivation are expected of the employee. Within a given bureau, however, are many types of officials—ranging from those who are motivated by self-interest ("What's in it for me?") to those few motivated by loyalty and self-sacrifice.

4 It tends to perpetuate itself, to expand, regardless of whether or not there is any real need for its services. This phenomenon is aptly described in C. Northcote Parkinson's famous first law: "Work expands so as to fill the time available for its completion." [17] An organization's propensity to expand is in direct proportion to its ability to attract and retain capable personnel. An expanding organization normally provides its leaders with increased

[16] Davis, *op. cit.*
[17] C. Northcote Parkinson, *Parkinson's Law and Other Studies in Administration,* Houghton Mifflin Company, Boston, 1962, p. 2.

power, income, and prestige, so that leaders encourage growth. The growth of an organization is also a deterrent to internal conflict since it enables the new members to improve their status without lowering that of the old.

ORGANIZATION SIZE   Increasing the size of an organization may very well improve the quality of its performance and its chances for survival. Therefore, the organizational leaders may seek expansion to reduce internal dissension and improve the morale of the organization. The advantages of being a large organization, in terms of continued life, are pointed out by William H. Starbuck in his analysis of organizational growth:[18]

> Large organizations have a better chance to survive than small ones. Large organizations are harder to destroy and harder to change than small ones (because they embody greater sunk costs); so they tend to be more resistant to external pressures. They also spend more on research and development (both in total and per employee), hence they can better develop new techniques useful in augmenting their power.
> Very large organizations can impose a certain degree of stability upon their external environment, whereas smaller ones cannot. Increased environmental stability reduces uncertainty and anxiety and solidifies the control of high ranking officials.

Other characteristics of bureaucracies can be summarized as follows:

1   A bureaucracy does not outlive its usefulness. It shifts its functions in order to survive and thus perpetuates the need for its existence.

2   There is a heavy dependence on formal policies and rules to motivate and guide behavior. An informal authority structure and an informal communications network, however, may exist side by side with the formal network, and this informal structure may result in the development of intense personal loyalties and deep involvements among the members, particularly among officials in the higher echelons of the hierarchy.

3   Officials near the top of a bureaucracy have a greater breadth of information about affairs in the organization than those below. Individuals at lower levels, however, have more detailed knowledge about their particular activities. Therefore, no one knows everything about what is going on in the organization.

Questioning the traditional model

The organizational characteristics of bureaucracy trace back to the church and military organizational models. Central to the bureaucratic form is the pyramidal organizational structure and the idea that authority is delegated

---

[18] William H. Starbuck, "Organizational Growth and Development," in J. G. March (ed.), *Handbook of Organizations,* Rand McNally & Company, Chicago, 1964.

downward. Many of the principles rest on speculation rather than empirical research and fall considerably short of being like the laws of the physical sciences. Unity of command may be essential on the battlefield, but it becomes unnecessary in many of our contemporary organizations when the environment is not so "crises centered," but rather resembles a society of coequals working in "knowledge-centered" organizations.

CRISES-CENTERED ORGANIZATIONS [19]   An executive in a crises-centered organization (for example, a military unit in combat conditions) uses direct command authority to effect management control. There may be little opportunity for judgment on the part of the subordinates except within the narrow definition of the objective. While the subordinates are expected to display initiative, there is less opportunity for the free discussions necessary for participative management. Crises-centered management is usually related to the military organization; yet only a very small proportion of the military forces engage in combat with the enemy. In recent years the impact of technology has been felt in military weapons. The result has been the emergence of a military leader who is a manager-technologist and whose management techniques are very similar to those found in industrial and educational organizations. To an increasing extent, the military organization is faced with a management situation where the problems are the same as those found in knowledge-centered organizations. The coexistence of a crises-centered and a knowledge-centered organization in the military establishment has resulted in a modification of the image of a military officer; rather than a decisive, intuitive person who must cope with his environment under adverse conditions, he is now conceived as an individual who must also use deliberate analysis to deal with the environment.

The present-day military organization is necessarily composed of varied forms, ranging from pure military complements to those made up of military and civilian personnel in varying proportions. In these mixed organizations, and in many pure military organizations as well, the management techniques must be designed to reflect a knowledge-centered environment.

KNOWLEDGE-CENTERED ORGANIZATIONS   In the knowledge-centered organization, such as a project team whose goal is to develop and produce a weapons system, there are closely coordinated, integrated teams that circumvent chains of command and depend on a high degree of reciprocity between the participants. In this type of organization, the traditional functional theory has some application, but if followed slavishly, it results in an authoritative

[19] This discussion of crises-centered organizations and knowledge-centered organizations is based on Suojanen, *op. cit.*, pp. 108–111. Used by permission.

environment which can offend and stifle the creative bent of the members. The knowledge-centered activity is more participative—there is greater reliance on peers and associates within a complex of organizations, and there is more colleague authority and responsibility.

GOING BEYOND TRADITIONAL THEORY   For many years, the traditional theory of management was the model taught in management courses. Today, however, traditional theory serves merely as the point of departure in the development of a philosophy of management. The textbook principles of organization—hierarchical structure, authority, unity of command, task specialization, span of control, line-staff division, parity of responsibility and authority, the sanctity of the superior-subordinate relationship, etc.—comprise a complex of assumptions which have had a profound influence on management thought over several generations. Many of the principles were derived from the military and church establishments, which differ from modern business organizations in many respects, particularly in that they ignore the political, social, and economic realities of this changing environment. An example is the traditional principle of operating by the organizational chart, which is, at best, a picture of how the organizational groups relate to one another at a given moment in time. In spite of the organizational chart, managers at all levels find their behavior and their *modus operandi* controlled by many others in the environment besides their superior(s). The traditional theory assumes some factors about human behavior and organizational interdependency that are not as true today as they were in the simpler organizations of the past, when the system of rewards and punishments provided for more negative than positive motivation. There has been insufficient attention given to the interdependencies that exist between organizations and individuals in their environment. More and more attention must be paid to the management problem of providing an environment in which the contributors can support one another in a reciprocal arrangement. The principles of the feudal hierarchy, the military authority, and the patriarchy of the church were transferred to Max Weber's bureaucracy, where public and private business is carried out "according to calculable rules and without regard for persons." The realities of modern industrial competition cause serious doubt about the universality of the traditional ideas.

For some time it has been realized that the flow of work and the use of authority have significant lateral and horizontal relations. The role of the superior has changed from that of a powerful executive who controls the people to that of a manager who provides an environment in which his people can work with the many different groups in the total environment.

Bureaucratic theory considers that the main problems of management exist only within the boundaries of the parent organization. Little attention has been given to the manager's effect on contacts and negotiations outside the company. These contacts (with bankers, suppliers, customers, and civic organizations, to name just a few) can be time consuming and limit the time available to him for internal company affairs. The success of a company may well depend on its executives' accepting their role in the environment in which the company competes and on their relating that role to the company's needs.

THEORY X AND THEORY Y   The traditional view of management was seriously challenged by Douglas McGregor in his discussion of two managers, one of whom operates under *Theory X* and the other under *Theory Y*. According to McGregor, behind every managerial decision or action are assumptions about human nature and human behavior; for Theory X these assumptions are: [20]

> The average human being has an inherent dislike of work and will avoid it if he can.
>
> Because of this human characteristic of dislike of work, most people must be coerced, controlled, directed, threatened with punishment to get them to put forth adequate effort toward the achievement of organizational objectives.
>
> The average human being prefers to be directed, wishes to avoid responsibility, has relatively little ambition, wants security above all.

Theory Y assumptions about human behavior are in dramatic contrast to these: [21]

> The expenditure of physical and mental effort in work is as natural as play or rest. The average human being does not inherently dislike work. Depending upon controllable conditions, work may be a source of satisfaction (and will be voluntarily performed) or a source of punishment (and will be avoided if possible).
>
> External control and the threat of punishment are not the only means for bringing about effort toward organizational objectives. Man will exercise self-direction and self-control in the service of objectives to which he is committed.
>
> Commitment to objectives is a function of the rewards associated with their achievement. The most significant of such rewards, e.g., the satisfaction of ego and self-actualization needs, can be direct products of effort directed toward organizational objectives.

[20] Douglas McGregor, *The Human Side of Enterprise*, McGraw-Hill Book Company, New York, 1960, pp. 33–34.
[21] *Ibid.*, pp. 47–48.

The average human being learns, under proper conditions, not only to accept but to seek responsibility. Avoidance of responsibility, lack of ambition, and emphasis on security are generally consequences of experience, not inherent human characteristics.

The capacity to exercise a relatively high degree of imagination, ingenuity, and creativity in the solution of organizational problems is widely, not narrowly, distributed in the population.

Under the conditions of modern industrial life, the intellectual potentialities of the average human being are only partially utilized.

McGregor's contribution to the dynamics of human behavior leads to serious doubt about the ability of a traditional manager to get the maximum support of his people. It also points out vividly the inadequacies of a theory which limits human collaboration in the organization. The Theory Y approach implies that the failure to reach desired objectives lies in management's method of operation and motivation, rather than in an inadequate scalar organizational posture.

OTHER ALTERNATIVES   The organizational forms taken from the church and the military ought to be viewed for currency since many of them are outmoded. In fact, we might well examine the efficacy of the bureaucratic forms in contemporary business and military life in terms of the following questions:

What other management processes and organizational forms have been tried?

Has the climate in the business and military environment been sufficiently competitive so as to eliminate the more inefficient and unwieldy forms of organization?

Has the bureaucratic, pyramidal model of management been more successful than other forms would have been?

Has any real attempt been made to build the organization around the task without undue reliance on the principles of management?

Is it necessary to have all the work thoroughly organized and all assignments rigidly controlled?

Does each individual have to have a definite area to cover, definite data to work with, and a schedule to meet?

Does each individual require a superior who tells him what to do and subordinates whom he tells what to do?

Serious questions can be raised about the ability of traditional theory to provide a suitable answer to the complex industrial problems of today. We have seen remarkable economic and social changes, and these changes are forcing the development of new ideas about how to manage organized activity.

INTRODUCING PROJECT MANAGEMENT   In the management of complex *ad hoc* projects, project groups, possibly numbering in the hundreds, are formed to manage a specific project having a definable end and an organizational involvement. In this environment, the management process takes on a different pattern from what would have been found in an earlier industrial operation.

Project management

The form of a bureaucracy is almost universally hierarchical, reflecting the scalar principle referred to by Mooney and Reiley.[22] The management of project activities such as exist in a research and development organization, however, requires horizontal and diagonal relationships. In such an organization, managers and technicians deal horizontally with peers and associates at different levels in the same organization and with outside organizations. To follow the "chain of command" would be unwieldy, time consuming, and costly and would disrupt and delay the work. Horizontal and vertical contacts grow out of the necessity to get the job done; they are seldom charted, and yet they are necessary to a smooth flow of work in the organization. These relationships have been called the "informal organization," but this is a misnomer. There may be little informality; the standards of performance may be just as stringent as those in the formal (hierarchical) structure. In many cases, these relationships have sufficient strength and permanency to become *de facto* the *modus operandi* of the organization.

The acceptance of horizontal-vertical relationships between members of an organization requires changes in the organizational form. The realignment of tasks, the restructuring of the formal hierarchical structure, and the *de jure* recognition of a *hybrid* organizational form have been accomplished in many of today's corporations. In weapons-system management, rigid hierarchical structuring has been abandoned in favor of closely integrated project groups. An informal structure to manage the "stream of projects" has its pitfalls, however, since the administration of a project raises unique problems that preclude a laissez-faire coordination, communication, and control. As a project grows, the system of working through informal contacts becomes inadequate to cope with the severity and frequency of management relationships. Large projects require close coordination, since seemingly insignificant errors can boomerang into large costs and schedule slippages. The project organization must reflect how all things fit together, but this fitting together must not become a sacred organizational chart, with

[22] James D. Mooney and Alen C. Reiley, *Onward Industry*, Harper & Row, Publishers, Incorporated, New York, 1931.

its job descriptions and task divisions, that turns into a *fence* rather than serving as a *guide* for accomplishing the job. Too often the manager thinks of his organization as an independent entity, completely self-sufficient in its environment. The manager of large projects must have a new approach to his job:

> His way of thinking must permit him to utilize new knowledge in management literature which recognizes that a strictly vertical approach to management is not necessary.
>
> He must become reoriented away from the purely functional approach to the management of human and nonhuman resources.
>
> He must be able to visualize his role beyond his company's internal operations and to understand how the project relates to its environment and to other projects in it.
>
> He must understand that purposeful conflict may very well be a necessary way of life as he manages his project across many vertical organizational lines.
>
> He must recognize that project management is a dynamic activity where major changes are almost the order of the day.

Many companies now derive a considerable part of their total income from products that did not exist a few years ago. Other companies are changing in other directions; they are revising their organizational structure, eliminating unprofitable products, or opening new facilities. A company in a growth situation is constantly reshuffling facilities, markets, and products in an effort to remain competitive. Inevitable as these changes may be, they nevertheless cause anxiety and disrupt the established order of business. A project approach to the organizational structure can smooth the path considerably in accomplishing these projects.

Project management and traditional management: a comparison

To understand the concept of project management, one must first understand the framework of the project environment and the phenomena found in it. This framework points up the salient differences between the role of the project manager and that of the traditional functional manager. While these differences are possibly more theoretical than actual, differences do exist, and they affect the manager's *modus operandi* and philosophy. The differences in the viewpoints of the *project* and the *functional* managers are outlined in Table 7-1. This comparison highlights a singular characteristic of the project manager; i.e., he must manage activities that include extensive participation by organizations and people not under his direct (line) control.

Table 7-1   Comparison of the functional and
the project viewpoints

PHENOMENA	PROJECT VIEWPOINT	FUNCTIONAL VIEWPOINT
Line-staff organizational dichotomy	Vestiges of the hierarchical model remain, but line functions are placed in a support position. A web of authority and responsibility relationships exists.	Line functions have direct responsibility for accomplishing the objectives; line commands, and staff advises.
Scalar principle	Elements of the vertical chain exist, but prime emphasis is placed on horizontal and diagonal work flow. Important business is conducted as the legitimacy of the task requires.	The chain of authority relationships is from superior to subordinate throughout the organization. Central, crucial, and important business is conducted up and down the vertical hierarchy.
Superior-subordinate relationship	Peer-to-peer, manager-to-technical-expert, associate-to-associate, etc., relationships are used to conduct much of the salient business.	This is the most important relationship; if kept healthy, success will follow. All important business is conducted through a pyramiding structure of superiors and subordinates.
Organizational objectives	Management of a project becomes a joint venture of many relatively independent organizations. Thus, the objective becomes multilateral.	Organizational objectives are sought by the parent unit (an assembly of suborganizations) working within its environment. The objective is unilateral.
Unity of direction	The project manager manages across functional and organizational lines to accomplish a common interorganizational objective.	The general manager acts as the one head for a group of activities having the same plan.
Parity of authority and responsibility	Considerable opportunity exists for the project manager's responsibility to exceed his authority. Support people are often responsible to other managers (functional) for pay, performance reports, promotions, etc.	Consistent with functional management; the integrity of the superior-subordinate relationship is maintained through functional authority and advisory staff services.
Time duration	The project (and hence the organization) is finite in duration.	Tends to perpetuate itself to provide continuing facilitative support.

SOURCE: David I. Cleland, "Understanding Project Authority," *Business Horizons*, Spring, 1966.

WHEN TO USE PROJECT TECHNIQUES The environmental conditions where project-management techniques are required are many and varied. The more dramatic situations are found in the management of large and complex weapons systems—from their inception to their operation. One typical characteristic of all these projects is a long lead time; many years may elapse between the time the need for a product is perceived and the time such a product is finally in use.

Basic to successful project management is recognizing when the project is needed—in other words, when to form a project, as opposed to when to use the regular functional organization to do the job. At what point in time do the changes in the company add up to project management? The senior executives must have a basis for identifying undertakings which the regular functional groups cannot manage successfully. Of course, there are no simple rules to follow, but several general criteria, discussed below, can be applied.

MAGNITUDE OF THE EFFORT Project management is appropriate for *ad hoc* undertakings concerned with a single specific end product, such as a complex weapons system for the government, a move to a new plant site, a corporate acquisition, or the placing of a new product in the market.

The question of size is difficult to pin down because size is a relative matter. When an undertaking requires substantially more resources (people, money, equipment) than are normally available in the business, project techniques are clearly required. Even though the functional elements for the end product are discernible in the organization, a function can be easily overwhelmed by the diversity and complexity of the task. In these cases, project management provides a logical approach to the organizational relationships and problems encountered in the integration of the work. For example, let us consider the move of a company from an Eastern city to one in a Southern state. This may appear to be a simple operation, but the endless development and correlation of plans, the coordination required in constructing the new site, and the task of answering numerous inquiries about the new site can easily swamp the existing organizational structure. These difficulties are compounded by the fact that the company must continue its normal operations during the period of the move. In such a situation, managing along traditional lines would be difficult, if not impossible.

The development and production of a weapons system shows a growth and decline pattern. Initially, the Department of Defense requests organizations throughout the defense establishment to conduct feasibility studies and advanced planning. As the studies progress, the cost, technology, schedule, supportability, maintainability, and many other areas related to the project are added. Key Department of Defense officials enter the planning activities, funds are allocated, and contracts are awarded. As the project matures, widening circles of people throughout the defense-industry complex enter the project to identify the resources and organizational changes needed to satisfy it. Once a prototype is developed, the user (e.g., the Strategic Air Command), the producer (the aerospace company), and many other government and industrial representatives test the entire system. Throughout the life of the project, therefore, there is a continuous meshing of the philosophies, policies, structures, procedures, and resources of all the participating organizations, which requires the active involvement of thousands of people. Eventually the project is completed: a weapons system capable of performing an operational mission has been created. In one sense, the project has reached an end; in another, it has only begun, for the system still has to be supported, and this may also have to be done on a project basis.

UNFAMILIARITY   An undertaking is not a project unless it is something out of the ordinary, different from a normal, routine affair in the organization. For example, an engineering change to an existing product could be conducted without setting up a project, although there would probably be a loss of overall efficiency in accomplishing the objective. The overhaul of a major product, on the other hand, would probably require project management. In the first instance, each of the functional managers could draw on his past experience to accomplish the work. In the latter case, however, the changes in cost, schedule, and technology would require a central management office (a project office) to bring together the functional activities required and relate them for compatibility.

INTERRELATEDNESS   Another decisive criterion for establishing a project is the degree of interdependence existing between the tasks of the effort. If the effort calls for many functionally separated activities to be pulled together, and if these activities are so closely related that moving one affects the others, project techniques are clearly needed. Consider the development and introduction of a new product. The early planning would require sales forecasts to be completed before plans for manufacturing processes, industrial facilities, special tooling, and marketing strategy could be developed. Sales promotions cannot be completed until the marketing research points the direction for the promotions. Performance and technical specifications must be resolved, as well as the many interdependencies between the production, marketing, finance, advertising, and administration groups. Provincialism cannot be tolerated. If no one agency can pull all the separate parts together, if the functional groups fail to make credible estimates, or if the plans submitted by the different departments cannot be reconciled, the activity needs the singleness of purpose of project management.

Projects are characterized by strong lateral working relationships requiring continuing coordination and decisions by many individuals, both within the parent organization and in outside companies. During the development of a major product, there will be close collaboration between the process and design engineers, and perhaps even closer collaboration between the individuals of a single department. These horizontal relationships do not function to the exclusion of the vertical relationships. The technicians and managers who make project decisions must also seek guidance from their supervisors.

ORGANIZATIONAL REPUTATION   The organization's stake in the undertaking is a crucial factor in the decision of whether or not to use the project techniques. For instance, if a failure to complete the contract on time and within the cost and performance limits would seriously damage the company's image and result in stockholder dissatisfaction, the case for using project management is strong. In the final analysis, a company's financial position can be seriously damaged if its performance on a contract fails to meet standards. In the case of defense contracting, the company faces a single, knowledgeable customer, and failure to perform successfully can be catastrophic in terms of obtaining further contracts with the government.

Project management is no panacea, but it does provide a means for controlling the undertaking. A project manager who sees his role as that of an integrator-generalist, responsible for meeting time, cost, and quality objectives, can do much to lessen the dangers inherent in a large undertaking. The project-management techniques concentrate into one man the attention demanded by a complex and unique undertaking. Before any recommendations are made concerning whether to use project techniques or not, the effects of the unique environment on the project must be weighed and evaluated. First, the objective of the undertaking must be considered. Possible improvements in methods that might take some time to implement would require considerable thought. The size and complexity of the project must be considered, since too much sophistication is also an ever-present danger. Other factors which merit consideration are the number of current projects in the company, the number in prospect for the organization, and the length of time remaining to complete the project. For example, establishing project management would be more appropriate at the start of an undertaking or at least early in its life, before large expenditures of manhours and resources are made. Each situation is unique, and whether to manage by a project or a functional approach should be resolved on the basis of specific problems found as well as present concepts of organization.

No company management takes a purely project or a purely functional approach. All companies combine the two, although one form may predominate. If the company's undertakings are small, there would be a series of small, one-man projects. If the undertakings are large, as in the case of a new product development or an acquisition of a major weapons system, the project group would be large and might exist over a period of several years. A project group in a development laboratory may be responsible only for development, although it might ultimately become responsible for production and marketing planning. In some cases, a project takes on the characteristics of a permanent functional organization.

There are many other circumstances under which project techniques are desirable:

> A multilateral objective exists, toward which many people and many relatively independent organizations work together.
>
> There are pressures to improve the product and advance the state of the art.
>
> Plans are subject to change, requiring organizational flexibility.
>
> The risks are high, and the uncertainty factors make prediction of the future difficult.
>
> Project integration requires the concurrent contribution by two or more functional elements and(or) independent organizations.
>
> The project is a type requiring advanced feasibility studies and development.
>
> The government procurement agency requires a project-oriented approach.
>
> A management climate exists which permits the temporary "shorting" of reporting relationships within the organization.

Frequently, the traditional vertical relationships of an organization prove inadequate to cope with the technology for a singular undertaking, and the horizontal relationships arising out of that technology must be considered. Project management requires new organizational setups and permits horizontal and diagonal relationships which are not patterned or clearly defined. Some sort of balance between the functional and the project organizations is required, however, even when the need for a project approach is clear.

Summary

Project management, particularly the management of major R&D projects, is undoubtedly one of the most complex and demanding management concepts in existence. A project in the R&D field has all the elements of an enterprise which has been conceived and built, reaches maturity, completes its mission, and phases out, all in a period of three to five years. The project manager's task is enormously complicated and diverse; he ties together the efforts of prime contractors, associate contractors, and subcontractors, who on some projects number in the hundreds. He deals with technical and administrative disciplines in pulling together a project team to act as a team rather than as a fragmented group of functional experts.

The project manager deals with the concepts of management in general. Many of the classical management principles apply; many project techniques may be used to relate these principles. Careful attention must be given to the division of tasks among the project participants. That division of work should be made which offers the fewest technical and contractual interfaces between the participants.

A proper line organization does not provide the environment essential to project success. In the most flexible of traditional line organizations, it is difficult to maintain a large number of men working in close harmony on creative, abstract work. Creative people do not fit into a precise and orderly line organization where all work is thoroughly organized and all assignments are rigidly controlled; where each individual has a definite area to cover, definite information to work with, and a definite schedule to meet; where bosses must be reported to and subordinates directed. Such an organization may soon have only the few creative men who lead the others. Innovations are difficult to come by since each one must be introduced and explained in detail at every one of the successive levels of the hierarchical chain.

Project management is an outgrowth of the need to develop and produce large projects in the shortest possible time. It has been developed from a need, but with little theoretical formulation. Project management is necessary for government contracts and subcontracts and is being used more and more for other purposes. An individual placed in the position of a project manager will find little in the literature to clarify his role because it has as yet very few theoretical foundations. Several organizational variations of project management are in vogue, however, which depend on the balance desired between the project and the functional organizations.

Recommended readings

Cleland, Maj. David I., and Maj. David C. Dellinger: "Changing Patterns in Management Theory," *Defense Industry Bulletin,* January, 1966.

Fisch, Gerold G.: "Line-Staff Is Obsolete," *Harvard Business Review,* Sept.–Oct., 1961.

Johnson, Richard A., et al.: "Systems Theory and Management," *Management Science*, January, 1964.

Litterer, J. A.: "Program Management: Organizing for Stability and Flexibility," *Personnel*, September, 1963.

McGregor, Douglas: *The Human Side of Enterprise*, McGraw-Hill Book Company, New York, 1960.

March, James G., and Herbert A. Simon: *Organizations*, John Wiley & Sons, Inc., New York, 1963.

Mee, John F.: "Ideational Items: Matrix Organization," *Business Horizons*, vol. 7, no. 2, Summer, 1964.

Mooney, James D., and Allen C. Reiley: *Onward Industry*, Harper & Row, Publishers, Incorporated, New York, 1931.

Peck, Merton J., and Frederick M. Scherer: *The Weapons Acquisition Process: An Economic Analysis*, Harvard University, Division of Research, Graduate School of Business Administration, Boston, 1962.

Ramo, Simon: "Management of Government Programs," *Harvard Business Review*, July–August, 1965.

Shull, Fremont A.: *Matrix Structure and Project Authority for Optimizing Organizational Capacity*, Southern Illinois University, Business Research Bureau, Carbondale, Ill., October, 1965.

Wittner, Howard M.: "R&D Project Managers: What and Who Are They?" *Armed Forces Management*, March, 1962.

CHAPTER 8
Organizational Concepts of Project Management

The reorganization of tasks, the
restructuring of formal organizational
relationships, and even the phasing
out of some aspects of the traditional
hierarchical form of organization
have already been accomplished in a
few of the more technologically
advanced U.S. corporations.[1]

Much of the confusion about project management centers around the interpretation of what is a "pure project" or a "pure functional" organization. Concepts of project organization vary from the form in which the project manager must have everyone associated with the project working directly for him to the form in which the title is mostly a paper gimmick and the project manager is largely a presentation maker and paper handler.

Management consists of performing certain functions—primarily those of planning, organizing, and controlling. Much of this work is actually performed concurrently at different levels of management, since the functions are closely linked and interdependent. The emphasis on a particular function is different at different levels of management, however, so the functions of the project manager vary according to his level in the organization.

The planning and organizing functions are closely related: planning con-

[1] William H. Read, "The Decline of the Hierarchy in Industrial Organizations," *Business Horizons*, Fall, 1965, p. 75.

cerns what is to be done, and organizing concerns the arrangements for getting it done. Planning for the organizing function requires answers to such questions as:

What is to be accomplished?

When is the work to be done and where?

Is there an acceptable way of classifying the work? If so, what are the classifications?

What overall organizational posture will provide the best arrangement of people and services to do the work?

Who will man the structure and do the work?

How will the functional and project groups be related?

What organizing philosophy will best reflect the total environment of the project?

What sort of charts will portray the desired organizational arrangements?

What principles should be used in planning the organizational structure(s)?

What role will the informal organization play?

Selecting the organizational structure

Selecting an organizational structure requires an understanding of the work and the kinds of activities required to reach the organization's objective. The project manager must visualize the total project environment in selecting an organizational philosophy, not just the locale of his project office, and visualizing the total project environment will require an identification and alignment of the relative roles of all the project participants. The project participants include any individuals or assembly of individuals in the project office, in the parent organization, or in an outside organization that has a vested interest in the project affairs. They may be involved with any of the total array of systems, subsystems, sub-subsystems, etc., required to complete the project.

This concept of organizational environment highlights an interdependency between people with a common objective. Fox, in defining an organization, distinguished between the *formal* and the *informal* organization: [2]

The "formal" organization structure of a company comprises the authority, responsibility, and communicative relationships among functions, physical factors, and personnel that are prescribed by owners or

[2] William M. Fox, *The Management Process*, Richard D. Irwin, Inc., Homewood, Ill., 1963, pp. 66–67.

their delegates for the achievement of organizational objectives. "Informal" organization structure comprises the authority, responsibility, communicative, and associative relationships among functions, physical factors, and personnel that are supplemental to the "formal" organization and structure and may be "for," "against," or "neutral" with regard to the achievement of organizational objectives.

The organization can be viewed as a continuous interaction between the formal and the informal organization. This interaction is a necessary part of the total organizational system and forms a part of the total environment in which the organization functions.

Organizations take many forms, from the pyramidal organization of the military and the church to the political or unstructured voluntary organization of a PTA or a businessmen's luncheon group. In any cooperative effort, the members have some common objective for joining together, and there is some definition of the authority relationships between them. These objectives and authority patterns may be either rigid or ill-defined.

In performing the organizing function, the project manager defines the tasks, suggests organizational alignments, and assigns activities so that the members of the organization can build, develop, and maintain a structure of working relationships to accomplish the project objectives. The project organization, in its broadest sense, becomes the structural and authority framework through which all the project efforts are coordinated and integrated into the common objective. The project organization, however, is not an independent entity operating in a vacuum; it is part of a larger system.

Why project organization?

Project organization is more than just an academic curiosity—it is a practical necessity. The project manager accomplishes the project objectives by working with functional groups of the company and with outside organizations. The total project organization has no discrete boundaries; it is a complex structure that facilitates the coordination and integration of many project activities. While the project manager uses many traditional organizational principles in planning his structure, he must be guided by some considerations that go beyond traditional theory, such as:

> How shall the parent and outside organizations be aligned to accomplish the multilateral objectives of the project?
>
> How applicable are traditional principles of organization such as span of management, the scalar principle, unity of command, parity of authority and responsibility, unity of direction, and functional homogeneity?

Are the authority and responsibility relationships subject to alignment in a scalar chain, or will the flow of authority and responsibility form a "web of relationships" in the total project environment?

As project manager, will his first responsibility be to plan and to organize and control his subordinates, or to provide the environment in which others can accomplish the project objectives successfully?

How should the organization be aligned to give contributors due recognition?

What will the organization consist of—the blocks on the organizational chart or something greater?

Are conditions such that a simple bureaucratic organization will not suffice for the technological progress and the interdependencies between complex organizations?

What effect will technology have on the project organization structure?

Industrial processes have been developed in which technology and organization form *linked pairs* that operate interdependently. The interdependency of technology and organization is a way of introducing the importance of an organizational technique which complements the forming of a mutually supporting, integrated team that will ensure a continued capability between organizational structures and the technological needs. Jasinski highlights the need for a proper organization-technology relationship by stating: [3]

> Frequently, the traditional, formally defined vertical relations in business and industrial organizations prove inadequate to cope with modern technology. New technologies require new organizational setups and it is being found increasingly that industrial processes require horizontal and diagonal relations which are not patterned or clearly defined.

Whatever fundamental organization theory is used, today's project manager must go beyond existing setups and find new organizational forms suitable for exploiting new dimensions in aligning human and nonhuman resources in an advancing, technological environment. The need for new forms of organizational alignment is evident in the environment where project management had its genesis.

Emergence of the project organization

As companies have grown, their top managers have found it increasingly difficult to keep abreast of all the major business affairs, much less attending

[3] Frank J. Jasinski, "Adapting Organization to New Technology," *Harvard Business Review,* January–February, 1959, p. 86.

to the routine ones. The future of the business is a major concern of these top managers; in the long-range planning activity, the risk and uncertainty associated with the future require considerable time to evaluate. The execution of major decisions in the organization can often be relegated to lower-level managers. The routine execution of decisions will not normally require much attention from the principal managers. This is not the case with major projects, which require both a long-range view and close day-to-day management that are different in nature from the routine, recurring activities of the business organization. It is in these organizations that we find a new organizational structure reflecting major work relationships rather than traditional work alignments. This new organizational structure contains four major elements: functional support, project management, routine administration, and research and development (long-range planning).

FUNCTIONAL SUPPORT   Functional support consists of facilitative technology provided for the company by various groups. In a manufacturing organization, this element would be supplied by three groups, designated "production," "marketing," and "finance." Functional support is provided for all projects in the organization as well as for the advancement of the state of the art in a particular discipline.

PROJECT MANAGEMENT   Project management is carried out by a set of managers acting as *unifying agents* for particular projects in respect to the current resources of time, funds, materials, people, and technology. The project managers act as focal points for their project activities through a unique organization superimposed on the traditional functional organization structure. The project managers are, in effect, the general managers of the company for their particular projects. They actively participate in planning, organizing, and controlling those major organizational and extraorganizational activities involved.

ROUTINE ADMINISTRATION   Routine administration involves the accommodating services provided for mission-related activities. These services include the centralized activities required to keep score on the business as a whole, as well as the routine administration and accounting of funds, people, materials, and ideas. Examples are the personnel function, repetitive business data processing, and recurring logistic support.

RESEARCH AND DEVELOPMENT (LONG-RANGE PLANNING)   Research and development activities are those concerned with advancing the *strategic* state of the art in the functional areas and with developing a system of plans for the company's future. This group is less concerned with accomplishing current work than with obtaining future work and finding new uses for existing resources; consequently, their work is more conceptual and abstract than that of other elements.

Contemporary managers face the problem of keeping themselves up to date on the many *ad hoc* activities needed to complete a project within time, cost, and technological boundaries. These projects may be in varying degrees of maturity; some may be merely concepts, while others are nearing completion and phase-out. This stream of projects, encompassing a number of different products, each of which requires considerable effort and attention, first manifests itself in the R&D function. The R&D functional manager cannot stay on top of all the development efforts for which he is responsible. To assist in these developments, a project engineer (project manager) is assigned to each of the major projects to achieve, first of all, unity of communication and coordination across the disciplines of the organization, as well as within the engineering discipline. He becomes a source of integrated information concerning his particular project and an interaction point for coordinating the diverse organizational and extra-organizational activities involved. This communication function, coupled with the coordinative function, enables him to exercise control over many aspects of the project.

As more and more projects are added, the functional managers depend increasingly on the project engineers to keep them informed, to manage their projects, and to coordinate action, as necessary, among the functional groups within the organization. The functional executives further depend on a "purposeful conflict" between project managers, on the one hand, and functional managers, on the other, as a means of evaluating relative trade-offs for the time, cost, and technical parameters of a particular project, with the line and staff groups becoming very much involved. The chief executive expects his project and functional managers to resolve daily operating problems among themselves and to bring only major unresolved question to him. Management by exception is the objective.

Rarely does the project manager find that the project activities are limited to his own organization; he usually must work with participants (or contributors) outside the company. He therefore has superior knowledge of the relative roles and functions of the individual parts of the project which makes him a logical person to take part in major interorganizational decisions affecting the project.

The project manager's role varies from one company to another, however. In some cases, he has influence and responsibilities cutting across many or all of the company's semi-independent divisions. In other cases, he operates merely as a project representative for the several functions within his own facility. In either case, his position is at the focus of an organizational relationship with unique work patterns. In conventional business circles, the project manager is thought of as a rather exotic figure, perhaps because overzealous writers of position descriptions have sometimes made him sound like a cross between a Ph.D.-level engineer and a Ph.D.-level manager, with the added ability to walk on water! Many executives consider project management to be unique to the defense business. They feel it is inappropriate to their own, even though one would usually find a project structure established and project-management techniques employed for any temporary task requiring management across many organizational lines.

A systems view of an organization

An understanding of the systems concept is necessary to a discussion of project-management organization. The concepts of *organization* and *system* have been associated together since the beginning of the scientific management era. Kendall, writing in 1912, perceived this relationship and spoke of the need to be organized so that ". . . separate processes and unit members are brought *into systematic* connection and operation as efficient parts of the whole." [4] In a more recent period, Barnard built his theme around the equivalency of systems and organizations by stating: [5]

> It is the central hypothesis of this book that the most useful concept for the analysis of experience of cooperative systems is embodied in the definition of a formal organization as a *system of consciously co-ordinated activities or forces of two or more persons.*

Barnard's view of the organization as a system related to larger systems in the environment implied reciprocal activities between the organizations in a particular sphere of activity. In Barnard's view, the organization has multidimensional characteristics with interrelated goal-seeking subsystems.

The systems concept appeared in management literature approximately fifty years ago, but it has only recently gained any degree of acceptance in the study of organizations. One can very easily question the usefulness of the concept. What can be done to further show the usefulness of the systems approach to a manager in managing his internal and external organizational affairs?

One reason why practitioners have hesitated for so long to accept the sys-

---

[4] Henry P. Kendall, *Scientific Management: First Conference at the Amos Tuck School,* The Plimpton Press, 1912, p. 113.
[5] Chester I. Bernard, *The Functions of the Executive,* Harvard University Press, Cambridge, Mass., 1962, p. 73.

tems approach is that it is based on analogical reasoning rather than on empirical verification. In addition, there was no real need for it in the past, and now that the need has arisen, the development of techniques has lagged far behind, as usual.

THE COMPONENT VIEW   In the past, management education and practices have emphasized a component view; accounting, production, marketing, finance, and human relations were taught as unrelated subjects. It was assumed, perhaps naïvely, that experience would give top-level managers the ability to integrate these disciplines in a practical management situation. The systems approach to management has gained in favor because it considers the interdependencies of today's industrial system. The interconnections and interactions between the components of the system are often more important than the separate components themselves.

Not only large and complex companies need project management; some small companies with relatively stable environments need it too. Small, stable companies that have an unchanging product or service can operate very well on a vertical management philosophy, except that they have a role in the larger scheme of things. All companies, both large and small, are part of their environment, and the extent to which a company is integrated into its environment can be a good measure of its success.

The boundaries of a company are not simple. The operation of a company from a systems view requires people and groups that never appear on the organizational charts. Seymour Tilles has written of the systems approach: [6]

> Many organizations have a management team that includes individuals—auditors, lawyers, bankers, brokers, and a variety of other specialists—who never appear on the organization chart. In some cases, these outside experts are consulted with such regularity that they are really a part of the management system. In fact, the extent of the management system is frequently an indication of the manager's ability.

Viewing the manager's job as Tilles has done may lead one to conclude that managers have been using the systems concept all along. Perhaps the use of coordination as a managerial technique qualifies as the systems approach; coordination—the synchronizing of activities with respect to time and place—entails working with many individuals outside the scalar chain.

Coordination is necessary to the management process—it can do much to assure the timely accomplishment of objectives. But coordination per se

[6] Seymour Tilles, "The Manager's Job: A Systems Approach," *Harvard Business Review*, Jan.–Feb., 1963, p. 75.

lacks the inherent integration implied by the systems approach, which requires interrelatedness and organizational reciprocity.

AN INTEGRATED SYSTEM   The organization must be aligned so that the individual functions are brought together into an integrated, organized system with the parts related to the common goal. The systems approach to the organization of human and nonhuman resources includes the basic ideas that:

1   An organization is composed of many subsystems, within the parent company and the general environment.

2   The organization is not an entity in itself, but must interface with other groups (public organizations, customers, suppliers, unions, creditors, bankers, stockholders, governments, etc.) to survive in its environment.

3   Subordinates are only part of the personnel groups that work for the supervisor.

4   The legitimacy of the task may sometimes dominate the vertical hierarchies.

5   Each person in an organization has a mix of roles in the total system, not a narrow specialization.

6   Individual managers do not occupy a single, central fixed position in the organization; rather, managers must have considerable organizational mobility to maintain the necessary relationships in the environment.

7   The manager must understand the relationships between the parts of the system as well as the specific requirements of his job.

Planning the project organization

Any undertaking requires some degree of organization; in some instances, the organization may be informal but inherent to the situation. As the number of individuals engaged in an enterprise increases and interorganizational and interpersonal complexities increase, more formality is required to achieve the desired objectives. Project management is not unlike other management in this respect. Organization is necessary to establish a framework, not only to produce the desired results, but also to clarify individual responsibilities, privileges, and authority. Certain key requirements are essential to any posture of project organization:

1   Clear-cut requirements must be established to provide the framework of the objective.

2   The *modus operandi* should be established.

3   The human and nonhuman resources should be aligned to aid the overall operation.

4 Feedback techniques should be established such that the overall effectiveness of the operation can be sensed and, if necessary, modified to meet changing demands.

Accomplishing the above destroys certain of the old tenets of organization and administration—clear lines of command and responsibility, clearly defined duties and functions, and a clear division between line and staff, to name a few. For instance, an organization that is concerned with the development and acquisition of a new product and is organized along the lines of a factory or the military can be inefficient.

The plans for the project organization should include some type of formalized structure for efficient collective action. The formal structure reflected on the organizational chart, although static and perhaps not representative of the way operations are carried out, does have value in defining the relationships between individuals and the organizational elements. The conventional project organization is more situational and dynamic than contemporary organizations, however, and the interfacing in project affairs should be designed, but from an understanding of the task. Project managers who get the best results frequently deviate from traditional theory. These organizations look less like a military hierarchy and more like a partnership of professionals.

The project team

The most effective project organization would be developed by assigning a project manager with perfect qualifications and giving him clear-cut authority and responsibility. This situation would be ideal, but probably is not realistic. The best manager available should be assigned, and the necessary human resources to support him should be provided. To select the human resources requires that the overall project be divided into subtasks, and so on, until the project is represented by an alignment of rational, related, recognizable work units. This dividing should be accomplished by the project manager in collaboration with the functional managers who will be supporting the project. For example, in the development and production of a large project such as a ballistic missile, the makeup of the team to support the project activities would include functional groups with the responsibility for:

1 Developing the general requirements of the project, i.e., establishing the overall organizational strategic plan.

2 Preparing the *general* and *technical* specifications of the product or project. In this context, the general specifications express the customer needs and desires, while the technical specifications designate product parameters.

3   Fabricating, testing, and evaluating the prototype and production models.

4   Establishing the reliability, maintainability, and supportability requirements for the overall system and for individual equipments.

5   Identifying and selecting sources for the items of the project which are to be procured.

6   Negotiating and administering all contracts consummated with suppliers and participants in the project effort.

7   Developing, coordinating, and maintaining the master and supporting schedules required to produce the product within the time restraints.

8   Creating, publishing, and distributing technical manuals and reports required for the product in its intended operational environment.

9   Planning for, and subsequently installing, operating, and maintaining, the completed product.

10   Providing operational logistic concepts required to assure the supportability of the product after it is produced. This group includes those individuals who are charged with the responsibility for providing a pool of spare parts, specialized supporting equipment, and trained personnel necessary to maintain the product.

11   Making a cost analysis to develop original costing and a method for continually tracking the product (or system) cost. This includes the financial management required to determine subsystem and system profitability and to develop a management information system for the project manager to use in maintaining surveillance of the schedule, cost, profitability, and technology of the project.

12   Establishing the product configuration and performance characteristics and tracking these characteristics throughout the project's life.

13   Providing technical leadership for the product line and maintaining the maximum state of the art in the project within the cost and schedule restraints. This is accomplished on the existing product generation, under the jurisdiction of the product manager, and is not to be confused with the overall R&D function to be carried out for the company as a whole.

14   Identifying and developing the personnel skills necessary to use the product.

The definition of organization implied here is broad, since it includes both technical and social structures. The groups required to work on the project are not reflected in a neat pyramidal way, but are concentrated around the project as the need arises. Authority and responsibility patterns are important, but not so important as to require an arrangement in some descending order. In our concept of organization, we mean not only tasks, jobs, or positions—the traditional formal organization—but the informal relations between the members and in the peer-associate work structure. The project manager is faced with constantly changing events, outside his office as well as within it.

The project organization may be too parochial for the man who wishes to maintain his technical status and his identification with his technical reference group. These are important to the development of a technical capability in the organization, since the functional organization is where functional know-how is advanced, expertise is developed, standards of performance are established, and manpower and facilities assignments are made.[7] The project staffs can be drawn from the functional departments and are returned to them when the project or task is completed.

Organizational alternatives

The organization for project management can take many forms. At one extreme is the pure project organization, where the project manager is given full authority to run his project as if it were a one-product company; at the other is the pure functional organization departmented on a traditional basis, reflecting the traditional hierarchy. In the middle lies an infinite variety of project-functional combinations. Each of these forms has certain advantages and disadvantages; no one form is best for all projects, or even best for one throughout its entire lifetime. The essence of project organization is versatility—the project can be built around the task; as the task changes, so must the scope of the organization.

The characteristics of the different organizations are discussed below.

PURE FUNCTIONAL ORGANIZATION   The pure functional organization provides flexibility in the use of manpower. Personnel can be used on many different projects; specialists can be grouped so that knowledge and experience gained on one project are transferred to another. The company has a broad manpower base to work with, and a continuity exists in the functional disciplines, procedures, and policies from one project to another. One disadvantage of the functional organization acting alone, however, is that it does not provide the project-oriented emphasis necessary to accomplish project tasks. No one individual is responsible for the total project; there is no customer focal point. Since no one person functions as the "champion" of the project, responsibility will be difficult to pinpoint, coordination unduly complex, response to customer needs slow, and motivation and innovation decreased. Ideas may tend to be functionally oriented, and approaches to the management process will tend to perpetuate the functional organization without regard for ongoing projects.

[7] This refers to all technical groups—cost, schedule, personnel, etc.—as well as to the better-known scientist and engineer groups. Each of these individuals has a technical liaison to maintain with his peers in his parent unit.

PURE PROJECT ORGANIZATION   The major advantage of the pure project organization is that it provides complete line authority over the project; the project participants work directly for the project manager. One of the strongest disadvantages to this type of organization is that the cost in a multiproject company would be prohibitive because a duplication of effort and facilities would be required among the projects. Since there would be no reservoir of specialists in a functional element, there might be a tendency to retain personnel on the project long after they were needed. Then, too, there would be no functional group to look toward the future and work to improve the company's capability for new programs.

MATRIX ORGANIZATION   A mixed project and functional structure, or *matrix* organization, is desirable for producing large projects within desired cost, schedule, and performance standards. The mixture can lie anywhere between the two extremes, the exact structure being determined by the particular task requirements. The matrix, or mixed, organization has many advantages:

1   The project is emphasized by designating one individual as the focal point for all matters pertaining to it.
2   Utilization of manpower can be flexible because a reservoir of specialists is maintained in functional organizations.
3   Specialized knowledge is available to all programs on an equal basis; knowledge and experience can be transferred from one project to another.
4   Project people have a functional home when they are no longer needed on a given project.
5   Responsiveness to project needs and customer desires is generally faster because lines of communication are established and decision points are *centralized*.
6   Management consistency between projects can be maintained through the deliberate conflict operating in the project-functional environment.
7   A better balance between time, cost, and performance can be obtained through the built-in checks and balances (the deliberate conflict) and the continuous negotiations carried on between the project and the functional organizations.

There are some disadvantages to a mixed organization. The balance of power between the functional and the project organizations must be watched so that neither one erodes the other. The balance between time, cost, and performance must also be continually monitored so that neither group favors cost or time over technical performance.

Each of the forms of organizational structure has certain advantages, but none can be considered best for all applications. The form to be used depends on the environmental requirements, which change continually as the project goes through its life cycle and as the number of projects and the product mix of the company change. The organization must be changed as the environment changes; two types of changes can be effected: (1) People can be reassigned from one position to another without changing the organizational structure, and (2) the organizational structure can be changed as dictated by the project-functional interface.

Rotating personnel between projects and functions can be a valuable technique in executive development. Individuals gain perspective in the project and functional ways of thinking; they develop an understanding of the other fellow's problems.

Changes in organizational structure are often necessary and can have a more far-reaching effect than merely rotating people from one position to another. Structural changes sometimes affect the human element adversely, however; they strike at the core of human motivation—status, security, acceptance. Informal working arrangements can be broken up and morale damaged, to the extent that the general efficiency of the organization declines. Regardless of these problems, change is necessary, and a degree of change is desirable.

The need for flexibility

The organizational structure must be dynamic and flexible enough to meet the needs of a continually changing project environment. Organizing is a dynamic process. Factors such as customer response, the number and complexity of projects, and the life-cycle phase of the projects are dynamic processes which contribute to this changing environment. The need for flexibility is well illustrated in the comments of a vice-president of a large aerospace company in a letter to the Director of NASA: [8]

> In order to sense and react quickly and to insure rapid decision-making, lines of communication should be the shortest possible between all levels of the organization. People with the most knowledge must be available at the source of the problem, and they must have decision-making authority and responsibility. Meaningful data must be available on a timely basis and the organization must be structured to produce this environment.
>
> In the aerospace industry, it is a serious weakness to be tied to fixed organization charts, plans, and procedures. With regard to organization, we successfully married the project concept of management with a central function concept. What we came up with is an organization within an organization—one to ramrod the day-to-day problems; the other to provide support for existing projects and to anticipate the requirements for future projects.

[8] Letter from J. Donald Rath, vice-president of Martin-Marietta Corporation, Denver Division, to J. E. Webb, of NASA, Oct. 28, 1963.

The project system is essential in getting complicated jobs done well and on time, but it solves only part of the management problem. When you have your nose to the project grindstone, you are often not in a position to see much beyond that project. This is where the central functional organization comes in. My experience has been that you need this central organization to give you depth, flexibility, and perspective. Together, the two parts permit you to see both the woods and the trees.

Initiative is essential at all levels of the organization. We try to press the level of decision to the lowest possible rung of the managerial ladder. This type of decision-making provides motivation and permits recognition for the individual and the group at all levels. It stimulates action and breeds dedication.

With this kind of encouragement, the organization can become a live thing—sensitive to problems and able to move in on them with much more speed and understanding than would be normally expected in a large operation. In this way, we can regroup or reorganize easily as situations dictate and can quickly focus on a "crisis." In this industry, a company must always be able to reorient itself to meet new objectives. In a more staid, old-line organization, frequent reorientation, usually accompanied by a corresponding shift of people's activities, could be most upsetting. However, in the aerospace industry, we come to expect those things. There will always be fire drills. We must be prepared for change. The entire picture is one of change.

The business organization must accept change. In the project environment, little in the way of a static system is found—the environment demands change and evolution.

Selecting the project organization

The organization of industrial projects varies considerably. The different types of organization represent varying degrees of authority and responsibility which are assumed by the project manager and which have been splintered from, or are shared with, the functional manager. Project managers are located at different levels in the organization and direct varying numbers of people temporarily assigned to them; the amount of the work done in the functional areas also varies.

The typical arrangement is to have a standard functional organization, with a project manager who reports to the company president or general manager in a staff capacity (Figure 8-1). In this setup, the project manager acts more or less as an assistant to the chief executive in matters involving the project, relieving him of some of the burdensome details. The project

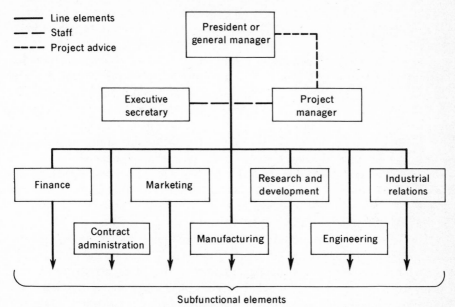

Figure 8-1   Functional organization with project manager acting as an assistant in a staff capacity.

manager may be provided with some nontechnical (clerical) personnel, but he usually has no direct control over the work which is done in the functional units. He plays the role of a staff officer: he investigates, researches, analyzes, recommends, and coordinates matters relative to the project. He also serves as an expediter of the project activities by dealing directly with individuals in the coordination of project affairs. Keith Davis has described this type of project manager well: [9]

> This reflects his [the project manager's] second function, that of serving as a center of communication to be able instantly to report to general management on the *whole* of the project and thus relieve general management of the tedious task of keeping up with all the details. Accordingly, he accomplishes unity of command, a key necessity in the complex world of advanced technology.

Most decisions are made by the chief executive, since the project manager has no real authority except to persuade and report results to his superior. He is a monitor who can "view with alarm" the adverse machinations of the project, but he is something less than a true coordinator or integrator

[9] Keith Davis, "The Role of Project Management in Scientific Manufacturing," *Arizona Business Bulletin*, May, 1965, p. 2.

of the project. Although he does not function in a line capacity, he usually has wide functional authority, and since he is in close organizational proximity to the chief executive, he has significant influence.

Placing the project manager in a staff capacity as an assistant restricts his freedom to function as a true integrator and decision maker. In management literature and in practice, an assistant is not considered to have the authority to act alone. Instead, he merely furnishes his superior with information and recommendations. In this arrangement, the project manager's responsibilities are likely to exceed his authority. In a staff position, his ability to act decisively would depend almost solely upon his personal persuasiveness and superior knowledge. While superior knowledge and persuasiveness are powerful additives to authority, his position would probably be weak because the role of a staff member, according to traditional theory, is restricted to giving advice and assistance.

The second organizational pattern is sometimes called *matrix* project management. In this type of structure (Figure 8-2), a functional organization exists in which the project manager reports to the chief executive in a line capacity. The staff of the project manager's office may vary in number from only the manager himself to several hundred people, depending upon the degree to which the project activities are centralized. As the project manager's responsibilities increase and more facets of the project are centralized under his control, the company may establish an organizational entity (a division) to manage the project independently. In this type of matrix organization, the project manager has authority over the functional managers regarding the "what" and "when" of the activities; the functional manager determines *how* the support will be given. The functional managers are responsible to both their functional supervisors and the project manager for support of the project. This situation, in which a line functional manager (such as a production manager) is placed in a position of providing advice, counsel, and specialized support to a project manager, who is concerned with unifying project activities across the company, represents a change in the authority relationships. This is a radical departure from the line-staff organizational dichotomy that has been the mainstay of management theory for decades. Also, it seems to be a violation of the scalar principle described by Henri Fayol.[10]

Authority patterns in the organization shown in Figure 8-2 flow both vertically and horizontally throughout the company. In addition, there is

[10] Fayol envisions the scalar chain as the chain of superiors ranging from the ultimate authority to the lowest rank, with the line of authority following every link in the chain. In today's large organizations, where lines of authority cross functional lines and extend into outside organizations, this principle requires some modification.

See Henri Fayol, *General and Industrial Management*, Sir Isaac Pitman & Sons, Ltd., London.

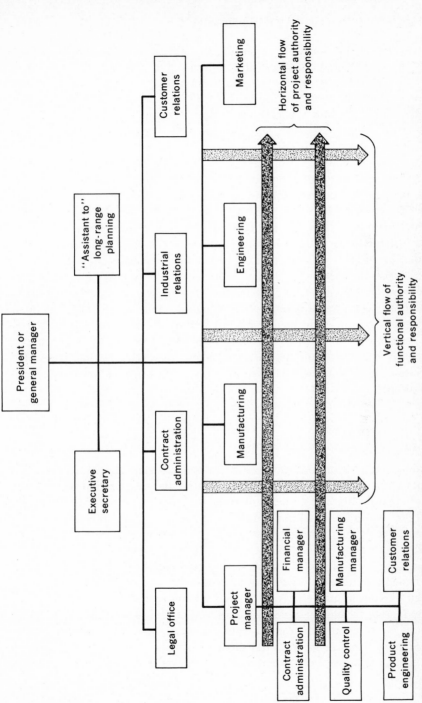

Figure 8-2 Functional organization with project manager in a line capacity. This organizational structure allows for vertical flow of the authority and responsibility of the functional managers, as well as horizontal flow of project authority and responsibility.

flow to outside participating organizations. Project organization frequently disregards levels and functions and superimposes the project structure on the existing organization. The structure depends, to a large degree, on the location of the project contributor, regardless of where that contributor is located. Thus, at times it is difficult, if not impossible, to chart the relationships; they will be discussed in connection with charting the project organization in a subsequent chapter.

Some form of matrix organization is established almost universally in companies engaged in developing, testing, and delivering large projects. In this dual management process, deliberate or purposeful conflict is recognized as a mechanism for achieving good trade-offs. Even though the organization is aligned in such a way that the conflict is required (and recognized), the chief executives expect the managers to work out their conflicts. In other words, the project manager and the functional managers must resolve the recurring conflicts that arise during the course of the project's life. Only truly significant disagreements should be brought up to a common superior for resolution; management by exception is the rule! Both project and functional managers have the right of appeal, but before any such right is exercised, two criteria should be met: (1) The issue is clearly drawn, with alternatives and costs described, and (2) it is a salient project-functional issue. The resolution of salient conflicts may determine the organizational placement of a project.

Additional organizational forms

Creating a matrix organization results in major organizational changes in a company. In general, these changes emphasize decentralization of authority and responsibility. The concept of project management also highlights the need for a top-level planning unit to study long-range requirements for future projects and to relate these needs to company capabilities. The trend in large aerospace companies is to set up divisions along product lines such as airframe, propulsion, electronics, and guidance—the typical components of a modern aeronautical weapons system.[11]

The organizational charts of a typical aerospace company show the normal vertical lines of authority and responsibility, but they also show lines of project authority and communication running across. For example, the organizational chart for TRW Space Technology Laboratories (Figure 8-3) shows that the Vela program office reports to the spacecraft systems

[11] F. Kast, and J. Rosenzweig, "A Survey of the Intra-company Impact of Weapon System Management," *IRE Transactions on Engineering Management,* March, 1962, p. 39.

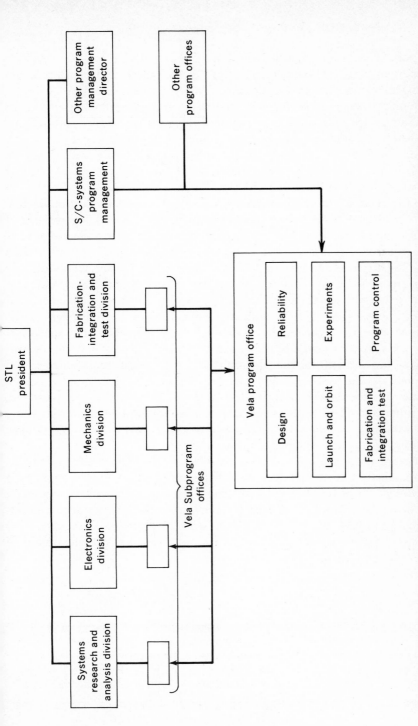

Figure 8-3 Organizational chart of TRW Space Technology Laboratories. Vela program office. (*From Englebert Kirchner, "The Project Manager," Space/Aeronautics, February, 1965, p. 58.*)

program office, a line element whose head is responsible for other projects in addition to the Vela project. The head of the spacecraft systems program management office reports to the president of the company. The Vela program office acts as a planning and supervising group coordinating the efforts of other groups within the company that do the actual design, production, and test work; administratively, these groups do not come under the project office. The engineer working on the Vela project attitude-control system, for example, is not under the supervision of the Vela project officer, but is part of the electronics division.

In the chart for the Radio Corporation of America, astro-electronics division (Figure 8-4), the project offices form one of the seven departments of the division. Lateral lines of communication, typical of a project organization, run from the project office to five other departments or groups within these departments. As an example, the Tiros project office works directly with groups in the engineering department responsible for spacecraft systems, spacecraft electronics, engineering test, engineering reliability, and applied physics, as well as with a technical staff. The influence of the project office also reaches down to the next level, where the spacecraft systems group of the engineering department works directly with the systems engineering section in the determination of design requirements and parameters. The systems engineering section acts as something of a consultant; it cannot issue orders to other groups in the engineering department, but submits its plans to the Tiros project office for approval. After checking and verifying the plans for total system compatibility, the project office releases them to the design groups as work orders.

The organizational chart depicts the way in which the company intends to function, but the actual operation of the project office and the supporting functional groups proves there is no magic formula for project management. The *modus operandi* can vacillate between the impersonal, formal organization and the interpersonal, informal network of peers and associates from various departments working together toward a common goal. As described by Englebert Kirchner: [12]

> In any case, whether the formal, permanent lines of communication are drawn more or less impersonally, they generally are used only so long as everything goes according to plan. Whenever a problem has to be solved, new, informal lines of communications are set up *ad hoc* and temporarily. In effect, an engineering task force is created with very little regard to the boxes and lines on the organization chart. For example, an *ad hoc* working group set up at RCA–AED to work out the orbit necessary for a new Tiros mission might bring together a

[12] Englebert Kirchner, "The Project Manager," *Space/Aeronautics*, February, 1965, p. 59.

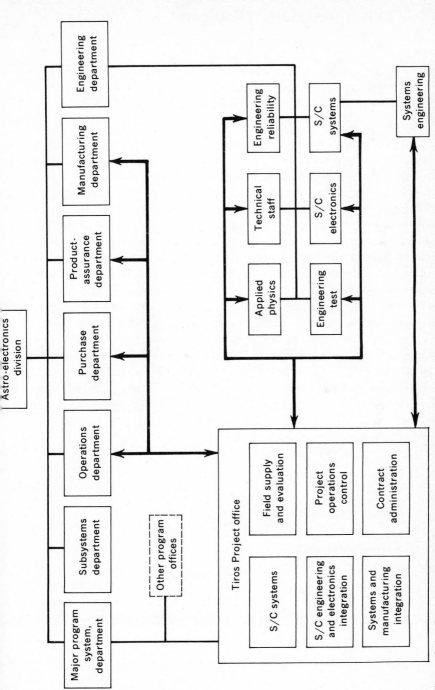

Figure 8-4 Organizational chart of Radio Corporation of America, astro-electronics division. (*From Englebert Kirchner, "The Project Manager," Space/Aeronautics, February, 1965, p. 59.*)

trajectory specialist from the Engineering Department's Technical Staff Group, several people from the same department's Spacecraft Systems Group (including someone from the Systems Engineering Section), a representative of the Spacecraft Electronics Group, and, of course, one or two engineers from the Tiros project office.

The tough technical jobs are given to such *ad hoc* groups in the company, rather than to an "official" group. For the most part, an official group under these circumstances would merely identify the existence of the problem, designate the group to handle it, and charge that group with the responsibility of reporting back on the problem resolution. This may appear to be an informal way of resolving problems, but standards of performance need not be lowered. Certainly, informal working procedures have inherent dangers, but as long as all reporting, reviewing, and supervising is accomplished through the formal channels, these dangers are slight.

Project managers may be differentiated on the basis of the degree of organizational involvement of the projects they manage. The size of the project is one distinction; i.e., does the project manager act as the focal point for a project that is being carried out only within the boundaries of a major functional unit, or does the project require cutting across the lines of several functional departments? Or is the project so small that its affairs can be conducted within the bounds of a major functional department? The organizational alignment of such a project is reflected in Figure 8-5. This

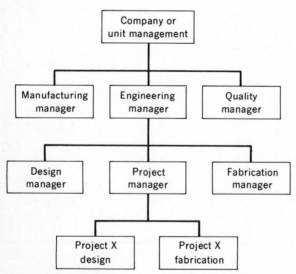

Figure 8-5   Project organization within a major functional department.

project manager has direct responsibility over the units doing the main work of the project. For the most part, the project affairs are conducted without any negotiation and coordination with outside organizations. This type of project organization is typical of many small affairs conducted in an organization which do not fit into any specific department, but require some degree of formality and central location to facilitate their performance.

Another type of a project organization functions within a given department, but has direct authority over the units doing the work. Such an organization is portrayed in Figure 8-6, where the project manager acts as an assistant to the department head. In this organization, the subordinate managers are, in effect, working for two people, i.e., the head of the engineering department and the project manager. People in this dual relationship report first through the traditional line organization and then through the project organization. The sphere of influence of the project manager is limited to the functional boundaries of the organization.

Another type of project organization is portrayed in Figure 8-7, where the project manager is placed in a line capacity with direct responsibility over the project affairs. In this case, the project manager would be a senior executive in the company and might bear the title of "vice-president" or

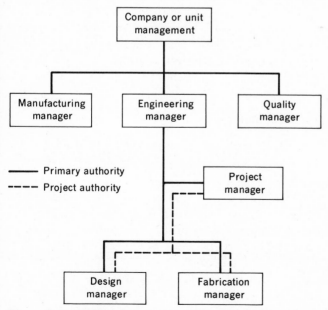

Figure 8-6   Project organization within a major functional department with the project manager acting in the capacity of "assistant."

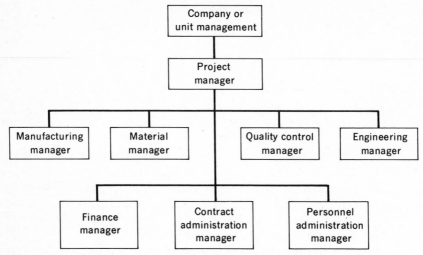

Figure 8-7 Project organization in which project authority and line authority are the same.

"assistant general manager." The range of the project manager's jurisdiction in this case would encompass most of the functional activities of the company. The project organization is similar to the traditional vertical model, with project authority and line authority being one. This project manager undoubtedly has authority and responsibility that cut across functional lines, although the chart does not depict a matrix relationship.

Other participating organizations

Organizational roles

Many different organizations play a role in the development and production of a major project. Consider, for example, the organizational relationships required between participants in the acquisition of a weapons system. The project manager's role as an integrator-generalist puts him in a focal position with respect to the many different participants in the project. This role is depicted in Figure 8-8. Herein lies one of the greatest challenges of project management: the design of a project organizational structure and information system which enables the project manager to maintain the necessary control over all the project participants.

Maintaining control can be most difficult, since many of the participants are not in the project manager's organization. In some cases, the organization

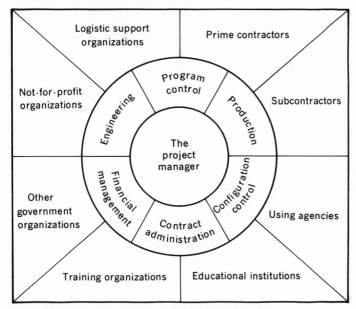

Figure 8-8   Focal position of the project manager.

that has a vested interest in the project is political in nature, for example, the Congress of the United States. These organizations, ranging from the project officer, per se, to Congress, play varying roles in the project effort.

The role of industry

The government itself does not develop and produce any of its systems. It plays the role of customer through working with industry to develop the systems concepts. Traditionally, industry supplies both concepts and systems hardware. A military project manager will often have to deal with many contractors or with a team of industrial contractors. A contractor for a particular system is selected through competitive procedures, contract terms and conditions are negotiated, and the desired system is then developed, produced, and delivered. Besides ideas, contractors provide guidance on the cost, technological, and scheduling feasibility of new concepts. Most major defense contractors have a systems-analysis group too, which studies the cost-effectiveness relationship of new weapons-systems possibilities. Out of these study efforts come the unsolicited proposals for many of our new weapons. Industry's role has grown from that of simply a hardware developer to that of a fully participating member during the conceptual, project definition, and production phases of the system development.

The role of Congress

The number and type of participants involved in the development of a major weapons system depend on the requirements of the particular system. As a minimum, these participants represent most of the major echelons of the Department of Defense as well as other agencies of the government. Congress itself plays a role significantly more vital than just interest. Congress has a constitutional right [13] to become involved in defense matters, which it does primarily through its committees. The committees investigate and gather facts, submit reports, prepare legislation, and determine what Congress will do in the defense field. Briefly, the role that Congress plays in weapons-system management includes authorization, appropriation, and surveillance.

AUTHORIZATION   Weapons systems and related defense projects must be authorized before they can be funded. This authorization or policy role is performed by the Armed Services Committee.

APPROPRIATION   After the authorization is enacted into law, the Appropriations Committee prepares the appropriation bills, which, when enacted into law, release money for use by the Department of Defense and, in turn, by individual services.

SURVEILLANCE   Congressional committees track the appropriate money to see that it is spent wisely. The Government Operations Committee has broad authorization to examine at all levels of government in the interest of efficiency and economy.

All major reorganization plans prepared by the executive office are referred to the Committee on Government Operations. Such key legislation as the National Security Act of 1947 was handled by a predecessor of this committee. The Armed Services Committee, however, wrote the requirement into the 1958 Defense Reorganization Act that certain kinds of reorganizations be referred to them before taking effect.

Congress, through its committees, keeps informed of and controls major changes in the defense organization and in the makeup of the major weapons-system complex in the military departments. Actually the investigating function is not a monopoly of a single committee; all the committees maintain a surveillance function, and every committee reserves the right to inquire into matters under its jurisdiction. The Armed Services Committee, the Appropriations Committee, and the Government Operations Committee

[13] Section 8, Article I, of the Constitution says, "The Congress shall have power to lay and collect taxes . . . to pay the debts and provide for the common defense and general welfare of the United States."

all investigate. The project manager must be exposed to congressional committees only during the initial evaluation of the efficacy of the particular weapons system. Congress does have the right to participate in the weapons-acquisition process, and project managers will do well to appreciate this right.[14]

The role of not-for-profit contractors [15]

In recent years, the military departments have depended more and more on not-for-profit corporations in engineering and scientific activities. The work of these firms varies considerably, from basic research to systems engineering and technical direction. Examples of these corporations are the Aerospace Corporation in Los Angeles, California, and the Mitre Corporation in Boston, Massachusetts.

The mission of these contractors is to provide scientific, engineering, and support personnel and facilities to military project managers engaged in weapons-system acquisition. In carrying out this function, these not-for-profit firms play a unique role:

> They act as privy council for the overall operation and management of the project development.

> They are authorized to participate in project-review meetings, to enter selected military contractor activities, and to review data that relate to a particular military contract.

> They provide specific consultation to the military project manager on systems engineering and project technical direction.

The role of trade associations

The total array of organizations that can become party to defense project management includes trade associations—for example, the Aerospace Industries Association of America Incorporated (AIA), which is a national trade association of manufacturers of aircraft; missiles; spacecraft; propulsion, navigation, and guidance systems; support equipment; and accessories used in the construction of aerospace products. The current membership consists of 61 aerospace manufacturing companies plus their corporate divi-

---

[14] For a full discussion of Congress's role in military project management, see Herbert Roback, "Congressional Interest in Weapons Acquisition," *Armed Forces Management*, February, 1963.

[15] The term "not-for-profit" as opposed to "nonprofit" is intended to convey that while profits are not a primary objective or motivating factor, the charging of fees for services rendered is justified. The fees vary somewhat, but are usually about 5 percent. For a discussion of this and of the future of the not-for-profit corporations, see Bruce L. R. Smith, *The Future of the Not-for-profit Corporations*, RAND Corporation, Report P–3366, Santa Monica, Calif.

sions. AIA achieves its objectives through a complex of committees, councils, panels, and other working groups, which keep the aerospace industry informed of new government procurement, R&D, and systems-acquisition policies. In addition, these working groups provide a sounding board for the aerospace industry's position on a particular government policy or procedure in the weapons-acquisition business.[16]

Committees of AIA are chartered by the Board of Governors and are supported by an AIA staff executive who has professional qualifications and experience. A committee typically includes representatives from member companies who are specialists in their fields and who have had considerable experience with the company they represent. The committees, in turn, are provided input from specialist groups appointed to deal with particular areas of subject matter. These groups vary in size and often meet with their government counterparts to discuss and attempt to resolve issues of mutual concern.

AIA does not become involved in a specific military project per se; rather, it conducts evaluation and review of policy matters pertaining to government procurement. AIA-government working groups provide valuable feedback in policy evaluation and critique for all the parties concerned. They are not a lobby group, although they undoubtedly influence government procurement law and systems-acquisition practices. AIA, therefore, is a force that can be an indirect participant (although informal) in a military project activity.[17]

Aligning the project organizations

A group of people in a work situation, a conceptual framework of the organization, and some type of organizational chart—are the necessary ingredients for a managerial environment. The organization is a composite of the physical layout of the resources, the documentation of existing policy and procedure, and the authority and responsibility relationships established between the participants.

Charting the project organizations

The organizational chart is a pictorial portrayal of the organization as it is envisioned at a given moment in time. At best, a traditional chart is an oversimplification of the organizational concept and is used as an aid in

[16] A discussion of an AIA–military department joint-venture product is contained in *Air Force Industry Follow-up Activities to the 1965 Data Management Symposium*, Air Force–Industry Steering Group, Washington, D.C., November, 1966.

[17] For a full discussion of the AIA's role, see *The Aerospace Industries Association Organization and Functions*, Aerospace Industries Association, Washington, D.C., n.d.

grasping the concept of the organization. Organizational charts sometimes become confused with organization theory. Management literature indicates various feelings about the value of the chart as an organization tool. For example, Cyert and March say: [18]

> Traditionally, organizations are described by organization charts. An organization chart specifies the authority or reportorial structure of the system. Although it is subject to frequent private jokes, considerable scorn on the part of sophisticated observers, and dubious championing by archaic organizational architects, the organization chart communicates some of the most important attributes of the system. It usually errs by not reflecting the nuances of relationships within the organization; it usually deals poorly with informal control and informal authority, usually underestimates the significance of personality variables in molding the actual system, and usually exaggerates the isomorphism between the authority system and the communication system. Nevertheless, the organization chart still provides a lot of information conveniently—partly because the organization usually has come to consider relationships in terms of the dimensions of the chart.

Jasinski is critical of the traditional, pyramidal organizational chart because it fails to display the nonvertical relations between the participants in the organization. He says: [19]

> Necessary as these horizontal and diagonal relations may be to the smooth functioning of the technology or work flow, they are seldom defined or charted formally. Nonetheless, wherever or whenever modern technology does operate effectively, these relations do exist, if only on a nonformal basis.

Can these charts of formal organizations be changed to reflect the horizontal and diagonal relations required in the management situation?

Charting horizontal relationships [20]

Traditionally, organizations are described by means of an organizational chart. The desire to retain a simple idealistic *concept* of an organization probably accounts for the durability and venerability of the pyramidal chart. The growing realization that organizations have internal and external

[18] Richard M. Cyert and James G. March, *A Behavioral Theory of the Firm*, Prentice-Hall, Inc., Englewood Cliffs, N.J., 1963, p. 289.

[19] Frank J. Jasinski, "Adapting Organization to New Technology," *Harvard Business Review*, January–February, 1959, p. 80.

[20] The material to follow in this chapter is an extension of the articles by David I. Cleland and Wallace Munsey, "Who Works with Whom," *Harvard Business Review*, September–October, 1967; and "The Organization Chart: A Systems View," *University of Washington Business Review*, Autumn, 1967. Used by permission.

modes which are neither simple nor idealistic probably accounts for much of the criticism of these charts. This observation leads to the generalization that the vertical organizational chart is a graphic portrayal of the traditional school of organization theory.

Today's organizations are considerably more complex than those of earlier times; this implies that the organizational chart should go beyond the limits of classical or traditional doctrines. A method of charting is needed which recognizes the role of the many organizations, in addition to the parent organization, that play a role in company fortunes. Consider again for a moment the words of Seymour Tilles:

> Many organizations have a management team that includes individuals—auditors, lawyers, bankers, brokers, and a variety of other specialists—who never appear on the organization chart. In some cases, these outside experts are consulted with such regularity that they are really a part of the management system. In fact, the extent of the management system is frequently an indication of the manager's ability.

What Tilles seems to be saying is that an organization is a complex of interpersonal relationships existing in the total systems environment and having tying bonds of reciprocity.

The lack of an organizational chart which can be used to analyze the environment can be a matter of frustration and consternation to managers. One project manager in a space missile organization, when asked to diagram his organization on the blackboard, replied, "It would be impossible to show a meaningful diagram of the organization. The work load weaves back and forth between the two branches of the division and other agencies in such a way that there is no practical way to tell anyone just how we go about getting our work done." To this successful project manager, the principal usefulness of the vertical organizational chart was in establishing superior-subordinate responsibilities in his organization and in showing the relative alignment of the various departments under his jurisdiction. Although this project manager could draw from memory numerous system schematics of the missile with which he worked, he could not draw a schematic of the organization he managed. He readily acknowledged that conceptually his organization was a system, but he had not developed any sort of schematic to analyze the interrelatedness of the project.

Usefulness of the traditional chart

The organizational chart is a means of visualizing many of the abstract features of an organization. The possible value of the organizational chart as a way of depicting organizational relationships has not been fully exploited in contemporary literature. A possible exception is Terry, who devotes most of a chapter to the subject.[21]

In summary, the organizational chart is useful in that:

It provides a general framework of the organization.

It can be used to acquaint the employees and outsiders with the nature of the organizational structure.

It can be used to identify how the people tie into the organization; it shows the skeleton of the organization, depicting the basic relationships and the groupings of positions and functions.

It shows formal lines of authority and responsibility, and it outlines the hierarchy—who fills each formal position, who reports to whom, and so on.

Limitations of the traditional chart

The organizational chart is something like a photograph. It shows the basic outline of the subject, but tells little about how he functions or relates to others in his environment. The organizational chart is limited in that:

It fails to show the nature and limits of the activities required to attain the objectives.

It does not reflect the myriad of reciprocal relationships that exist between peers, associates, and many others with a common interest in the project.

It is a static, formal portrayal of the organizational structure; most charts are out of date by the time they are published.

It shows the relationships that are supposed to exist, but neglects the informal, dynamic relationships that are constantly at play in the environment.

It may confuse organizational position with status and prestige; it overemphasizes the vertical role of managers and causes parochialism, a result of the blocks and lines of the chart and the neat, orderly flow they imply.

Alternatives to traditional organizational charting

The usefulness of organizational charts, together with their limitations, suggests that new means for graphically displaying the interactions between people and functions in an organized activity should be sought. The charts should be constructed in such a way that their limitations, which seem to be universally recognized, are reduced, thus making the charts more useful.

Introducing new techniques of charting will be difficult because people are so resistant to change. The popularity of the pyramidal organizational chart is probably due to its simplicity and ease of preparation. For many

[21] George R. Terry, *Principles of Management,* Richard D. Irwin, Inc., Homewood, Ill., 1964, pp. 443–462.

executives, reorganizations are brought about by changing the alignment of the blocks and lines on the chart. This is the most drastic form of reorganization because it breaks up patterns of formal and informal authority and responsibility and disrupts the prevailing procedures and policies. Dalton E. McFarland's statement illustrates the problem: [22]

> Innovations in organization charting can be expected from time to time, but so far none has appealed widely to executives. Principal reliance must continue to be placed on standard top-to-bottom charts. Custom and habit support their use. These represent the basis upon which other types of charts are made. The standard charting procedure is realistic in the sense that most business organizations actually are set up so that authority resides at the top and flows in a downward direction. Charting procedures that are in the nature of euphemism provide no enduring practical value.

Perhaps the greatest threat to new methods of charting is the feeling of some executives that they will lose prestige if their relative positions on a hierarchical chart are changed. There is a tendency to equate the ascending levels of an organization with gradations of talent and competence.[23]

In selecting a new means of charting an organization, one should consider the purpose for which the charts will be used: (1) information display and (2) organizational analysis. Both are required, but can one chart satisfy both needs? If the organization is simple in concept, structure, and environmental relationships (i.e., if there is very little interdependency between functions and organizations), perhaps the traditional chart will adequately portray organizational information. However, if the organization is a complex system that fits into a larger system, the organizational chart that displays the skeletal formal structure is far from being adequate for organizational analysis.

If the organizational chart is intended as a means of communicating information, then its use as an analytical tool is an unintentional by-product. The creation of the chart itself is a way of forcing planning and analysis; its greatest value may be the analysis required for its preparation. In this respect, it is like systems analysis and the network planning and control techniques to be discussed in a later chapter.

Our discussion has centered around the assumption that the chart, derived as a result of some organizational analysis, has been subsequently used for communications purposes. If the chart is intended primarily as a vehicle

---

[22] Dalton E. McFarland, *Management Principles and Practices*, The Macmillan Company, New York, 1958, p. 288.
[23] See William H. Read, "The Decline of the Hierarchy in Industrial Organizations," *Business Horizons*, Fall, 1965.

for the dissemination of information, it must of necessity be simple in format and devoid of detail. On the other hand, if it is to be used for detailed fact gathering, analysis, and correlation, something more than conventional techniques are required. This reasoning might well lead to the conclusion that two organizational charts are needed in certain organizations, one to show the intended legal or formal overall structure of the organization (the picture) and the other to portray the manner in which the day-to-day details of the organization are carried out (the schematic diagram).

Linear responsibility charting

The linear responsibility chart (LRC) is a recent innovation in management theory that goes beyond the simple display of formal lines of communication, gradations of organizational level, departmentation, and line-staff relationships. In addition to the simple display, the LRC reveals the task–job position couplings that are an *advisory, informational, technical,* and *specialty* nature. The use of this approach as a facilitative charting tool in project management will be discussed in detail in the next chapter.

Summary

Man could probably devise more varied organizational arrangements than there are companies or projects. Varied as these arrangements might be, they would all be based on the concept of pulling together technical and managerial talents into a team to operate without limits of disciplines or product lines in undertaking a project. The organization form that finally evolves out of the project requirements will undoubtedly be a compromise between pure project management and standard functional alignment.

Recommended readings

The Aerospace Industries Association Organization and Functions, Aerospace Industries Association, Washington, D.C., n.d.

Bennis, W. G.: "Evolving Organization Obsoleting Pyramid, etc.," *Steel,* Apr. 11, 1966, p. 28.

Bowie, Robert M.: "The Project Overlay System in Research Organization," *IRE Transactions on Engineering Management,* September, 1957.

Cherington, Paul W., Merton J. Peck, and Frederick M. Scherer: *Organi-*

zation and Research and Development Decision Making within a Government Department, Harvard University Press, Cambridge, Mass.

Cleland, David I.: "Organizational Dynamics of Project Management," *IEEE Transactions on Engineering Management,* December, 1966.

Davis, Keith: "The Organization That's Not on the Chart," *Supervisory Management,* July, 1961.

Davison, Roy: *The System View and the Disenchanted Executive,* Systems Development Corporation, Santa Monica, Calif., Nov. 16, 1965.

Establishing System Program Offices, Air Force Systems Command 375-7, Dec. 30, 1962.

Fenell, Klas K.: *Multiple Program Organizations,* Air Force Institute of Technology, Dayton, Ohio, October, 1964.

Fuchs, G. J., and G. C. Thompson: "Management of a New Product Development," *Conference Board Business Record,* October, 1960.

Higgans, Carter C.: "The Organization Chart: Its Theory and Practice," *Management Review,* October, 1956, pp. 889–893.

Janger, A. R.: "Organizing the Corporate Research Function," *Management Records,* December, 1960.

————: "Anatomy of the Project Organization," *Business Management Record,* National Industrial Conference Board, Inc., New York, 1963.

Jasinski, Frank J.: "Adapting Organization to New Technology," *Harvard Business Review,* January–February, 1959, pp. 79–86.

Johnson, Samuel D., and Conrad Jones: "Organizing for Development," *Harvard Business Review,* May–June, 1957.

Kast, F., and J. Rosenzweig: "A Survey of the Intra-company Impact of Weapon System Management," *Harvard Business Review,* March, 1962.

Lanier, F.: "Organizing for Large Engineering Projects," *Machine Design,* Dec. 27, 1956, p. 54.

Lazar, R. G., and A. D. Kellner: "Personnel and Organization Development in an R&D Matrix-overlay Operation," *IEEE Transactions on Engineering Management,* vol. 2, June, 1964.

McWhinney, W. H.: "On the Geometry of Organizations," *Administrative Sciences Quarterly,* December, 1965.

Polaris Management, Department of the Navy, Special Projects Office, Washington, D.C., revised, September, 1962.

Ramo, Simon: "The Role of the Systems-engineering–Technical-direction Contractor in the Management of Air Force Systems Acquisition Programs," in *Science Technology and Management*, McGraw-Hill Book Company, New York, 1963.

Roback, Herbert: "Congressional Interest in Weapons Acquisition," *Armed Forces Management*, February, 1963.

Shepard, Herbert A.: "Patterns of Organization for Applied Research and Development," *The Journal of Business of the University of Chicago*, January, 1956.

Yosphe, Harry B., and Stanley L. Falk: "Organization for National Security," *The Economics of National Security*, Industrial College of the Armed Forces, Washington, D.C., Apr. 1, 1963.

CHAPTER 9
The Organizational Chart: A Systems Viewpoint [1]

This one fact—that the chart is
essentially a device for clarifying
authority relationships—goes a long
way toward explaining its usefulness.[2]

It is the purpose of this chapter to examine the linear responsibility chart
(LRC) and other charting techniques to arrive at a device that will be
useful in tracing authority relationships from the systems viewpoint. Such
techniques and charts will go beyond the usual practice of depicting only
the functional entities and the lines of delegated formal authority. The
charting techniques that we shall develop will also display the coordinative
and integrative requirements of a project manager's job.

The LRC has also been called the "linear organization chart," the "linear

---

[1] The authors are indebted to Maj. Virgil W. Munsey, United States Air Force, whose
thesis, *An Empirical Demonstration of the Systems Characteristics of Complex Organizations*, Air Force Institute of Technology, School of Engineering, 1966, provided the core
of thought for this chapter. In addition, this chapter is an extension of the articles by
David I. Cleland and Wallace Munsey, "Who Works with Whom," *Harvard Business
Review*, September–October, 1967; and "The Organization Chart: A Systems View,"
University of Washington Business Review, Autumn, 1967. Used by permission.

[2] Allen R. Janger, "Charting Authority Relationships," *The Conference Board Record*,
December, 1964.

chart," and the "functional chart." None of these names adequately describes the device. The LRC (or the table or grid, as Janger calls it) [3] shows who participates, and to what degree, when an activity is performed or a decision made. It shows the extent or type of authority exercised by each executive in performing an activity in which two or more executives have overlapping authority and responsibility. It clarifies the authority relationships that arise when executives share common work. The need for a device to clarify the authority relationships is evident from the relative utility of the traditional pyramidal chart, which (1) is merely a simple portrayal of overall functional and authority models and (2) must be combined with detailed position descriptions and organizational manuals to delineate authority relationships and work-performance duties.

It is the authors' contention that the typical pyramidal organizational chart is not adequate as a tool of organizational analysis. It is because of this inadequacy that a technology of position descriptions and organizational manuals has come into being. As organizations have grown larger and larger, personnel interrelationships have increased in complexity, and job descriptions and organizational manuals have grown more detailed. Typical organizational manuals and position descriptions have become so verbose that an organizational analysis can be lost in semantics. An article in *Business Week* reflected on the problem of adequate organizational tools in this manner: [4]

> The usual way to supplement it [the pyramid organization chart] is by recourse to a voluminous organizational manual prescribing the proper relationships and responsibilities. But the manuals—cumbersome and often outdated—rarely earn much attention.

Position descriptions do serve the purpose of describing a single position, but an executive is also concerned with how the people under his jurisdiction relate to one another. On many occasions, executives are confronted with the task of examining and explaining relationships. Project management, corporate staff organization, concepts of product planning, the development of a corporate plan—all these lead to highly complex working relationships. A dynamic organization is often—even continually—redefining large numbers of positions and establishing new responsibility and authority patterns. The basic question is: "When is it necessary to turn away from conventional devices used to describe an organization and seek out a new technique, such as an LRC?"

[3] *Ibid.*
[4] "Manning the Executive Setup," *Business Week*, Apr. 6, 1957, p. 187.

Structure of the LRC

Typically, the LRC shows these characteristics:

1 Core information from conventional organizational charts and associated manuals displayed in a matrix format [5]

2 A series of position titles listed along the top of the table (columns)

3 A listing of responsibilities, authorities, activities, functions, and projects down the side of the chart (lines)

4 An array of symbols indicating degree or extent of authority and explaining the relationship between the columns and the lines

Such an arrangement shows in one horizontal line all persons involved in a function and the extent and nature of their involvement. Furthermore, the one vertical line shows all functions that a person is responsible for and the nature of his responsibility. A vertical line represents an individual's job description; a horizontal line shows the breakout of a function or task by job position.

One potential value of such a chart is the analysis required to create it, i.e., the necessary abstracting and cross-referencing from position descriptions and related documentation manuals. The LRC in Figure 9-1 illustrates the authority interrelationships of a series of positions composing a definable unit. This chart conveys the same message provided by extensive organizational manuals, position descriptions, memorandums of agreement, policy letters, etc. It shows at a glance not only the individuals' responsibilities for certain functions but, what may be even more valuable, the way a given position relates to other positions within the organization. (The chart shown in Figure 9-1 was developed as a result of a corporate reorganization and served to integrate the corporate functions created as a result thereof.)

But why not use the more conventional procedure of position analysis and position description for this sort of thing? There are two primary advantages to this mode of presentation. First, position descriptions and position guides are better at laying down responsibilities and authority patterns than at *portraying relationships*. Second, this type of charting depicts the work of top management as an *integrated system* rather than as a series of individual positions. The chart makes it easy to compare the responsibilities of related executives; in the coordination of budgets, for example, six individuals share the responsibility, ranging from "must be consulted" to "may be consulted" and "must be notified." The filled-in chart provides a quick picture of all the positions involved in the performance of a particular function.

[5] For example, one writer proclaimed: ". . . on one pocket-size chart it shows the facts buried in all the dusty organizational manuals—plus a lot more." *Ibid.*, p. 89.

	Board	President	Vice president marketing-advertising	Vice president engineering and R & D	Vice president finance	Director of manufacturing	Secretary-treasurer	Vice president foreign operations
Establish basic policies and objectives	2	1	3	3	3	3	3	3
Direct operations, control and planning functions	2	1	4	4	4	4	4	4
Fix relationships between central office and operating divisions	2	1	3	3	3	3	3	3
Control expansion—merger—acquisition plans	2	1	3	3	3	3	3	3
Administer merger—acquisition operations		2	1	3	3	3	3	3
Establish marketing policies and procedures		2	1		4			4
Coordinate sales forecasts and projections	5	2	1		5			3
Coordinate advertising plans	5	5	1					4
Coordinate engineering, research and development	5	2	3	1	4	4		4
Coordinate new product programs		2	3	1	4	3		4
Administer research and development center		3		1				
Establish accounting policies and procedures		2			1			
Administer financing, borrowing, equity	2	2			1		3	
Coordinate Budgets	5	2	3	4	1	3		
Administer legal and tax matters		2			1			
Utilization of manufacturing facilities		3				1		
Coordinate training and safety programs		2	1			1		
Coordinate and Administer capital expenditures	2	2	4	4	3	1	3	
Administer insurance plans and stockholder relations		2			4		1	
Coordinate foreign and export operations		2	4	4				1

Code

1 Actual responsibility   2 General supervision   3 must be consulted

4 may be consulted   5 must be notified

Figure 9-1 Authority interrelationships in a unit. Allen R. Janger, "Charting Authority Relationships," *The Conference Board Record*, December, 1964.

In the words of Allen R. Janger, concerning the chart of Figure 9-1: [6]

> The top line . . . shows that the *president* is responsible for estab-
> lishing basic policies and objectives. He works under the general super-
> vision of his *board of directors,* and with the consultation of his
> corporate staff. Responsibility for coordinating engineering, research
> and development . . . is parceled out in a bit more complicated
> fashion. The *vice president, engineering, research,* and development
> carries the actual responsibility. He operates under the general super-
> vision of the *president,* but must carry on close consultations with the
> *vice president, marketing* and *advertising* and the *director of manu-
> facturing.* Consultation with the *vice president, finance* on R&D matters
> is not mandatory but may be required. It is also understood that the
> *board of directors* will be informed of significant developments.
>
> By reading down the chart it is possible to summarize rapidly a
> position's salient responsibilities: As depicted, the *president* has actual
> responsibility for establishing basic policies and objectives, direction of
> operating control and planning functions, fixing relationships between
> the corporate headquarters and the product divisions, and control of
> expansion, merger, and acquisition plans. Other top management func-
> tions are the direct responsibilities of other corporate executives, al-
> though the president generally exercises supervision over them. He
> must at least be consulted on the administration of the R&D center and
> the utilization of manufacturing facilities. The *vice president, market-
> ing* and *advertising* need only notify him about advertising plans.

Staff-line and project-functional relationships pose some of the more
challenging problems of project management, particularly in light of the
desirability of the deliberate conflict between the functional managers and
the project manager. The deliberate conflict must be planned so that respective prerogatives are recognized and protected. The use of a chart similar
to that shown in Figure 9-2 can do much to define and postulate the func-
tional-project relationships, as well as the staff-line, staff-staff interfaces in
the project environment.

The chart shown in Figure 9-2 is different from the chart for top management shown in Figure 9-1 in that the starting point is different. Figure 9-2
shows the work, i.e., the purchasing function and its subfunctions. The
essence of the analysis is the determination of the sphere of each executive's
authority in each of the key purchasing activities and of the extent of that
authority. When these facts are ascertained, the relevant positions are listed
at the top of the chart, and the appropriate symbols are added. The chart
shows the roles of the various executives in manufacturing-related purchasing activities.

[6] *Op. cit.*

Figure 9-1 does more than clarify authority relationships; it can double as a collection of position guides. Its perspective is adequate to permit it to be used as an organizational chart of the top management of the organization. Figure 9-2, on the other hand, cannot serve as an organizational chart since it is not possible to get an overall picture of a position or a unit and its responsibilities from the chart. Figure 9-2 shows only the purchasing activities related to manufacturing; the nonpurchasing activities of the positions, which could be significant, are not shown.

Limitations of LRCs

Charts such as those shown in Figures 9-1 and 9-2 are not a panacea for all organizational difficulties. The LRC is a pictorial representation, and it is subject to the characteristic limitations and shortcomings of pyramidal organizational charts. The LRC does reveal the functional breakout of the work to be done and the interrelationships between the functions and the job positions; however, *it does not show how people act and interact*.

It is doubtful that any contemporary management theorists would deny that organizational effectiveness is as dependent on the informal organization of human actions and relations as it is on the structured, formal organization. The LRC, as we have so far discussed it, is limited to showing the man-job relationships that constitute the formal organization; it does not purport to reveal the infinite number of variations in human relations arising out of the informal organization. The LRC technique simply extends the scope of charting formal organizations wherever they are located in the hierarchical order. Thus, a note of caution is in order about the LRC. But, as Karger and Murdick have implied, we still must give it a vote of confidence: [7]

> Obviously, the chart has weaknesses, of which one of the larger ones is that it is a mechanical aid. Just because it says something is a fact does not make it true. It is very difficult to discover, except generally, exactly what occurs in a company—and with whom. The chart tries to express in specific terms relationships that cannot always be delineated so clearly; moreover, the degree to which it can be done depends on the specific situation. This is the difference between the formal and informal organizations mentioned. Despite this, the Linear Responsibility Chart is one of the best devices for organization analysis known to the authors.

The LRC is a useful device for charting organizational relationships.

[7] Delmar W. Karger and Robert G. Murdick, *Managing Engineering and Research,* The Industrial Press, New York, 1963, p. 89.

Corporate   Division   Plant

PURCHASING ACTIVITIES	Director of purchasing	V. P. manufacturing	Manager, engineering	Controller	Manager, trade relations	General manager of division	Division purchasing	Division engineer	Manager construction	Plant purchasing	Plant manager	Plant purchasing agent	Plant controller	Plant engineer
PURCHASING-OPERATIONS														
A. Raw materials (controlled commodities)														
1. Development of annual plan for purchases of major raw materials.	○	▲				△	●							
2. Purchase or requisition of raw materials according to annual plan.							○			△	●			
3. Revisions in annual plan as to supplier, quantity, and (or) price.	○	▲				△	●			○	○			
4. Selection of appropriate suppliers.	○	△			○		●			○	○			
5. Conducting of any contract or other negotiations with suppliers.	○	▲			○	△	●							
B. Maintenance contracts														
1. Under $10,000 and on standard contract form.												△	●	●
2. Over $10,000 or a nonstandard contract (also approved by Legal Department and Trade Relations Department).	○	▲						△			▲	●	○	●
C. Surplus disposal														
1. Request for disposition of fixed assets.	▲	▲	▲	▲		▲	○			▲			▲	●
2. Disposition of surplus construction materials, equipment, and supplies.	▲		▲			▲				▲	▲	●	○	○
3. Disposition of self-generated scrap (other than metal), supplies, and waste materials up to $100,000.	▲		▲			▲				▲	▲	●	○	○
D. General stores and supplies														
1. Determination of minimum inventory requirements.							○			△	●			
2. Ordering of stores and supplies.							○			△	●			
E. Rental agreements—equipment (under the authorization to execute contracts and purchasing policy).	▲	▲				▲	▲			▲	●			
PURCHASING-CONSTRUCTION														
A. Buildings and equipment														
1. Development of process designs and equipment specifications.		○		△					▲	○	○			●
2. Request of and appropriation of capital funds (RFI procedure in accordance with dollar authorizations).	▲	▲	▲			▲		▲		▲	○	●	●	
3. Determination of the bid list—items over $10,000.	▲	▲				▲			▲	▲	▲	▲	●	
4. Selection of the successful bidder—items over $10,000.	▲	▲				▲			▲	▲	▲	▲	●	
5. Follow up on the rate and amount of expenditures of the appropriated capital funds (capital expenditures report).		○		▲		○			●		○		●	●

KEY:

△   Authorizes and (or) actuates   ○   Recommends and (or) reviews and counsels

▲   Approves   ●   Does the work. (personally or within the department)

Figure 9-2   Functional authority relationships. Allen R. Janger, "Charting Authority Relationships," *The Conference Board Record*, December, 1964.

However, its use can be extended if we combine it with some charting techniques which have developed from the systems view of management.

The systems view

In recent years, management theorists and practitioners have supported the idea that an organization operates as a system. Although this concept has only recently been popularized under such labels as "matrix organization," "program management," and "project management," it was known and discussed as early as 1911: [8]

> Any manufacturing or mercantile business made up of different processes more or less interdependent must, to secure the best results, be so organized that the separate processes *and the unit member* within these will be brought into systematic connection and operation as efficient parts of the whole (italics supplied).

The important point made in this excerpt, from an address by Henry P. Kendall at the First Conference on Scientific Management at Dartmouth College in 1911, is that the unit members as well as the processes must be "brought into systematic connection and operation as efficient parts of the whole." During the ensuing years, Gantt charts, operation and process flow sheets, PERT [9] and other graphic aids were devised to assist managers in the planning and control of processes and activities to ensure their proper interconnection into a systematic whole.

The only graphic means of showing the interconnections between members of the organization, however, has been the pyramidal chart. Such charts depict only the *vertical* interconnections of formal authority. This limitation has restricted the manager in his use of the charts and has permitted him to show only how his organization is divided, so that he can determine who works *for* whom; he has not been able to show how his organization is interconnected, so that he can determine who works *with* whom.

The systems concept of the organization—a view that emphasizes the operating interconnections between people—provides the means for struc-

[8] Henry P. Kendall, *Scientific Management: First Conference at the Amos Tuck School,* The Plimpton Press, Norwood, Mass., 1912.
[9] In 1903, the Polish engineer Karol Amamiecki described a graphical device called a "harmonogram," which was the precursor of the present-day PERT concept. See John F. Mee, "Pioneers of Management," *Advanced Management-Office Executive,* Oct., 1962, pp. 26–29.

turing the members of the organization into an integrated entity. This concept cannot, however, become useful until it is translated into an operable technique. Just as Gantt charts, flow diagrams, PERT, and other graphic devices have been developed to implement the systems concept in organizational *activities,* so must a charting technique be developed for the organizational *system.*

The universal subsystems of management

Let us assume that the organizational system can be subdivided into three subsystems:

> The *technical subsystem,* which has as its component parts the *things* or services that constitute the objectives of the organization.
>
> The *work subsystem,* which has as its component parts the *activities* and *tasks* that produce the technical subsystem and its parts. Included in this subsystem are the facilities and equipment required to perform such activities and tasks.
>
> The *managing subsystem,* which has as its component parts the *members* of the organization who perform the activities and accomplish the tasks structured by the work subsystem.[10]

The technical subsystem of an organization consists simply of the products produced and services furnished by the organization—television sets, tractors, fire-protection services, etc. This subsystem is the basis of the other two, but it does not actively enter into this discussion of organization charting and will not be considered further.

The work subsystem is the task structure adapted to facilitate the economic processes of planning for and executing the development, financing, manufacturing, and marketing of the technical subsystem. The diagrams of the work subsystem are the process and operations flow sheets, the schematic layouts of general task areas, and the activity sequences with their time and functional interrelations. These graphic displays are an analytical and systematic description of *what* the organization does, and *when,* as it works on the technical subsystem. The component parts of the work subsystem are the activities and tasks of the oganization.

The managing subsystem is that system of interrelationships between people required to tie together, adjust, regulate, redirect, evaluate, expedite, limit, and otherwise breathe life into the total organizational system. It is the subsystem through which a change in production rates, an entrance into

---

[10] The basic idea of this classification is described in Joseph A. Litterer, *The Analysis of Organizations,* John Wiley & Sons, Inc., New York, 1965, pp. 299–304.

a new marketing area, the redesign of a product, and countless other unplanned, nonprogrammable tasks are integrated into, and assimilated by, the work and technical subsystems.

The managing subsystem describes how people interact, not how things and activities interact. The managing subsystem is people centered in that the inputs, outputs, environmental factors, and external considerations are molded into the work and technical subsystems through the continuing, conscious actions of the people in the organization. The point of view that *people* are the component parts of the managing subsystem and that the interactions of the system are therefore the interpersonal relations between the people provides the basis for structuring the organization as a system of people and not as a system of activities.

It is the managing subsystem for which charting techniques have not as yet been developed. We believe, however, that managing subsystems can be described by schematic diagrams in much the same manner as other systems.

Systems characteristics of a managing subsystem

A person's job performance is analogous to the operation of an electronic tube amplifier system. First, the tube must be designed and constructed so that it will function in a specific way. Second, its design and operating features must be compatible with the environment in which it is placed, Third, a source of power has to be provided that will be suitable for the tube's capabilities and the anticipated input signals. Finally, the tube must be connected to a source that will furnish the input signal, and to an element that will receive the output signal.

Satisfying the first three of these conditions places the system in a static or quiescent state. Not until the fourth step is taken is the system raised to its dynamic state. The tube's basic internal structure, and its intercoupling with a power source and an environment are the determinants of its *potential* performance, but its input and output intercouplings and the input signal combine to form the *actual* output performance.

Analyzing job-performance capabilities and the actual job performance requires that we consider many factors like those discussed in the example of the electronic tube. The person must be intrinsically capable of performing the job to which he is assigned. The social, physical, psychological, and other environments in which he exists must be inherently compatible with his basic needs. The proper authority must be delegated (and responsibility exacted) to serve as the power motivating him to accomplish the job specifications. Lastly, the person must be provided with the necessary couplings for incoming information (input signals) and output decisions (processed output signals).

Note that this description covers the two basic aspects of a system description: (1) what the system is capable of doing, as determined by the design of its component parts and the intercoupling of its component parts with its environment and power source, and (2) what the system actually does as determined by its input-output intercouplings and its input signal.

ORGANIZATIONAL INTERCOUPLINGS   Our next step is to fit the "how," "when," and "what" of the worker's task accomplishment (analogous to the amplifier function of the electronic tube) and administrative needs (the tube's environmental requirements) into a systems scheme. How a worker does his job or accomplishes a task is a composite of his personal capabilities, the extent of authority delegated to him, the influence of his supervisor, and the framework of policies, rules, and procedures within which he must work. The operation of the "how" factor is based on a vertical intercoupling between a worker and his supervisor.

A second type of intercoupling between a worker and his supervisor relates to his administrative needs—not as a worker, but as a person! This is the same as saying that an amplifier tube must have its environmental needs satisfied as a tube, as well as its functional needs as an amplifier. If managers recognized and provided for human environmental needs to the same extent that engineers recognize and provide for mechanical environmental needs, the social and material well-being of workers would be vastly improved.

The person, the functional supervisor, the environment, and the intercouplings and interrelations between these elements are the determinants of how—and how well—a worker does a job; these are the features of the vertical flows that form the basis of classical management doctrine; these are the ingredients of activity specialization; and these are the structural aspects and the static-state factors of the managing subsystem.

But what about the *horizontal* flows of interpersonal relations that form the basis of both project management and activity integration? These are the flows which raise the managing subsystem to its dynamic state. These are the input flows of "what" and "when" that are combined with the vertical power flows of "how" to produce a useful output.

The vertical flows arise from division of labor, activity specialization, and formal authority. The horizontal flows originate from such considerations as regulating, phasing, integrating, coordinating, and otherwise facilitating a task as it proceeds from job to job.

The interpersonal relations between the persons of the managing subsystem have been identified as the intercouplings between the component parts of the system. The vertical intercouplings provide for the vertical flows of formal authority over jobs and other factors, while the horizontal intercouplings serve to link the jobs into the tasks that the organization must accomplish. The vertical intercouplings are represented by the lines on the pyramidal organizational chart. Where on the chart are the horizontal intercouplings shown?

USEFULNESS OF ANALOGIES   We have attempted to develop an analogy between an electronic system and the managing subsystem of an organization. Given that the analogy is apparent, two questions must be asked: "Is it *valid?*" "Is it *useful?*" William G. Scott flashes a warning signal to those who attempt to use poorly founded analogies: [11]

> Thus, certain forces of cybernetic models could be generalized to human organization. Considerable danger, however, lies in poorly founded analogies. Superficial similarities between simpler system forms and social systems are apparent everywhere. Instinctually based ant societies, for example, do not yield particularly *instructive* lessons for understanding rationally conceived human organizations. Thus, care must be taken that analogies used to bridge system levels are not mere devices for literary enrichment. For analogies to have *usefulness* and *validity,* they must exhibit inherent structural similarities or implicitly identical operational principles.

Bearing this note of caution in mind, let us examine the analogy critically as it relates to the diagramming of systems, whether physical or social systems. We shall show that the difficulties in drawing a useful schematic diagram arise more from the *complexity* of the system than from its *type.*

The usefulness of a schematic diagram in describing an electronic system depends largely on the correspondence between the diagram and the actual system. For example, a rectangle on a diagram might stand for an electronic package, and a line between two symbols within the rectangle might depict a wire between two components within the electronic package. If we lifted the cover of the electronic package, we would see wires connected between the two component parts as depicted in the schematic diagram (Figure 9-3). In this case, there is close correspondence between the system and the diagram.

Unfortunately for the manager, there is no such clear-cut one-to-one correspondence between his organizational charts and his managing sub-

[11] William G. Scott, "Organization Theory: An Overview and an Appraisal," *Journal of the Academy of Management,* vol. 4, no. 1, April, 1961.

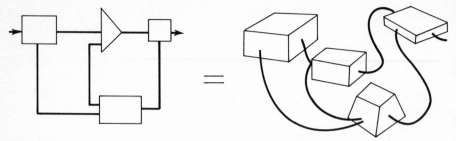

Figure 9-3   Schematic diagram: physical-system equivalency.

system. The manager's world has no neatly constructed organizational package that can be touched, looked at, or otherwise verified as being the physical counterpart of the rectangle on the chart. How can he show a line of authority connecting two persons as it was drawn on the chart, e.g., as reflected in Figure 9-4?

Does this enigma mean that the engineer can go on drawing and using schematic diagrams, while the manager can draw organizational charts, but *not use* them?

Both the engineer and the manager work with systems; both draw charts to help describe their respective systems. The former finds charts extremely useful, while the latter may find them more disadvantageous than otherwise. The answer to this dilemma does not necessarily lie in a different way of drawing the charts—although this is a part of the manager's problem. Instead, it requires that we look beyond the charts to the differences between the systems.

CLOSED VERSUS OPEN SYSTEMS   The engineer's system—i.e., the electronic tube system—is a structured, closed system, It is structured because it was synthesized from component parts having characteristics that were carefully

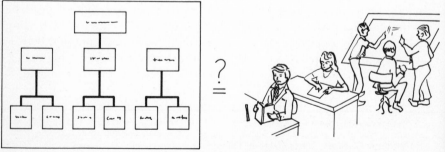

Figure 9-4   Organizational chart: social-system equivalency.

chosen to function in accordance with the designer's intent. The parts were manufactured and assembled so that their individual performance and the overall system performance would be as predicted, given the type of power supply, the range of inputs, and the environment as specified.

The engineer's system is closed because it will produce the specified output *only* when all conditions and factors that were anticipated and provided for in the design, manufacture, and operation are present and none others have interfered. Thus, if the power supply falls below acceptable limits, if the range of signal inputs is wider than provided for, if the environment is more severe than anticipated, if the characteristics of its parts change, or if some other adverse condition exists, the output probably will not be as intended, or the system itself might not survive.

The key factors in a structured, closed system are thus *predictability* and *conformity*. All future situations and conditions must be predicted and provided for (or protected against) by the designer, and all events must conform to the limits of the predictions. (A house heating system incorporating a thermostatic device is a familiar example of a closed, structured system.)

The managing subsystem, in contrast to an engineer's system, can be viewed as an unstructured, open system. The component parts are the members of the organization. A person is not "structured" in accordance with a set of specifications so that he will perform in some characteristic manner, given a set of specified conditions and inputs. Nor can the manager appraise the risks and uncertainties associated with a task to the extent that he can determine all the salient features in the makeup of the organizational system that must be accommodated or anticipated in his design.

The managing subsystem is viewed as being unstructured and open only in relation to the more simple technical subsystems. There is, of course, some structure to an organization; if there were not, one could hardly call it an organization. An organization is also, to some extent, a closed system. For any given task and any given set of environmental factors, the efficiency of an organization is largely a measure of the extent to which it is structured and closed. However, concern with present efficiency of operations is offset by the need to consider future effectiveness in being able to respond to, and deal with, change. To satisfy this organizational necessity, the manager seeks *not* the engineer's closed system, but the open system of the biologist Ludwig von Bertalanffy,[12] i.e., that system which can maintain a dynamic equilibrium within its changing and unpredictable environment.

---

[12] Ludwig von Bertalanffy, "General System Theory: A New Approach to Unity of Science," *Human Biology*, December, 1951, pp. 303–361; and Kenneth Boulding, "General Systems Theory: The Skeleton of Science," *Management Science*, April, 1956, pp. 197–208.

COMPLEX VERSUS SIMPLE SYSTEMS   Suppose now that the manager and the engineer find themselves in reversed roles insofar as the relative complexity of their respective systems is concerned. The engineer is constructing a diagrammatic representation of a physical system made from component parts which have a rather wide variability in behavioral characteristics and which must perform a multiplicity of transformations as determined by some external control switch. This system is to operate over a very wide range of environmental conditions. It must accept a large variety of inputs, and its power supply may vary from exceedingly weak to very strong. From all this must come some steady-state output with a profile and substance that can vary only slightly from its design goal. Can an understandable diagram be drawn which will depict the makeup and functioning of this system at one instant in time or over a period of time? It would be a most difficult challenge to produce a meaningful and useful schematic diagram of such a system.

The manager, on the other hand, has a little more luck in diagramming his system. Each person—each component part—in his managing subsystem has a rather well-defined and narrow set of characteristics that are matched to the one and only job he performs. The jobs are all horizontally decoupled and the formal authority is strong and clear-cut. The environment is both predictable and stable for long periods of time and is compatible with the optimum mode of operation of the system. The inputs are always of the same nature, and the output need not be exceedingly uniform or steady. A few straight lines interconnecting a number of rectangles should be sufficient to depict adequately the nature and workings of this manager's *system of persons*.

So far, we have discussed engineers, managers, systems, and diagrams. More explicitly, we have attempted to show that engineers are managers, managers are engineers, systems are systems, and system-diagraming techniques are not dependent upon whether the component parts are human beings, activities, or physical things. Now we shall describe a way in which the managing-subsystem concept can be translated into a managing-subsystem schematic *diagram* that will portray the horizontal as well as the vertical intercouplings between the members of an organization.

Systems charting

The linear responsibility charting idea was first introduced in this country by the Serge A. Birn Company in the early 1950s. Since that time, it has been adopted to perform many analytical tasks in addition to organizational analyses. Justifying new equipment, manpower planning, realigning and smoothing out work loads, and cutting overhead costs are but a few of the uses which have been described.[13]

An input-output device

The LRC can be visualized as an input-output device. For example, if the job positions of the managing subsystems are considered to be the inputs, task accomplishments the outputs, and matrix symbols the specific task-to-job relationships, then the overall LRC can be looked upon as a diagram of the managing subsystem from a systems viewpoint (Figure 9-5 diagrammatically illustrates this idea).

If two additional steps are added to this charting scheme, the systems

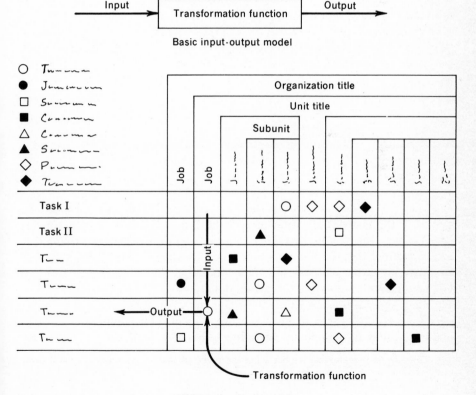

Figure 9-5   Input-output-device schematic.

[13] "Linear Responsibility Charting," *Factory,* vol. 121, pp. 88–91, March, 1963.

viewpoint can be made more explicit. First, if systems terminology is used to structure the LRC matrix symbols and if the personnel affected are indoctrinated in the philosophy of an LRC, then many of the facets of the informal organization [14] can be formalized and assimilated along with the formal organization into the managing-subsystem structure. The second step is to use the *systems symbols* from one row (one task) of the LRC to draw a schematic diagram, as indicated by the symbols of that row; this would show the interrelationships or intercouplings between the persons involved in accomplishing a task (see Figure 9-6).

The organization's work-subsystem chart could yield another advantage if the titles for the tasks and activities of the LRC were used. If this were done, the managing-subsystem schematic could also be used for diagrammatically integrating the work subsystem and the managing subsystem. A third step would be to superimpose a string of managing-subsystem schematics on the *total* work-subsystem chart to give an overall analytical view of how the organization operates; this would show the stream of interpersonal relations that serve to control, change, and otherwise facilitate the accomplishment of the tasks essential to the realization of the organizational goals.

The systematized LRC

A systematized LRC could be structured to serve as the basis for drawing a managing-subsystem schematic diagram by following the three steps described below.

ARRANGEMENT AND FORM OF INPUTS: JOB POSITIONS   The job positions involved in the analysis are listed across the top of the LRC matrix. As can be seen from the sample in Figure 9-6, these job positions are arranged in such a manner that the line structure around them indicates the administrative ordering of the job positions. This method of showing job positions provides a means of integrating the pyramidal organization chart into the LRC.[15] The chart should show only the jobs being analyzed. If the analysis concerns only the executives and engineers of an organizational unit, for example, nothing would be gained by including jobs such as those of secretaries,

---

[14] The informal organization is not what the name implies, i.e., a casual, loosely structured community of people who have similar interests. The informal organization can be most demanding on its members. Its standards of performance and loyalty and its authority patterns can be anything but loose. It can be the most powerful of alliances existing between people having vested interests.

[15] Compare the top portion of the LRC in Fig. 9-6 with the organizational chart in Fig. 9-7 for a one-to-one correspondence in information.

clerks, and draftsmen, even though they are vital parts of the organizational effort. The LRC, like any other chart, must be brief and simple to be effective.

LISTING OUTPUTS: TASKS AND ACTIVITIES   The tasks and activities related to the job positions are listed on the left side of the matrix. These tasks and activities should be listed in groupings and subgroupings that would facilitate the analysis and enhance the perspective view of the chart. If the tasks are extracted from the organization's work-subsystem chart, this scheme would enable the work subsystem to be integrated into the managing subsystem. Whether this method or some other is chosen, it is very important that complete, accurate, and agreed-upon descriptions of the tasks are selected. The relative ease of accomplishing the analysis and the subsequent usefulness of the LRC will depend strongly on the adequacy of the task statements.

DESCRIPTION AND DEFINITION OF MATRIX SYMBOLS: TASK-JOB RELATIONSHIPS There are a number of ways in which a person (a job position) can be related to a task. For example, he may be the person who takes some direct action concerning the task, he may be that person's supervisor, or perhaps he is an adviser on how to do the work. Perhaps he advises as to what needs to be done from a standpoint of intertask sequencing, e.g., as a production scheduler. He may even be someone in the system who only needs to be notified that an operation on the task has been completed. In each case, there exists what may be called a *task-job relationship* (TJR).

From a systems viewpoint, each TJR can be visualized as falling into one of three major categories: (1) transfer function, (2) control loop, or (3) input-output stream. The LRC shown in Figure 9-6 for the equipment test division of an electrical equipment company uses the eight TJRs defined below. The first three of these are usually found in papers and articles about the LRC; the other five have been retitled and changed so as to be more meaningful for a systems treatment.

TRANSFER FUNCTION: WORK IS DONE/TJR (WID/TJR)   The WID/TJR is the transfer-function aspect of the managing-subsystem model. It is the actual juncture of the managing and the work subsystems. The given inputs of information, matter, and energy (i/m/e) are transformed into predetermined outputs of i/m/e in accordance with the program of instructions (policies, rules, procedures) furnished to the person for this job position.

CONTROL LOOP: DIRECT SUPERVISION/TJR (DS/TJR)   The DS/TJR constitutes

Task-/Job Relationships
Symbol titles

- ○ Work is done
- ● Direct supervision
- □ General supervision
- ■ Intertask integration
- △ Occasional intertask integration
- ◀ Intertask coordination
- ◇ Occasional intertask coordination
- ◆ Output notification mandatory

Major functional area: test program activities	Division manager	Test management and plans branch					Test operations branch										
		Branch manager	Test-activity integrator	Test-facility manager	Test-data planner	Test and documents coordinator	Branch manager	Data A & A section Section supervisor	Instrumentation engineer	Elec. mach. testing section Section supervisor	Test-equipment engineer	Test-article engineer	Electronic testing section Section supervisor	Electrical-systems engineer	R.F. systems engineer	Cmd and C+I systems engineer	Test-equipment engineer
Approve test-program changes	○	◀					◀	◇									
Define test objectives	●	○	○				■	◀		◀			◀				
Determine test requirements	□	●	○	◀			■	◇		◇			◇				
Evaluate test-program progress	●	○	◀	◇			◀										
Make test-program policy decisions	○	◀			◀	◀	◀										
Write test-program responsibility doctrine	□	●	○				■			◇			◇				

Equipment-test division

Major functional area:
integration of test-support act

- Chair-test working group
- Prepare milestone-test schedules
- Write test directive

- Write detailed test procedures
- Coordinate test prepartions
- Verify test-article configuration

Major functional area:
all systems test

- Certify test readiness
- Perform test-director function
- Perform test-conductor function
- Analyze test data
- Resolve test anomalies
- Prepare test report

Figure 9-6 Systems LRC for equipment test division.

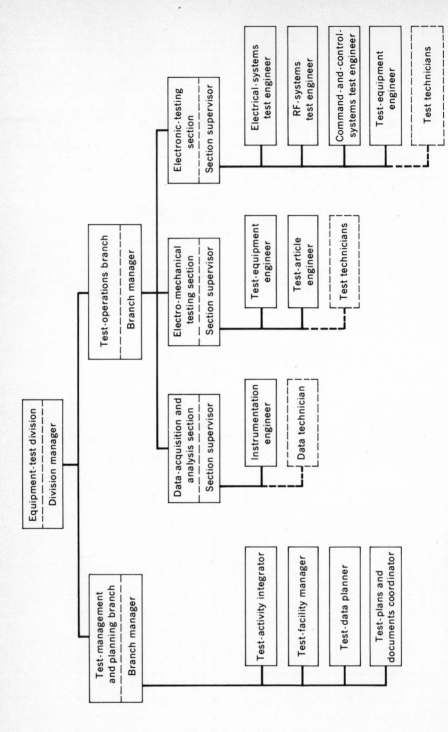

Figure 9-7 Organizational chart for equipment test division.

the prime operational control element in the WID/TJR control loop. The person in the DS job position is considered to be the administrative supervisor of the person in the WID job position. The DS/TJR evaluates the quantity, quality, and timeliness of the WID/TJR outputs through the use of policy-guidance information, program directives, procedures, WID input-output comparisons, schedules, and other managerial feedback, measurement, and control devices. The omission of this TJR from a row (task) indicates that the WID/TJR is of such a routine, stable nature that frequent contact with the DS/TJR is not normally required in operation of the transfer function.

GENERAL SUPERVISION/TJR (GS/TJR)   The GS/TJR is a second-order operational-control element and a first-order or prime source of policy guidance for the WID/TJR. The person in the GS job position is the administrative supervisor of the person in the DS job position. The primary role of the GS/TJR is to furnish the DS and WID job positions with a framework of policies and guidance of a scope that permits as much *closed-loop* decision-making flexibility as possible in attainment of the desired WID/TJR outputs. The exclusion of the GS/TJR from a given WID/TJR control loop indicates that WID actions are seldom taken that involve questions of conformance to, or exceptions from, existing GS policy.

INTERTASK INTEGRATION/TJR (II/TJR)   The II/TJR is placed in the WID/TJR control loop to indicate the need for consideration of functional compatibility between this WID/TJR and other WID/TJRs. The extent of the involvement of the II/TJR in the control loop is the extent to which the transfer functions of the tasks concerned are interlocked or functionally interdependent. The person in the II job position does not have an administrative role in the WID/TJR control loop.

OCCASIONAL INTERTASK INTEGRATION/TJR (OII/TJR)   The OII/TJR is similar in concept and definition to the II/TJR, discussed above. The principal difference is the specialty nature of this TJR as opposed to the general or routine nature of the II/TJR. The omission of this TJR and(or) the II/TJR from a control loop indicates that the WID/TJR is, as a rule, functionally independent of, and hence decoupled from, other transfer functions in the work subsystem.

INPUT-OUTPUT STREAM: INTERTASK COORDINATION/TJR (IC/TJR)   The IC/TJR is an information *input* to the WID/TJR and hence does not appear in the control loop; it has nothing to do with the "shape" or "how" of the transfer function. Intertask sequencing, schedule compatibility, quantities, qualities, and other matters of a "what" and "when" nature are indicated by the use of the IC/TJR.

OCCASIONAL INTERTASK COORDINATION/TJR (OIC/TJR)   The OIC/TJR is similar to the IC/TJR, discussed above, except that its use indicates only specialized instances of coordination instead of being a routine input.

OUTPUT NOTIFICATION MANDATORY/TJR (ONM/TJR)   The ONM/TJR is placed in the *output* of the WID/TJR transfer function when it is essential or critical that the ONM job position receive some specialized, exact, or timely information concerning the WID/TJR outputs. The concept of this TJR is one of passive transmission of information only and is not coordinative.

The LRC format, as discussed to this point, consists of job positions administratively ordered, tasks and activities grouped in some meaningful way, and TJRs defined along the lines of systems terminology. The subsequent analytical process involves the findings and determinations that lead to inserting the TJRs in the boxes of the LRC matrix. If a TJR symbol does not appear in a box, the analyst has concluded that the job position is not intercoupled with the WID job position of the task.

The completed analysis is then a systematized LRC model of the managing subsystem. This model displays the following characteristics of, and information about, an organizational unit:

> The pyramidal organizational chart is incorporated into the top of the matrix through the use of lines to partition the job positions administratively.
>
> The tasks and activities of the work subsystem are listed according to some functional flow plan.
>
> The TJR symbols in the LRC matrix show the types of intercouplings between the person that offsets the work subsystem—the WID job position—and other persons with an interest in the task.
>
> The TJRs also serve to show how the managing and work subsystems are integrated.
>
> The overall model yields a perspective view of how the *static* formal organization is combined with the *passive* work subsystem to become a *dynamic* functioning entity that maintains a continuous balance with its environment while transforming its information-matter-energy inputs into the outputs that satisfy the ever-changing goals and objectives of the organization.

System model schematic diagrams

One additional diagram can be constructed that will further illustrate the systems nature of the managing subsystem. If a WID/TJR and its associated task title are combined in one rectangle and the remaining TJRs are inter-coupled with that WID/TJR and each is enclosed in separate rectangles arranged about, and interconnected with, the WID in accordance with their respective TJRs the resulting schematic diagram will convey a systems concept of the interpersonal relations involved in accomplishing a given task. Figure 9-8 shows the arrangement of TJRs in a system model schematic format. Figure 9-9 is a system model schematic of the task "Write detailed test procedures," which appears in Figure 9-6. If all tasks of the organization's work subsystems are properly analyzed and charted and if the system model schematic for each task is shown with its respective tasks and interconnections with the other schematics, the results should give an overall portrayal of the organization's integrated work subsystem and managing subsystem, such as is shown by the sketch in Figure 9-10.

Summary

Systems engineering evolved from an awareness of the interrelatedness of organizational activities. During the last few years, a systems-management philosophy has evolved in response to a growing recognition of this inter-

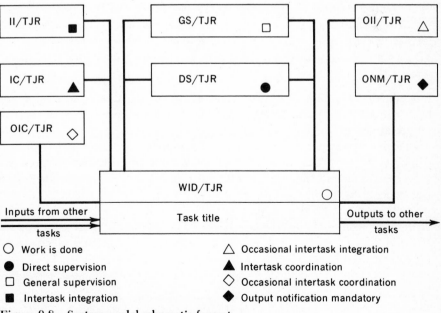

Figure 9-8   System model schematic format.

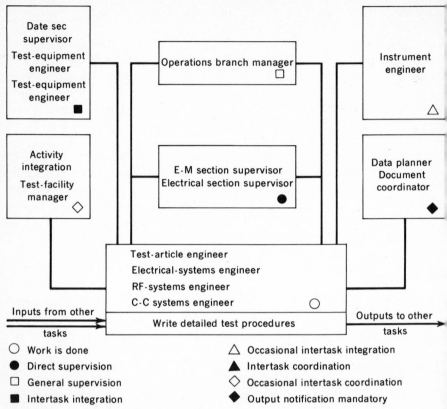

○ Work is done   △ Occasional intertask integration
● Direct supervision   ▲ Intertask coordination
□ General supervision   ◇ Occasional intertask coordination
■ Intertask integration   ◆ Output notification mandatory

Figure 9-9   System model schematic of the task "Write detailed test procedures."

relatedness. This philosophy can also be used to show the interrelatedness between people. We have here described a technique for charting this interrelatedness.

One of the authors, in an earlier writing, took the position that project management is a "theoretical framework for viewing the internal and external environmental factors as integrated into the whole. . . . Explicit in this concept, is the interdependency of decisions between all parts of components of the management problem." [16] By adding people to the concept of the organization as a system, we can define an organization as an assemblage of persons, each of whom carries out assigned tasks and all of whom are interrelated in such a way as to obtain a particular goal.

The concepts of *technical* subsystems, *work* subsystems, and *managing*

[16] David I. Cleland and David C. Dellinger, "Changing Patterns in Management Theory," *Aerospace Management*, General Electric Company, vol. 1, Spring, 1966, p. 4.

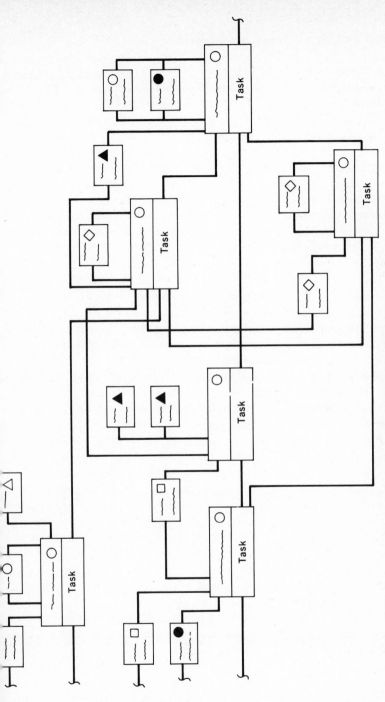

Figure 9-10 Integration of an organization's work and managing subsystems.

subsystems are part of an interdependent whole. Systems engineering and technical subsystems are joined in the industrial process of understanding physical phenomena and using material resources to achieve economic purposes. Managing subsystems and work subsystems are also linked pairs which treat the decision process and execution process in such a way as to make beneficial use of the technical subsystem. Systems organization and managing subsystems are concerned with the underlying structure of human interrelationships. The use of system schematic models and linear responsibility charts is a step forward in management, therefore since it provides a means of charting the interrelationships between human beings.

In this chapter, and in the two preceding chapters, we have analyzed the organizing function of project management. We started off by asking questions about the alignment of the human and nonhuman resources required to do the job, and we ended up by describing some charting techniques to analyze the interactions between the *people* components of the system. We have ranged far and wide in our deliberations; our analysis has gone beyond the concept of a simple pyramidal type of organization. We have structured our concept of an organization in terms of a total environmental system with no organizational or functional constraints. In this light, our organization grows until it encompasses virtually every individual having an interest in the system. Has our concept of the organization grown until it is too unwieldy for analysis? Perhaps so, but a less comprehensive concept would be artificial, and its analysis would lack reality.

One of the more important points we make is that a "going concern" faces a continuous stream of projects flowing through it and that such an organization requires different management techniques from those needed for a functional element alone. We have augmented this stream of projects with supporting elements, such as functional support, routine administration, and research and development organization. In so doing, we preserve a remnant of the traditional management model with the hope that it will make this new organizational concept more palatable to the traditional manager. Our approach has conceived of the organization as a part of a larger system, but also identifies the differing subsystems of the organization—its technical, work, and managing aspects.

From the organization planner's point of view, the project organization is superimposed on the existing functional structure. The resulting matrix organization creates unique authority and responsibility patterns—which become a web of relationships rather than a discrete line-staff dichotomy. The project organization is a means of getting a product delivered on time within allowable cost; it provides the desired performance characteristics without creating a full-scale product division. The project manager becomes, in effect, the general manager of the project for the company. Thus, the project organization offers an organizational alternative without upsetting the existing functional alignment.

As we have seen, the project manager is a distinct type of specialist, a man with a broad perspective of the total organizational system and the ability to unify the many activities involved. He tends to abandon the hierarchical model of management and to establish closely coordinated and integrated teams or task forces to circumvent chains of command; these teams may contain personnel with a heterogeneous collection of skills and thus may be almost complete within themselves. The project organization is indeed a radical departure from Max Weber's bureaucracy, where business was carried out "according to *calculable rules* and 'without regard for persons.'"

Recommended readings

Allen, Louis A.: *Charting the Company Organization Structure,* Studies in Personnel Policy, no. 168 (New York: National Industrial Conference Board Inc.) 1959.

Barnard, Chester I.: *The Functions of the Executive,* Harvard University Press, Cambridge, 1938.

"Changing the Company Organization Chart," *Management Record,* November, 1959.

Cooper, W. W., et al (eds.): *New Perspectives in Organization Research,* John Wiley & Sons, Inc., New York, 1964.

Dale, Ernest: *Planning and Developing the Company Organization Structure,* American Management Association, New York, 1952.

Higgans, Carter C.: "The Organization Chart: Its Theory and Practice," *Management Review,* October, 1956.

Janger, Allen R.: "Charting Authority Relationships," *The Conference Board Record,* December, 1964.

Karger, Delmar W., and Robert G. Murdick: *Managing Engineering and Research,* The Industrial Press, New York, 1963.

Landsberger, Henry A.: "The Horizontal Dimension in Bureaucracy," *Administrative Science Quarterly,* December, 1961.

"Linear Responsibility Charting," *Factory,* vol. 121, March, 1963.

Litterer, Joseph A.: *The Analysis of Organizations,* John Wiley & Sons, Inc., New York, 1965.

"Mapping the Executive Setup," *Business Week,* Apr. 6, 1957.

Mesarvoic, Mihajlo D.: *Views on General Systems Theory,* John Wiley & Sons, Inc., New York, 1964.

Munsey, Virgil W.: *An Empirical Demonstration of the Systems Characteristics of Complex Organizations,* Research Report, Air Force Institute of Technology, School of Engineering, 1966.

Patton, John A.: "Make and Use an Organization Chart," *Business Management,* May, 1963.

Randall, Clarence B.: "The Myth of the Organization Chart," *Dun's Review and Modern Industry,* February, 1960.

Terry, George R.: *Principles of Management,* 4th ed., Richard D. Irwin, Inc., Homewood, Ill., 1964.

CHAPTER 10
Project Authority

The project manager who fails to
build and maintain his alliances will
soon find indifference or opposition
to his project requirements.[1]

Authority is necessary if one is to get a project completed on time and within the cost and performance requirements. However, a degree of personal freedom is required in the project environment—particularly for the professional people. Balancing these two conditions of freedom and authority, which are both contradictory and complementary, is one of the more challenging problems facing the project manager.

In this chapter we should outline a conceptual framework for authority, its limits, and its needs. One might say that the practically oriented project manager has no concern for the philosophical niceties of authority, that his greatest concern is the management of the technical affairs of the project. This is truly not the case. However complex the technology, and great the magnitude of the material resources, project management is still a function of executive leadership acting through organized groups.

[1] Lieut. Col. David I. Cleland, "Understanding Project Authority," *Business Horizons*, Spring, 1967. The present chapter is an extension of this article.

What is authority?

Authority is a conceptual framework and, at the same time, an enigma in the study of organizations. The authority patterns in an organization, most commentators agree, serve as both a motivating and a tempering influence. This agreement, however, does not extend to the emphasis that the different commentators place on a given authority concept. Early theories of management regarded authority more or less as a gravitational force that flowed from the top down. Recent theories view authority more as a force which is to be accepted voluntarily and which moves both vertically and horizontally.

Defining authority

Although authority is the key to the management process, the term is not always used in the same way. Authority is usually defined as a "legal or rightful power to command or act." As applied to the manager, authority is the power to command others to act or not to act. The manager's authority provides the cohesive force for any group; it comes into being because of the group effort. In the traditional theory of management, authority is a right granted from a superior to a subordinate.

Authority, at least formal authority, is the right of a person to be listened to and obeyed. But where does this "right" originate? Every manager obtains his formal authority as a delegation from the next higher level. In this view, therefore, the ultimate source of authority (i.e., hierarchical authority) is the right to private property [2] in our society or in the charismatic power of hierarchical role. [3] In theory, authority is still concentrated at the top of the organization and is delegated in the scalar chain to subordinate organizational elements. This hierarchical authority exists primarily as a contingent force, to be used in resolving intraorganizational disputes, in making basic strategic decisions affecting the whole organization, and in establishing overall policy for the organization.

Barnard tempers the traditional view of authority by recognizing the right of the "contributors" to, or members of, a formal organization to accept or reject an order given by a higher official. [4] Traditional theory has never considered that the *sources* and *uses* of authority are ever manifested outside the boundaries of the parent organization. This traditional viewpoint therefore ignores the authority patterns that exist between managers and technicians in different organizations. Nor does the traditional view recognize the impact of the reciprocal authority relationships existing between

[2] Ralph C. Davis, *The Fundamentals of Top Management,* Harper & Row, Publishers, Incorporated, New York, pp. 281–322.
[3] Victor A. Thompson, *Modern Organization,* Alfred A. Knopf, Inc., New York, p. 77.
[4] Chester I. Barnard, *The Functions of the Executive,* Harvard Business Press, Cambridge, Mass., 1938, p. 163.

peers and associates. With the exception of functional authority, the traditional view presupposes some superior-subordinate relationship in the organizational arrangement.

Power

Power is a concept frequently associated with authority and is defined as the ability to unilaterally determine the behavior of others, regardless of the basis for that ability.[5] Authority provides that power which is attached to the organizational position; it is delegated through the media of position descriptions, organizational titles, standard operating procedures, and related policies. Authority as influence, however, may be assumed by individuals without the legitimacy of an organizational position. An individual may exercise influence in his environment simply because he has knowledge and expertise, and without documentation of authority. There is little doubt that a duly appointed superior has power over his subordinates in matters involving pay, promotion, and effectiveness reports. This delegated power functions unilaterally, from the top down. A manager's authority, however, is a combination of his power and his influence, such that subordinates, peers, and associates alike willingly accept his superior judgment. To conceive of this combination of power and influence is to take an *integrative* approach to a discussion of the project manager's authority, emphasizing both the legal grants and the personal effectiveness of his organizational position. Fayol may be taken to favor this integrative approach. He explained that: [6]

> Authority is the right to give orders and the power to exact obedience. Distinction must be made between a manager's official authority deriving from office and personal authority, compounded of intelligence, experience, moral worth, ability to lead, past services, so forth. . . . [Personal authority] is the indispensable complement of official authority.

How much project authority?

The project manager manages across functional (parent company) and organizational (outside organizations) lines to bring together activities required to accomplish the objectives of the specific project. In the traditional bureaucratic organization, business is conducted up and down the vertical

---

[5] For example, see James D. Thompson, "Authority and Power in 'Identical' Organizations," *The American Journal of Sociology*, vol. 60, November, 1956.

[6] Henri Fayol, *General and Industrial Management*, Sir Isaac Pitman & Sons, Ltd., London, 1949, p. 21.

hierarchy. The project manager, on the other hand, is more concerned with the flow of work in horizontal and diagonal directions than he is with flows in the scalar chain. Problems of motivation exist for the traditional vertical manager, but these problems are compounded for the project manager because the traditional leverages of hierarchical authority are not at his disposal. He must act as the focal point for major project decisions and considerations, however, so he must be given adequate authority to accomplish these objectives.

Several authors have commented on the efficacy of the project manager's authority. His authority is described by Peck and Scherer as having no legal basis for the resolution of interfunctional disagreements.[7] Ramo adds to this viewpoint by reflecting that project managers do not have substantial, well-delegated, clearly defined responsibilities or commensurate authority.[8] These views, while only a sample, reflect the consensus about the project manager's authority. These observations are not an accurate reflection of the project manager's authority, however, since they consider only the legal aspect. This is, admittedly, an important factor, but it is not the only one. He has another source of authority, the *de facto* or political source, that is of equal or perhaps even greater importance.

What is project authority?

The manager must have authority in order to accomplish his work. No philosophy of authority, however, is going to tell him how to exercise his authority in specific cases; what a philosophy can do is give him a conceptual framework as a base for his thinking about it. Authority has not, says Golembiewski, enjoyed "conceptual unanimity."[9] The concept of authority is in a period of transformation, from the bureaucratic hierarchical force to a participative and persuasive one. The elements of participation and persuasion in the authority relationships are products of our modern organizations and reflect the influence of the democratic and scientific revolution in contemporary society.

The exercise of authority in the execution phase of a project is far removed from the organic power of the chief executive. Decisions are made constantly by the functional and the project managers, and the success of these decisions depends upon the successful integration of these managers'

---

[7] Merton J. Peck, and Frederick M. Scherer, *The Weapons Acquisition Process,* Harvard University, Division of Research, Graduate School of Business Administration, Boston, 1962.

[8] Simon Ramo, "Management of Government Programs," *Harvard Business Review,* July–August, 1965, p. 7.

[9] Robert T. Golembiewski, "Authority as a Problem in Overlays: A Concept for Action and Analysis," *Administrative Science Quarterly,* June, 1964, p. 24.

delegated and assumed authority. In the project environment, the real basis of a man's authority (or, perhaps better, his influence) is his professional reputation among his peers and associates. A man gains this type of authority only through recognition of his accomplishment by the other members of his environment and not by policy documentation, however extensive.

A significant measure of the project manager's authority springs from his function and the style with which he performs it. The project manager's authority is neither all *de jure* (having specific legal foundations) nor all *de facto* (actual influence exercised and accepted in the environment). Rather, his authority is a combination of *de jure* and *de facto* elements in the total project environment. Taken in this context, the project manager's authority has no organizational or functional constraints, but rather diffuses from his office throughout and beyond the organization, seeking out the things and the people it wishes and needs to influence and control.

Project authority

In its total sense, project authority is the legal and personal influence that the project manager exercises over the scheduling, cost, and technical considerations of the project. Project authority manifests itself within the legitimacy of the project; it extends horizontally, diagonally, and vertically within the parent organization and radiates to outside participating organizations. The traditional line-staff relationships are modified in the project environment since a line functional manager (such as a production manager) in the project environment gives advice, counsel, and specialized support to the project manager. Project authority provides the "way of thinking" required to unify all organizational activities toward accomplishment of the project end, regardless of where they are located.[10]

Project authority also determines how project requirements are to be met within the planned scheduling, technological, and cost restraints. The work of the project manager varies in accordance with the type and degree of authority vested in him. At one extreme, the project manager may serve as an assistant to the general manager and, as such, plays the role of a project coordinator. At the other extreme, he may run his program with a line type

[10] One derivative of formal authority is functional authority. At first glance, it might appear that functional authority and project authority are one and the same. Functional authority is defined as the manager's legal right to act or command with respect to specific activities or processes in departments other than his parent department. It is a small slice of the authority of some line manager and relates to particular phenomena in the organization, for example, the authority of the personnel officer to prescribe certain grievance procedures. The project manager's authority vastly exceeds any that could be delegated under the concept of functional authority.

and degree of authority that denies the functional executive any significant right of appeal.

Contemporary theory

Contemporary management theory identifies three basic kinds of authority: formal line authority, staff authority and functional authority.

FORMAL LINE AUTHORITY   This is the right, derived from a legitimate source, to command, act, or direct. This formal authority flows from the right of private property, conferred by the society, through the owners of the business and their delegates. The formal line authority is based on some enforceable contract. The use of formal authority in contemporary organizations is backed by long-standing custom and certain basic values in our society.

STAFF AUTHORITY   The legal authority of the staff official is derived from his appointment as a staff member to assist, advise, and counsel the line official to whom he reports. The staff official may have *line* authority over his subordinates, but he does not have command authority over other people in the organization except as it operates through his superior knowledge.

FUNCTIONAL AUTHORITY   As described earlier, this is the legal right to act with respect to specific activities or processes.

These three concepts of authority—line, staff, and functional—and their relationship to *project* authority can be understood better by thinking of them in terms of organizational parameters. This is illustrated in Figure 10-1, where the four types of authority are depicted as having an *internal* force in the organization, while only project authority operates outside the boundaries of the parent organization.

Authority through negotiation

The project manager does not have unilateral authority in the project effort; he frequently negotiates with the functional manager.[11] These negotiations provide an opportunity to achieve trade-offs (checks and balances) between project performance, delivery, and cost objectives. The flow of the project manager's authority departs from the vertical structure of the organization.

[11] This may be described as a deliberate conflict; i.e., the project manager determines the "when" and the "what" of the project activities, whereas the functional managers, in supporting many different projects in the organization, determine *how* the support will be given. Heretofore, the functional manager has tended to have total authority within his function, except, of course, when specific restrictions are imposed by his superiors.

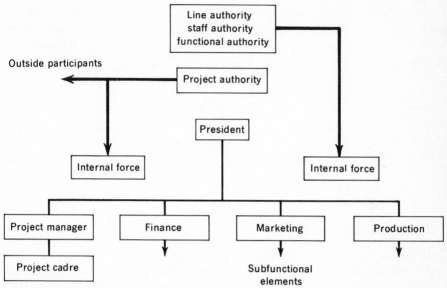

Figure 10-1   The project manager's authority.

This flow of authority (influence) is more a network of alliances between the project participants than a recurring delegation of power between the chain of superiors and subordinates in the various hierarchies. This network of alliances depends heavily upon the reputation of the individual as reflected in his professional achievements. The character of project authority is supportive, with more reliance on peers, associates, and a consensus thereof than on the customary manifestations such as organizational position descriptions and policy documentation.

Current literature in organizational theory has noted that informal and persuasive processes modify bureaucratic authority today. Authority systems have become less arbitrary, less formal, and less direct. Under the bureaucratic theory, there was assumed to be one center of authority—the line. In the project environment, no such clear-cut line of authority exists except for nonprofessional support people. The professionals do not form into an authority structure in the regular sense of the term.[12] Various modifications of the formal authority structure exist, even in those organizations considered to be bureaucratic. Hence, effective authority in the project environment depends on manifestations other than the legal ones. The effective

---

[12] For a discussion of the authority structure in professional organizations, see Amitai Etzioni, "Authority Structure and Organizational Effectiveness," *Administrative Science Quarterly,* June, 1959.

authority of the project manager is seldom autocratic. His most meaningful authority may be based on his ability to build reciprocity in his environment, to create and maintain political alliances, and to resolve conflict between the functional managers. Unilateral decisions, dogmatic attitudes, and the *resort to the authority of a hierarchical position* are inconsistent with the analysis of technological phenomena that occurs in the project environment. Instead, the project manager's job is to search for points of agreement, to examine the situation critically, to think reflectively, and only then to take an authoritative position based on the superiority of his knowledge. This, rather than his organizational position, is the basis for his authority.

What place hierarchy?

Adequate authority to accomplish project objectives cannot be created by rearranging the compartments and shifting the lines on the organizational charts. Participants in the project organization at all levels must modify, negate, supplement, and reinforce the legal authority which emanates from a given arrangement of positions. The project manager accomplishes his objectives through working with personnel who are largely professional. Consequently, his use of authority (both *de jure* and *de facto*) must be different from what one would expect to find in a simple superior-subordinate relationship. For professional people, project leadership must include explaining the rationale of the effort as well as the more obvious functions of planning, organizing, directing, and controlling.

Authority in project decisions may be indifferent to the hierarchical order of affairs. In many cases, the decisions that executives in the higher echelons reserve for themselves amount to nothing more than approving the proposals made by the project manager. The role played by these line and staff managers can easily deteriorate to that of delayers, debaters, investigators, coordinators, and vetoers, and such parochial views may work to the managers' own disadvantage.

Upper-echelon executives may be in a more precarious position than they realize. One of the folklores of functional management is the powerful executive who sits at the head of a highly organized, tightly run organizational pyramid, running things from the top down. In project management, the vertical organization still plays an important role, but this role is concerned largely with facilitating project affairs and ensuring that the proper environment is provided for those participating in the project. George Weissman, president of Phillip Morris, Inc., has said that his role is "to carry the oil can." [13] Concerning the operation of Phillip Morris brand (product) managers, *Business Week* has said that ". . . the basic moving parts are the brand managers. . . . They run the show. Within corporate budgetary limitations, they control packaging, promotion, sales effort, and advertising for their brands." [14]

Project management proves one thing about management theory, and that is that ". . . simply being in an executive hierarchy does not mean that one can freely direct those below him." [15] The higher-level officials in an organization are more dependent on their subordinates and peers than traditional theory will admit. The decisions made in the course of a large project are of considerable complexity; so many of them must be made that one individual, acting unilaterally, cannot hope to have sufficient time to make a thorough analysis of all the factors governing his decisions. The decision maker in project management must depend on many others to provide analysis, alternatives, and a recommended course of action.

Project authority depends heavily on the personality of the project manager and on how he sees his role in relation to the project environment. His authority is not necessarily weak because it is not thoroughly documented and because it functions outside the parent organization, between the participating organizations. The project manager is in a focal position in the project endeavors, and this focal position gives him the opportunity to control the flow of information and to have superior knowledge of the project. The scope of power and control exercised by the project manager may be virtually independent of his legal authority.

Documenting project authority

The project manager should have broad authority over all elements of the project. Although a considerable amount of his authority depends on his personal abilities, his position will be strengthened by the publication of documentation to establish his *modus operandi* and his legal authority. As a minimum, the documentation (expressed in a policy manual, policy letters, and standard operating procedures) should delineate his role and prerogatives in regard to:

1 His focal position in the project activities
2 The need for a deliberate conflict between the project manager and the functional managers

[13] Quoted in *Business Week*, Mar. 4, 1967, p. 94.
[14] *Ibid.*
[15] Herbert A. Simon, Donald W. Smithburg, and Victor A. Thompson, *Public Administration,* Alfred A. Knopf, Inc., New York, 1950, p. 404.

3   The need for his influence to cut across functional and organizational lines to achieve unanimity of the project objective

4   Active participation in major management and technical decisions to complete the project

5   Collaborating (with the personnel office and the functional supervisors) in staffing the project

6   Control over the allocation and expenditure of funds and active participation in major budgeting and scheduling deliberations

7   Selection of subcontractors to support the project and the negotiation of contracts

8   Rights in resolving conflicts that jeopardize the project goals

9   Having a voice in maintaining the integrity of the project team during the complete life of the project

10   Establishing project plans through the coordinated efforts of the organizations involved in the project

11   Providing an information system for the project with sufficient data for the control of the project within allowable cost, schedule, and technical parameters

12   Providing leadership in the preparation of operational requirements, specifications, justifications, and the bid package

13   Maintaining prime customer liaison and contact on project matters

14   Promoting technological and managerial improvements throughout the life of the project

15   Establishing a project organization (a matrix organization) for the duration of the project

The publication of suitable policy media describing his *modus operandi* and his legal authority will do much to strengthen his position in the total project environment.

Examples of (de jure) authority

In practice one finds varying degrees of *de jure* (legal) authority delegated to project managers. In the Department of Defense, policy governing the use and application of project management is contained in a DOD directive. In this directive, the project manager's *de jure* authority is defined as: [16]

> *Responsibility and Authority.* A System/Project Manager shall be responsible for successful accomplishment of his System/Project. He shall exercise executive authority over the planning, direction, and control of the approved system/project, and over the allocation and

[16] Department of Defense Directive 5010.4, May 4, 1965. Subject: System/Project Management.

utilization of all resources approved . . . and authorized for obligation for the execution of the approved System/Project.

The aerospace industry has responded and contributed significantly to the evolving project-management thought and theory. One of the major contributions that individual companies have made is in the creation of policy documentation which establishes the *modus operandi* and authority of the project manager. For example, in the military communications department of the General Electric Company, the project managers are appointed by the department general manager to manage a given program (or a group of closely related programs) on a full-time basis. Appointment of these individuals is done in the preproposal, proposal, or contract stage of a program. Although project managers may be located in various departments of the company, it is expressly intended that a project manager represent the general manager on all facets of the project, regardless of where he may report. Each project manager has the following documented responsibilities and authority: [17]

1   He will act for the Department General Manager in providing guidance to all elements of the Department on any and all aspects of the Program(s).

2   He is authorized to represent the Department to the customer on all matters concerning the Program (but with the exception of the negotiation of strictly contractual terms and conditions which will continue to be the full responsibility of Marketing). This is to be done through established Marketing channels including coordination . . . where appropriate.

3   He will define the requirements of the program (for contracts, these will be consistent with contractual terms) in relation to each element of the Department. He will define the work to be performed by each functional element in terms of cost, delivery, and performance. During the life of the contract, he will be responsible for auditing the relationship of these factors. If any of them deviate in such a way that the overall program commitments will be jeopardized, he will immediately make this fact known to the Functional Managers involved and the General Manager.

4   He will utilize the services of the Financial Section for all program financial information and will obtain all other services from appropriate functional components.

5   He will review manning of the program by each element of the Department. If in the Program Manager's opinion manning is not

[17] General Electric Company, Military Communications Department Policy 51.1, Nov. 4, 1963. Subject: Program Manager.

adequate or is excessive in relation to the task to be performed, he will immediately notify the Functional Managers involved and the General Manager.

6 He will determine types and details of various management controls and reports to be used at program level, and insure that they are consistent with Department policy. (Functional elements will contribute to these controls and reports as requested; may utilize other techniques within their functions as are currently in use, but will not generate any other information at program level.)

It is the intent that individual Program Managers will integrate their Program reporting methods to achieve uniformity between programs to the maximum extent feasible and to facilitate aggregating.

7 He will schedule and hold a design concept review(s) covering all aspects of the design concept at a very early stage in the proposal or contract. He will determine the complete agenda and will determine who will make the presentations. He will recommend attendance by reviewers and will solicit additional recommendations for reviewers from Section Managers concerned. Those he selects will participate in the review and take any follow-up action as may be requested or appropriate.

8 For contracts, he will schedule and hold at least one design review at appropriate stages of the program covering all aspects of the design. He will determine the complete agenda and will determine who will make the presentations. He will recommend attendance by reviewers and will solicit additional recommendations for reviewers from Section Managers concerned. Those he selects will participate in the review and take any follow-up action as may be requested or appropriate.

9 He is authorized to approve or disapprove all changes in the program, changes in planning, changes in specifications, major personnel changes, etc. He will normally establish change control procedures for administration through normal functional channels, and monitor such activity for compliance with policies, but may enter directly into the approval routine at his discretion.

10 For proposals, he will schedule and hold at least one pre-cost meeting with regard to costing and will establish guidelines for the program costing.

11 For contracts, he will control the dollar resources and will allocate appropriate amounts to each element of the Department through requisitions issued at his direction by Contract Administration and through Shop Orders issued at his direction. He will determine the degree to which the program is to be segregated by Shop Orders, consistent with the PERT controls and with existing Department

Policy and machine accounting capability. Cost performance of each functional manager will also be reported.

12 For contracts, he will schedule and hold expected cost-performance reviews at the initiation of each contract and actual and projected cost-performance reviews at significant stages of the contract. He will schedule these reviews at the beginning of the programs and publish the schedule to all concerned.

13 He will be chairman of a make-or-buy and source-selection board. He will constitute the(se) board(s) in close cooperation with functional managers and as approved by the General Manager.

14 He is authorized to make decisions consistent with Department Policies and Procedures for any aspect of this program including all functional areas. Where such decisions would appear to be in conflict with the overall objectives and goals of functional elements, the Program Manager will pursue resolution of the matter up to and including the functional Section Managers. If concurrence cannot be achieved at this level, they will bring the matter to the attention of the General Manager. Pending resolution, however, the Program Manager's decision will be followed. The Program Manager will, of course, delay implementation of the decision until resolution is achieved in all cases where in his opinion the time schedule permits.

15 He will be responsible for the preparation of a monthly Report.

16 He will report regularly the status of the program to the Department General Manager, and will bring any unusual items to his attention as they occur.

Dual reporting in project management

Within the project-management concept, organizational assignments result in dual-reporting relationships. The existence of this dual reporting creates the strong need for clarifying the authority and responsibility relationships between the project manager, the functional managers, and others concerned with the project. Clarification of these relationships will help to create the management climate for the deliberate conflict so necessary for successful project management. Rocketdyne, a producer of rocket engines for the Department of Defense, recognizes this dual-reporting relationship and has published an operating policy which details the administrative responsibilities of project and functional organizations: [18]

[18] "Program/Project Management," Rocketdyne Operating Policy A–577, Oct. 27, 1966, pp. 2–3.

A. *Program Organization*

Approval of the Program Manager will be required for assignments and subsequent changes of those functional organization personnel who report directly to the Program Manager as reflected on authorized formal Rocketdyne organization charts.

Salary changes for the above personnel will require Program Manager approval. Where Program Representatives serve two or more programs, the salary changes will be approved by the Product Division Head rather than the Program Managers involved. The Program Manager may recommend salary changes.

Functional organizations will be responsible for obtaining the approvals specified above. Such approvals will be obtained by signature on authorizing documents.

The above approval requirements will not apply for subdivision of work managers. Instead, functional managers will request and receive from Program Managers a performance rating before initiating salary changes for subdivision of work managers.

The Program Manager is responsible for issuance of a performance rating for the Program Representatives and subdivision of work managers upon the conclusion of their assignment to the program. This rating will be forwarded to the employee's functional organization where it will become a part of the employee's departmental record.

Travel Authorizations involving program activities will require the approval of the Program Manager. Trips of Program Organization personnel, which are for purposes other than program activities, and periods of absence (vacations, etc.) require Program Manager concurrence to ensure program continuity.

B. *Functional Organization*

1   The functional organization manager is responsible for administrative control of the functional personnel assigned to the program. Such administrative control includes: (1) Maintenance of departmental personnel records; (2) Initiation and approval of personnel paperwork involving requisitions, transfers, status changes, and merit increases . . . and (3) Approval of Travel Authorizations, expense reports, and special buys.

2   The functional organization is responsible for assuring the technical excellence and quality requirements of assigned tasks, for providing policy and procedural guidance, and for the support necessary for the successful accomplishment of the program.

3   Personnel assigned to specific programs will retain the department number of the functional organization.

The project manager has been described as that individual who is appointed to manage a specific project in order to deliver the product within the scheduling, cost, and performance requirements. Since he manages across organizational lines, he must have the advantage of every bit of authority "leverage" available since many of the people supporting him owe allegiance to their functional superiors. The Rocketdyne operating policy, quoted above, gives the project manager considerable leverage since the functional managers are required to request and receive appropriate recommendations on salary changes and performance ratings from the project manager before administrative or personnel actions are undertaken. Such a policy might be repugnant to the functional manager because it seems to violate the traditional, venerable superior-subordinate relationship. However, there is a direct correlation between the project success and the efficacy of the functional support; consequently, a project manager should be given the greatest possible policy support to enhance his role as the integrator-generalist of the project.

The foregoing examples of project-authority documentation reflect the care that is being taken to delineate the legal position of the project manager. This constitutes an obvious source of power in the project environment. While this gives the project manager the right to exercise that power, the significance of authority under the deliberate project-functional conflict cannot be understated. While the project manager may have the final, unilateral right to order affairs in the project, it would be foolhardy for the project manager to substitute his view without fully considering the "crystallization of thinking" of the other participants in the project. The project manager will rarely hope to gain and build alliances in his environment by arbitrarily overruling the other managers who contribute to the project.

An alliance

The authors have taken the position that one of the project manager's greatest sources of authority involves the manner in which he builds alliances in his environment—with his peers, associates, superiors, subordinates, and other interested parties. The building of alliances supplements his legal authority; it is the process through which the project manager can translate disagreement and conflict into authority (or influence power) to make his decisions stand. Sometimes the power and control of the project manager represent a subtle departure from this legal authority. Consider, for example, the decision process at the national level in the selection of a major weapons system.

Project-management decisions at the national level require an economic as well as a strategic view. Within the Department of Defense, there are critical decisions to be made concerning the development and subsequent production of a major weapons system, such as a ballistic missile or a bomber. The final decision is made by the Secretary of Defense and, in some cases, by the President. The competitive struggle for the selection of a particular weapons system, and of a contractor to develop and produce it, creates political forces in the economy and in the government itself. The need for the creation and maintenance of alliances is nowhere more dramatically illustrated than in the gamesmanship displayed during a House Armed Services Subcommittee meeting conducting hearings on a new manned strategic bomber. The interchange, as reported by Frederick Taylor in the *Wall Street Journal,* goes as follows: [19]

Who's We? McNamara Provides the Answer
By Frederick Taylor

WASHINGTON—A House Armed Services subcommittee, which wants a start made on a new manned strategic bomber is piqued at Defense Secretary McNamara, who doesn't. When he met with the subcommittee, Mr. McNamara told its members ". . . we still cannot see a clear need for a new strategic bomber. . . ."

The subcommittee expressed itself as mystified about whom he meant when he said, "We still cannot see a clear need," and went to considerable lengths to discover who supported him in this opinion.

Witness, for example, this exchange between Rep. Alton Lennon (D., N.C.) and some top Air Force officers:

Rep. Lennon: "Who is he speaking for when he says 'we still cannot see a clear need for a new strategic bomber'? Will you answer that question, General Schriever?" General Bernard Schriever is commanding general of the Air Force Systems Command.

Gen. Schriever: "I do not know, sir."

Rep. Lennon: "Would you answer that question, General Ryan?" General John D. Ryan is commanding general of the Strategic Air Command.

Gen. Ryan: "I do not know, sir."

Rep. Lennon: "Would you answer the question, please, General Ferguson?" Lt. General James Ferguson is deputy chief of staff for Air Force Research and Development.

General Ferguson: "I do not know, sir."

Later, Rep. Lennon got into the subject with Dr. John S. Foster, director of Defense Research and Engineering for the Defense Department.

---

[19] Frederick Taylor, "Who's We? McNamara Provides the Answer," *The Wall Street Journal,* May 3, 1966, p. 18.

Rep. Lennon: "Well, who is it that is of a different opinion than the Secretary himself? Yet, he says, 'we' do not see the need?"

Dr. Foster: "I cannot tell you the people who are in complete agreement with the Secretary's position."

And still later:

Rep. Lennon: "We want that person here and we want to get their statement on the record as to why they think there is not a clear need. You tell us who that person is."

Dr. Foster: "I presume that those who say there is not a clear need are the Secretary of Defense and the other person or people to whom he referred when he said, 'we see no clear need.' "

Rep. Lennon: "Could you give us any idea to whom he may be referring?"

Dr. Foster: "No, I'm afraid I can't, Mr. Lennon."

At that point, Rep. Porter Hardy Jr. (D., Va). joined in.

Rep. Hardy: "He told us there are some. Why doesn't he tell us who are the 'some'?"

Rep. Lennon: "Who are the 'some'? Doctor, I think we are entitled to have those individuals come here and tell us they certainly don't see the need, so be gracious and kind and helpful enough to give us the names of these individuals so we may be able to ask them to come down here and put on the record their feelings."

Dr. Foster: "I will be glad to go back to the office and see if I can find people who think there is not a clear need."

Subcommittee members also asked General John F. McConnell, Chief of Staff of the Air Force, whether he wanted a new bomber.

Rep. Lennon: "In your judgment, is there a clear need for a new strategic bomber to replace ultimately the B-52Gs through Hs?"

Gen. McConnell: "Yes, sir."

And, Dr. Harold Brown, Secretary of the Air Force, agreed.

Dr. Brown: "I think that I have made it clear to this committee that I believe that the B-52Gs and Hs should be replaced by a successor."

Rep. L. Mendel Rivers (D., S.C.), Chairman of the House Armed Services Committee, dropped in on the subcommittee's hearings, and Rep. Edward Hebert (D., La.) filled him in.

Rep. Hebert: ". . . Mr. Rivers, this morning, although you were not here, we were trying to find out who 'we' is when the Secretary of Defense speaks. We cannot find 'we.' Everybody that has testified before our committee, Mr. Rivers, is in a part of the 'we.' They all have different opinions and are quite contradictory, and in contrast with the Secretary of Defense, and yet he tells us 'we.' We are still trying to find out who 'we' is."

The subcommittee completed its sessions without ever hearing the answer to that burning question. But, it had dark suspicions. The subcommittee report, in a special section entitled, "The Decision Making

Process (We)," comments, "So, the subcommittee never found who 'we' were. However, it ventures the opinion that the word 'we' is used to hide the essential singularity of the decision-making process in the Department of Defense."

Maybe because they were afraid of what the answer would be, members of the bomber-bent subcommittee—despite their professed anxiety to get to the bottom of the question—did not put it to the man most likely to have the answer: Secretary McNamara.

As a public service, then, the query was addressed to him at a news conference.

A Wall Street Journal reporter: "Mr. Secretary, the committee seemed highly concerned whether there was going to be one [a new strategic bomber] at all. They kept referring to your statement that 'we see no clear need for it' and . . . ."

Mr. McNamara (breaking in): "On the question of we see no clear need, let me comment on that since that was one of the major questions raised by the committee. The committee said they were unable to identify who 'we' was. . . . I will tell you who the 'we' was. The 'we' was the Chief of Staff of the Army, the Chief of Naval Operations, the Commandant of the Marine Corps, the Chairman of the Joint Chiefs, the Deputy Secretary of Defense—and the President of the United States."

"So the thought that 'we' was me is absolutely without foundation."

Mystery solved.

This episode demonstrates the power of alliances in the exercise of authority. The Secretary of Defense has the legal authority under the powers granted in the National Security Act of 1947 (as amended). This grant of authority is clear, but in this instance the alliances he built with the Chief of Staff of the Army, the Chief of Naval Operations, the Commandant of the Marine Corps, the Chairman of the Joint Chiefs, and the President of the United States made the decision stick. This kind of authority, the building of alliances, has to be developed; it cannot be given! This decision (this exercise of authority) was developed on the basis of *negotiation* rather than *through* independent action by the Secretary of Defense.

Look as you may for the traditional patterns of authority in this episode, you will not find them. There were simply evidences of the formal, pyramidal legal authority—with an enormous bargaining power. There was *real* authority demonstrated in this exchange in the House Armed Services Subcommittee, and yet few of us would recognize it. But then, before effective authority can be created and recognized, one must know of what it consists.

The ideas about project authority can be summarized through the use of

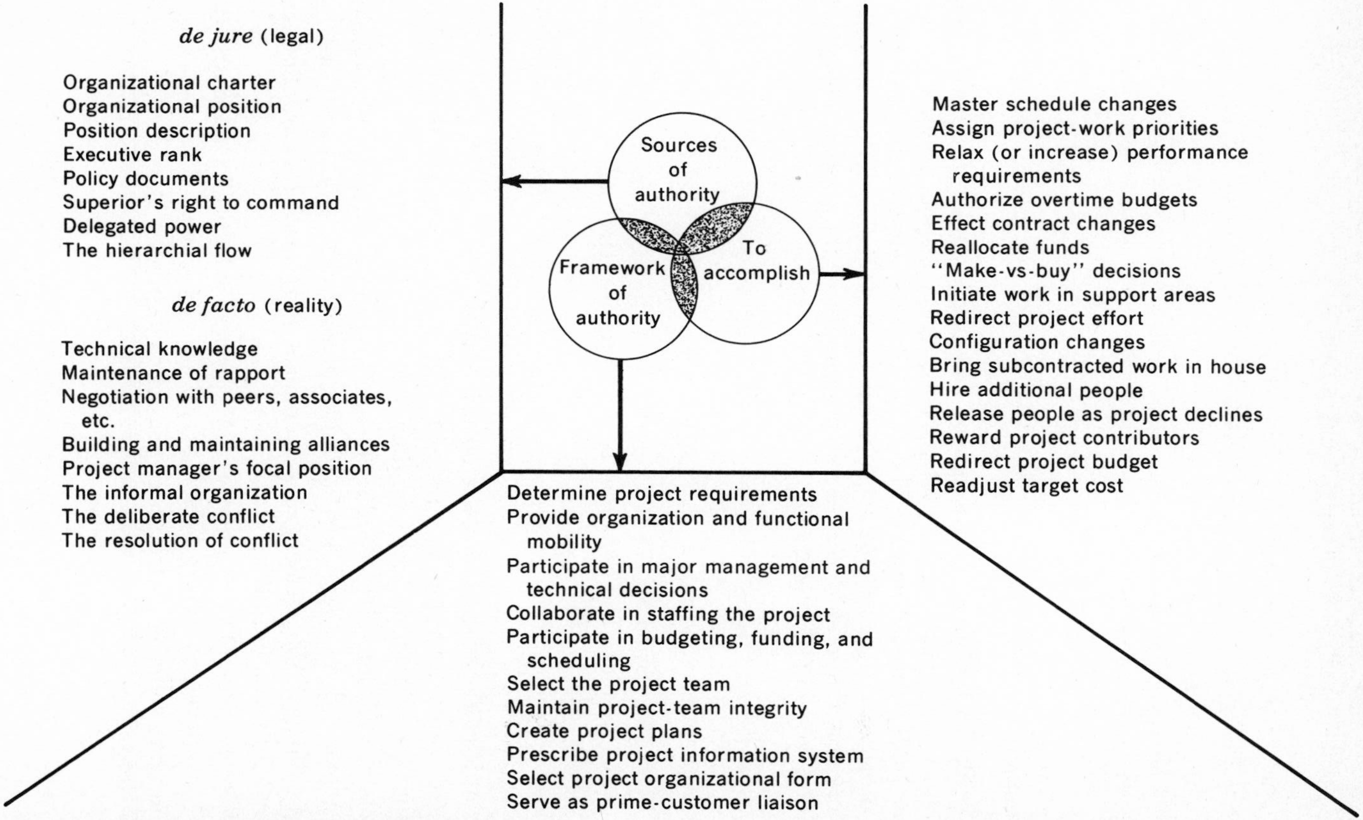

de jure (legal)

Organizational charter
Organizational position
Position description
Executive rank
Policy documents
Superior's right to command
Delegated power
The hierarchial flow

de facto (reality)

Technical knowledge
Maintenance of rapport
Negotiation with peers, associates, etc.
Building and maintaining alliances
Project manager's focal position
The informal organization
The deliberate conflict
The resolution of conflict

Sources of authority → To accomplish → Framework of authority

Master schedule changes
Assign project-work priorities
Relax (or increase) performance requirements
Authorize overtime budgets
Effect contract changes
Reallocate funds
"Make-vs-buy" decisions
Initiate work in support areas
Redirect project effort
Configuration changes
Bring subcontracted work in house
Hire additional people
Release people as project declines
Reward project contributors
Redirect project budget
Readjust target cost

Determine project requirements
Provide organization and functional mobility
Participate in major management and technical decisions
Collaborate in staffing the project
Participate in budgeting, funding, and scheduling
Select the project team
Maintain project-team integrity
Create project plans
Prescribe project information system
Select project organizational form
Serve as prime-customer liaison

Figure 10-2   A model of project authority.

a model, such as that in Figure 10-2. The authority relationships in the project environment show the essential reciprocal elements to be:

1   The sources of project authority
2   The conceptual framework
3   The results of project authority

Summary

Authority in the project environment flows horizontally, diagonally, and vertically. Technical competence, persuasion, negotiation, reciprocity, alliances, and the resolution of deliberate conflict are some of the means that the project manager can use to augment his legal authority to accomplish project objectives. Thus, the effective authority of the project manager is political as well as hierarchical.

Recommended readings

Air Force Regulation Nr 375–3, Department of the Air Force, Nov. 25, 1963.

Barnard, Chester I: *The Functions of the Executive,* Harvard Business Press, Cambridge, Mass., 1938.

Cleland, David I.: "Understanding Project Authority," *Business Horizons,* Spring, 1967.

Department of Defense Directive 5010.4, May 4, 1965.

Etzioni, Amitai: "Authority Structure and Organizational Effectiveness," *Administrative Science Quarterly,* June, 1959.

Golembiewski, Robert T.: "Authority as a Problem in Overlays: A Concept for Action and Analysis," *Administrative Science Quarterly,* June, 1964.

Ramo, Simon: "Management of Government Programs," *Harvard Business Review,* July–August, 1965.

Thompson, James D.: "Authority and Power in 'Identical' Organizations," *The American Journal of Sociology* vol. 60, November, 1956.

Thompson, Victor A.: *Modern Organization,* Alfred A. Knopf, Inc., New York, 1961.

CHAPTER 11
Project Control

In an undertaking, control consists
in verifying whether everything occurs
in conformity with the plan adopted,
the instructions issued and principles
established.[1]

The philosophy of control

In managing a project, the cost, scheduling, and technological factors must
be controlled within the established constraints. Control of the project requires that adequate plans be formed, suitable standards developed, and an
information system set up that will enable the project to be tracked during
its life cycle and supply sufficient data for comparing *expected* with *actual*
performance.

The definition of "control" varies, depending on the specific function or
area to which it is being applied. In describing the role of control in
project management, the emphasis may be on:

1   The organic function of management, e.g., the control elements of super-
    vision.

[1] Henri Fayol, *General and Industrial Management*, Sir Isaac Pitman & Sons, Ltd.,
London, 1949, p. 107.

2   The means for regulating an individual or organization, such as the specific tools a comptroller employs.

3   The restraining function of a system; i.e., control is the objective of feedback and is defined as the monitored state of a system.

Managerial controls, whatever the type, provide the project manager with the tools for determining whether or not the organization is proceeding toward the objective, as planned. Controls also advise the project manager of the extent of deviations and of the recommended corrective action or alternative course of action. Control has to do with making events conform to plans. It is an organic function of management which coordinates the project affairs so that the project objectives are achieved.

Control and the management process

Planning, organizing, staffing, and directing are steps taken in preparing to execute decisions, whereas control is the step taken in making certain that the decision is properly executed. Without control, the management job is not complete. Control is part of the management process, but the lines of demarcation between control and the other managerial functions are not clear-cut. Rather, at all levels of management, control and the other management functions should be considered to be in a constant, circular pattern with interplay between the functions.

Control is much like planning in the sense that it is forward-looking. Control procedures cannot be applied retrospectively, although, of course, the thoughtful manager learns by studying the past. Control uses information from the past to develop the necessary actions for the future. Since control is forward-looking, any deviations from the standard should be identified and reported to the manager as soon as possible. Control, therefore, must be established in terms of deviation from the plan early enough so that corrective action can be instituted before progress is impaired.

Prerequisites of a control system

The sophistication of the control system depends on the complexity of the project and the ability of the participants to administer it. A simple project may require only a few indicators to determine whether or not it is progressing on schedule and within the desired cost and performance constraints. On the other hand, a major project will require an extensive control system that will identify and report many conditions that reflect its progress. Regardless of the complexity of the project, however, certain basic conditions must be met in order to have a workable control system:

It must be understood by those who use it and obtain data from it.

It must relate to the project organization, since organization and control are interdependent; neither can function properly without the other.

It must *anticipate* and *report* deviations on a timely basis so that corrective action can be initiated before more serious deviations actually occur.

It must be sufficiently flexible to remain compatible with the changing organizational environment.

It must be economical so as to be worth the additional maintenance expense.

It should indicate the nature of the corrective action required to bring the project back into consonance with the plan.

It should reduce to a language (words, pictures, graphs, or other models) which permits a visual display that is easy to read and comprehensive in its communication.

It should be developed through the active participation of all major executives involved in the project.

The subfunctions of control

Control, then, has to do with making activities conform to the plan of action that has been established for the organization. It is a function of management which facilitates and coordinates the project affairs so that project objectives are achieved. Control consists of several subfunctions necessary for constraining activity. These subfunctions are discussed below.

ROUTINE PLANNING   This is the collection, classification, and presentation of the data required for the controlled execution of plans. It involves collecting the data from the project participants and restructuring it into a form that will portray conditions and trends. This function is largely routine; it should not be confused with other planning which is more creative and involves greater time periods.

SCHEDULING   This is the specification of *dates* and *times* for performing functions and implementing the many subplans of the project. Scheduling, in this context, consists of translating the schedule plan into actual calendar dates and times. It establishes specific calendar periods for the completion of the project and for the orderly integration of the complex of dates and times necessary for execution of the plan.

DISPATCHING   This is the release of authority to act—*how* to act, as well as *when* and *where*. Authority to act is communicated to those affected by means of written or verbal orders or standing orders expressed in policy or procedural documents.

COMPARISON　As a subfunction of control, this has to do with the evaluation of completed actions to see how they conform to the plans or standards. The comparison subfunction is carried out by observing data, physical activities, or the status of human and nonhuman resources. Thus, a quality-control inspector checking a manufactured part for conformance with quality specifications is performing the comparison function.

CORRECTING　Corrective action which follows some form of comparison is concerned with getting the project to conform to the goals which have been set—time schedule, costs, etc. For corrective action to be meaningful, a framework of realistic standards must be established and actual performance measured against these standards. Corrective action is the last step in the control cycle, as portrayed in Figure 11-1.

The role of standards

Standards are the criteria by which we evaluate past or present performance, objectives, policies, procedures, and rules. Such criteria become standards when they are related to the control function. The project cannot be successfully managed without standards, and the quality of the project will depend upon the realism and authenticity of its standards. Careful analysis of the standards required for a particular project in its unique environment will make them more realistic. The standards of performance used in developing a ballistic missile, for example, would be significantly different from those used in building a bridge. If the project participants take part

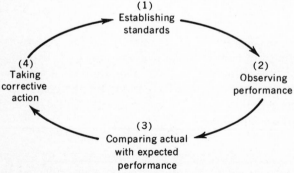

Figure 11-1　The control cycle.

in developing the standards, they will more readily accept and comply with them.

Standards used in project management are based on the basic parameters of *cost, schedule,* and *performance.* Each of these parameters is developed depending on the requirements of the project. From the perspective of the total organization, the network of standards to be developed should consist of standards such as the following:

1 Ethical standards. The expected behavior patterns of the project personnel.

2 Standard costs. Normative costs that are incurred in the performance of the functions or phases of operations.

3 Financial ratios. The *current ratio*—inventory turnover, for example—which shows the relationship between certain items of financial data.

4 Budgets. The cash budget, or forecast, is a tool of planning which becomes a standard when it is approved.

5 Return on investment. A control used in evaluating overall project performance.

6 Miscellaneous criteria. Standards that can be used to evaluate the long-term control and performance of the firm, such as:
(a) philosophy and quality of management; (b) market position; (c) corporate image; (d) organization viability; (e) organization morale; (f) customer and public relations; (g) personnel training and development; (h) innovation and research; and (i) conservation of assets.

The term "management controls" is widely used, but as it is usually applied, it is a misnomer. Management controls do not control at all, but are the methods and tools by means of which progress against objectives is measured, evaluated, and reported to management. The manager then couples this information with the authority granted him to establish control. Management-control systems require the manager to play an active part in the control function, particularly in deciding on the proper course to take in effecting corrective action.

Information to control the project

We mentioned earlier that the project manager requires information concerning the cost, schedule, and technology of the project. There are additional types of information which the project manager must collect so that he will be able to take appropriate action in managing his project.

First, he will need to assess the total project as it compares with other projects in the organization. Making this overall review while maintaining the proper balance in the daily routine of many competing projects is difficult. The situation should be reviewed often enough, however, so that the project manager and his team members remain aware of the total situation.

Second, the project manager must evaluate those areas which deviate from the plan. The control system must report exceptions, but it must pinpoint those commitment deviations which, when taken together, provide the greatest threat to the project objectives.

Third, the project manager must be given the best possible forecast for the immediate future—the overall view and the most meaningful exceptions in terms of their relation to the future. Whatever information is chosen for control must enable the system manager to forecast the future. The analogy of the aircraft stall-warning device is a useful one. One type of stall-warning device informs the pilot that his aircraft is going to stall at the instant the stall occurs; therefore, it simply verifies that he has gone into a dangerous situation. Another type of stall-warning device anticipates the stall sufficiently in advance that the pilot has time to take corrective action and prevent the stall; this control system's built-in "anticipation" calls attention to the need for corrective action. In the same manner, the information presented to the project manager must portray a variance in the rate of change; i.e., how rapidly is the actual performance diverging from the plan? A graph can show present status and previous status, but unless he knows the rate of change, the project manager cannot determine whether or not he is on schedule.

The best of information systems will not keep the project manager out of trouble, but it will keep him from being surprised when trouble comes. The information system is only as good as its inputs. A standardized reporting system can be set up that will give "visibility" to the project. Such a reporting system will make the delegation of authority easier because everyone can tell quickly who is in charge of each part of the project and where to reach him. Without an adequate information system, it can be difficult to tell who is responsible for a particular aspect of the project and *how that individual is doing in his work.*

Reports should be specified for each project and reviewed frequently for applicability and need. The use of existing information should be encouraged; only where a new problem exists or a new approach is being tried should new techniques be employed. The tendency to apply *all* currently popular administrative and control techniques indiscriminately should be resisted.[2]

---

[2] The proliferation of management-control techniques in the Department of Defense has led to some difficulties in completing projects. The recognition of these difficulties has resulted in an attempt to develop a "management system for management systems." See "The Pentagon Builds a Monster," *Business Week,* Feb. 18, 1967, pp. 198–199.

Design of the information system

A management information program for a particular project will have many overlapping phases. The following steps are suggested as a guide to designing the project information system:

Identify the long-range objective of the project.

Analyze the existing information system in terms of its suitability to assess project progress.

Identify and provide for interfacing of the project information system with the overall master information system for the company.

Establish a time plan for the development and implementation of the information system.

Accomplish the plan.

One of the problems in a large project involves coordinating the machines and materials and establishing suitable organizational relationships. The organizational relationships are important because they provide the links through which information is transferred for making and executing decisions. How the information flows and the role it plays can be seen in an assembly operation, where production control achieves coordination through the use of information.

It is virtually impossible to engage in project activities of any magnitude without establishing an information system. After a project is established, the information flows in accordance with established policies, procedures, methods, and organizational relationships. When outside organizations are involved, information is needed to coordinate the efforts of the suppliers and project contributors. This information may be very narrow (information for a specific purpose, for example, payroll accounting or record keeping) or very broad, completely integrating all the information on the project.

James Rosenzweig has drawn an interesting analogy between the basic functions required for mission accomplishment in a major weapons system and those required in a product mission for an electronic data-processing system. According to Professor Rosenzweig, there are five basic functions necessary for successful mission accomplishment: [3]

Perception of need

Design

Production

Delivery

Utilization

[3] James Rosenzweig, "The Weapons Systems Management Concept and Electronic Data Processing," *Management Science,* January, 1960, pp. 157–158.

These five functions have to be performed by someone—the producer, the user, or both. The overall system of information flow has four basic elements: collecting, processing, comparing, and selecting.[4]

The idea of a product mission provides for the procedural integration of interfunctional (and interorganizational) effort to develop a suitable management information system. In its simplest terms, the project-management information system should provide for the coordination, integration, and expedition of all the communications required to develop and produce the project.

An information system is a complex of formal and informal networks for the transmission of communications between the project participants. Information systems vary widely in degree of formality, ranging from a highly structured method such as Program Evaluation Review Technique (PERT) to the personal talks by project members. Communications networks between the project participants are of the three basic types discussed below.[5]

FORMAL COMMUNICATIONS NETWORKS   These are used to transmit those messages recognized as "official" by the organization. These official messages take many forms, such as organizational charts, standard operating procedures, formal orders, policy manuals, periodic reports, official correspondence, and so on. The formal communication channels of the organization coincide substantially with the formal authority structure.

SUBFORMAL (OR INFORMAL) COMMUNICATIONS NETWORKS   These are used to transmit messages through the informal authority structure. Every contributor to the project soon becomes acquainted with this informal route and learns what to communicate through these channels. The project members learn the rules through experience, since they are seldom written down.

The informal network in the management information system can create difficulties. Sometimes the system transmits information not intended to be transmitted. New ideas often arise out of the subformal communications route, since the route is not official and the idea can be withdrawn, altered, adjusted, magnified, or canceled without any official involvement. The channels spring up when there is a need for the people to communicate

---

[4] See Ned Chapin, *An Introduction to Automatic Computers*, D. Van Nostrand Company, Inc., Princeton, N.J., 1957, p. 42.

[5] This discussion of the basic type of communications networks is based on William M. Jones, *Decision Making in Large Organizations*, RAND Corporation, RM-3968-PR, Santa Monica, Calif., March, 1964.

but there is no existing formal structure. The formal channels are vertical, but the gap-filling, subformal lines are horizontal and diagonal, so that they connect peers, associates, and colleagues rather than superiors and subordinates. Even when officials in the organization are linked via the subformal channels, the informality of the messages tends to reduce the difference in rank and status. People are prone to speak more freely and openly to their peers or to people who act like their peers. Furthermore, the subformal system facilitates crossing functional and organizational lines. Therefore, these subformal, or informal, lines of communications should be encouraged.

The fact that subformal information networks exist makes it futile to design an information system that does not provide for informal messages. The structure of the organization and the *modus operandi,* however efficient, will not carry all the messages. Quite to the contrary, the more stringent the formal channels, the more opportunity there is for the subformal channels to flourish. Thus, project organization should lean toward a complete management information system that provides an environment in which each project contributor is able (and feels free) to communicate directly with the other members of the project team, all of whom are naturally linked together by reciprocal functions and interests. A complete communications network, therefore, need not be a complete network of formal channels.

Although the subformal network can work toward filling the gaps (and clarifying the overlap) of the formal system, the functional managers can severely restrict its development and value. Members can be directed, under threat of punishment, not to communicate about their affairs in the project. The flow of communications can be ordered by physically separating people, by placing security clearance requirements on the communications, or by requiring approval of the functional manager for any communications outside the organization. All these measures can seriously hamper the flow of communication, but they will not eliminate it altogether.

PERSONAL COMMUNICATIONS NETWORKS According to Jones, a personal communication is one in which ". . . an organization functionary, in communicating with an insider or an outsider, deliberately reveals something of his own attitude toward the activities of his own organization." [6] Jones elaborates further about personal communications:

> *a.* Personal channels are almost always used for reports rather than directives.

[6] *Ibid.*

   b. Personal messages are transmitted by officials acting as persons rather than as office holders, so they do not bear the responsible weight of the person's office. In this respect, they differ from subformal messages, which are transmitted by individuals acting in their official capacity but not for the record.

   c. The personal network can transmit messages with amazing speed because no verification mechanism slows down their dissemination.

   d. Before an official takes action on information received through personal channels, he will usually verify that information through either subformal or formal channels.

Formal communications between the project participants are often inappropriate for several reasons. First, with many matrix organizations involved, formal communications would require a long time to pass through the organizational levels to the designated official. Second, since the formal message is for the record, it must be prepared carefully and coordinated; the officials concerned may want to discuss the matter tentatively before they prepare the final message, all of which takes time. Third, an official may not want to disclose his idea to his superiors at that time, even in a draft form, but formal communications are all routed through the chain of superiors. Thus, the subformal and the personal communications networks play important roles in the relationships between the project participants. However, a project team member is rarely able to discern, much less become familiar with, the subformal and personal communications networks in other agencies involved in the project. (This fact often explains the reason why project contributors have difficulty in understanding the complex of communications in the project.) This difficulty can be alleviated if the project contributors feel free to participate in some type of subformal or personal relationship with other project people. This relationship can be through social as well as business activities. Often such communications result in identification of the proper individual to deal officially with the matter at hand.

Overall control of the project

The project manager will want to know several basic things about his project during its life:

   Will the product or service be delivered on time?
   Will the final cost be within the original budget?
   Will the product or service meet the desired performance characteristics?
   If not, what engineering changes will be required?

Where does the project stand in relation to cost, schedule, and expected performance characteristics?

What is the interrelationship of costs, schedules, and desired performance characteristics; e.g., what is the rate of fund expenditure relative to the passage of time?

What is the customer's evaluation of progress on the project?

One of the more distressing trends in project management is the tendency to overstress control. Various types of management information systems have been developed recently which can provide an abundance of data concerning the project. Many of the information systems extend through many management levels and require the project participants to report a large amount of data. Also, the number of groups seeking data is often large; in the case of a major project, there can be several dozen. This proliferation of requirements for information can generate a need for augmenting personnel assigned to the "doing" and "monitoring" groups, since the more time they spend providing data, the less time they have to perform their other tasks.

Another distressing trend is the current tendency to rely heavily on complicated, sophisticated management systems. There is a very real danger that the project manager can become so preoccupied with the system that he fails to exercise enough personal management of a project. Control is of a personal nature, so it is important that the project manager use control techniques that reflect his personality and are consistent with the complexity of the project. The use of PERT and PERT-Cost may be justified for large projects; less sophisticated methods may be adequate on smaller projects, however, where the interaction between the manager and technicians concerned is adequate to control the project. However, the greater insights into the structure of the project which may be gained through the use of a project network device such as PERT may well warrant its use. This is particularly true of the initial stages of planning a project, when such insights may be of great value. Here, we mean to imply only that a rigid adherence to such a system may severely compromise the very flexibility which is a virtue of a small project.

When to initiate control

Control begins when the first germ of an idea for a project appears in the organization—a discernible effort which will require an expenditure of organizational resources (human effort, time, money, physical resources) and lead to an organizational objective. After a project has been officially recognized, it should be reviewed, initially and during its life cycle, to determine:

Whether organizational resources are to be expended

Whether adequate progress is being realized in accomplishing the project goals

Whether the project should be continued, redirected, or terminated

Whether the project contributes to the overall organizational mission

Control continues throughout the life cycle of the project as one of the organic functions of the project manager. Project control is the nerve center of the project and provides a framework for decision making.

Basic elements of project control

Schedule, cost, and progress are the basic elements of project control. Each project is finite in duration. Ultimately, each project will be completed and replaced by an oncoming project. There is a definable end in terms of time and progress. An information system to appraise the schedule and cost parameters continually is necessary. But what form should this information system take? Are there any subtle schedule-cost interrelationships that can cause the project manager trouble? According to Baumgartner: [7]

Schedules may not be sufficiently detailed to afford a comparison of actual progress versus plan until it is too late to take timely action. This was a common deficiency prior to the general use of PERT.

The interrelationship and interdependence of work effort (task, subtask, black box) schedules may not be clearly perceived and documented, thereby tending to obscure the causes of slippages. PERT permits a clear portrayal of these relationships.

A schedule is only as firm as the esteem given it by people working on the project. When schedules change frequently, whatever the reason, or when there are doubts, second guesses about the "actual" schedule, the validity of the schedule as an element of control is weakened.

In projects whose deliverable item is a report rather than hardware, written schedules may be nonexistent due to the popular and fallacious belief, "you can't schedule study efforts."

Actual progress may be difficult to measure. One information indicator will not suffice for all purposes; a composite of project information is required.

[7] John Stanley Baumgartner, *Project Management*, Richard D. Irwin, Inc., Homewood, Ill., p. 34.

SCHEDULE CONTROL   Schedule control consists of integrating all the schedules in the project, including the overall schedule and the detailed schedules for each segment of work. These schedules may be integrated by means of PERT, Critical Path Method (CPM), or a variation of the Gantt chart.[8] The project control office will be responsible for seeing that the project proceeds in consonance with established schedules, and will keep the project director informed of potential and actual schedule slippages. Project control will coordinate all the schedules with the project participants and obtain the concurrence of the customer on any proposed changes.

The need for good scheduling can hardly be overstressed. Time is a most important resource, but it cannot be purchased. It is usually possible to get additional funds, facilities, or human resources, but time cannot be supplemented. When a schedule slips, the time lost to the project is costly, and it is difficult, if not impossible, to regain.

COST CONTROL   Cost control has to do with the organization, administration, and control of the cost procedures necessary for the project. This function integrates the cost proposals from the participating organizations into a central control file. They issue work orders authorizing the expenditure of funds which should be directed to specific project tasks and name specific project participants as responsible for the disbursements. They are responsible for accumulating all actual costs (engineering, development, manufacturing, support, subcontractor, etc.) and for monitoring and directing the activities of the financial management organization to ensure the timely and accurate accumulation of costs. The responsibilities of the cost function should include:

Conducting project audit

Preparing periodic (weekly or monthly) comparisons of actual versus programmed cost

Preparing comparisons of actual versus programmed manpower allocation

Updating the cost-to-complete projection reports and funding schedules

Facilitating the flow of funds from the customer and to and between the subcontractors

Providing a comparison of costs sustained by activity to the established cost standards

Sponsoring cost-improvement programs

The primary functions of cost control are to document historical costs and to compare these costs periodically with the original estimates. (Such com-

[8] These techniques will be discussed in Chap. 12.

parisons can be revealing.) [9] Other important activities are establishing proper costs, anticipating problem areas, and recommending corrective action.

The cost function includes the collection of cost estimates from the project participants. It also includes the determination of the realism of the estimates, to see whether there are any cost areas that have been overlooked and to ensure that the cost estimating is accomplished systematically.

CONTROL OF TECHNOLOGY   Technology is the most difficult parameter of the project to define and control. The "technology of the project" refers to the state of the art that results from the project endeavors and is often measured in terms of the item's performance characteristics. Performance is expressed in terms of such factors as speed, range, utility, endurance, limitations, reliability, maintainability, transportability, and technical goals.[10] A new product must have an element of utility greater than that of its predecessor, and the amount of added utility reflects the addition to the state of the art made by that project. But by what means do we measure that increment of added utility? Progress in schedule and cost can be measured and reported through the management information systems, but technology is more elusive. The most promising source of information is the technical personnel. The value judgments and opinions of the technical people involved in the project are the best sources of information concerning what technology advancements are represented by the product.

Project documentation and review

There are many forms of documentation for the management of a project. A myriad of policy instruments exists to establish the objectives, provide operating guidance, delegate authority, and compare performance with standards. Then, there is the system of plans drawn up for the project, as discussed in Chapter 5, which provides the basic framework for the project. Our intent here is to identify and discuss those forms of project documenta-

---

[9] For example, see A. W. Marshall and W. H. Meckling, "Predictability of Costs, Time, and Success of Development," in Richard Nelson (ed.), *The Rate and Direction of Inventive Activity: Economic and Social Factors*, National Bureau of Economic Research, New York, in press. Also, W. R. King and T. A. Wilson have reported on historical analysis of activity time estimates made in critical path project networks in "Subjective Time Estimates in Critical Path Planning: A Preliminary Analysis," *Management Science*, vol. 13, no. 5, January, 1967.

[10] These performance measures are the same as those called "outcome descriptors" in the discussion of systems analysis in Chap. 3.

tion required to control the project properly. We shall not be concerned with the detailed documentation, such as the many records required to track the cost of a project, but rather with the documentation that the project manager needs to provide overall control of the project, as opposed to control of a specific functional element.

Master project manual

The focus of the project documentation is the master project manual. This manual provides an unambiguous definition of the policy framework and many facts relating to the project. The master project manual should not be confused with the company policy and procedures manuals, although it may contain some of the same information. The master project manual expresses a policy framework for the project in terms of the interfaces between the project organization and the company operations. The content of the project manual will, of course, depend on the requirements of the particular project. Appendix 2 outlines what should typically be included in a project manual.[11]

Because each project is unique, some of the sections of the project manual described in Appendix 2 may be applicable, and some not. The manual is most useful if prepared in loose-leaf form, since its value depends heavily on its being kept current. If maintained properly, such a manual can be the primary means by which the project manager keeps up to date on major aspects of the project. The time and money such a manual would save would be difficult to measure. What would be the value of having timely information on hand to give a customer, for example, or a corporate official when he calls about a particular problem? Most routine questions can be answered by referring to the manual, and others can usually be answered by some person listed in it.

DEVELOPING THE MANUAL   The manual should be developed as the project grows. The initial distribution of the manual should precede initiation of work on the project, since the manual will play an integral part in the project's management. If the project manager and the key project participants work together in preparing the manual, important benefits can result; for example:

> The participants will be more apt to support it, since they have participated in its development and upkeep.

[11] The project-manual concept as presented in Appendix 2 is taken from L. H. Kurkjian, "Tools for Effective Project Management of Medium Size R&D Programs," *IEEE Transactions on Engineering Management*, June, 1963, with modifications by the authors.

The participants will be better informed, since they will be exposed to the project problems as they maintain the documentation.

The project will have more meaning to the participants, and thus they will be able to identify their own value systems and personal objectives with the project objectives.

In a sense, the project manual is the plan of the project since it summarizes all its major deliberations. This is the information the project manager requires to maintain activities in accordance with the plan. On small projects, he might be able to store this information in his head or in several other documents, but on a project of any complexity, he will need more formalized documentation to keep order in the project—hence the project manual.

Project review

Project review is an effective method of comparing the project progress with the progress plan. The purpose, in broad terms, is to:

Inquire into the effectiveness of the management of a project

Inquire into the *degree* to which the project's objectives have been accomplished

Determine whether the project should be accelerated, phased down, or disestablished

The project review can (and should) be accomplished by the project manager in collaboration with his key contributors. He may designate one individual from his staff to act as a central point of contact during the review. The areas to be examined during the project review should generally include the following:

Authority and responsibility of the project manager

Project charter

Project identification

Project priority

Dollar size and complexity

Applicability of project-management techniques

Project history

Project visibility

Project staffing

Communications channels

Reporting

Project status reviews and evaluations

Management information system

Financial management

Planning

Technical direction

Each of the foregoing major areas should be subdivided into specific questions, the answers to which would provide salient information on the project. If inconsistencies appear during the review, the specific area involved should be investigated further. All inconsistencies should be resolved or at least explained before a final report on the review is given to top management.

PROJECT-REVIEW TEAM   Project review should be conducted with as little disruption of the project effort as possible. The continuity of the project effort can be preserved by appointing an *ad hoc* team of qualified executives to head up the review. The skill mix of this team should be compatible with the organic activities of the project; specialists in cost, schedule, and technology (or performance) should be included. At the conclusion of the review, the team should present its *independent* findings, conclusions, and recommendations to the project manager, who, at his discretion, communicates the report with appropriate notations to the top-level managers.

The team's report should be given wide distribution in the project, particularly among the major contributors. This will provide cross-fertilization of ideas, which will contribute substantially to the overall understanding of the project problems and work. In one case in the Department of Defense, the project review served to confirm:

That the concept of using existing functional support to support the project was sound

That the project manager needed to execute careful, formal, explicit interface agreements since several DOD components and outside agencies were engaged in related work

That the project-review staff caused the project manager to identify his problems and request assistance of higher authority to solve them

That "closed-loop" communications were needed between the project manager and those to whom he was responsible

Project-management-review checklist

The project-review team needs some structure to follow in appraising the project. The questionnaire outlined in Appendix 3 can provide a framework against which to measure the status of the project. Of course, the checklist will vary depending on the project.

The checklist technique is used extensively to ensure the proper sequencing in complex jobs; it is used, for example, in the operation of a highly automated manufacturing shop. The best example of the value of a checklist is in the field of aviation, where it is used to ensure that the system is prepared for operation; the checklist with the proper sequencing is required for the human subsystem, as well as for the physical system. "Fasten seat belts" and "Start engines" are two separate actions in getting an airliner into operation, and they must be done in a predetermined order. In a sense, the checklist for the project is a summary of the documentation; it embodies the main features of the project manager's plans, policies, and management philosophy. At the same time, the checklist acts as a technique for identifying areas where all may not be well with the project and for causing them to be investigated.

Although the checklist implies a mechanistic approach, project participants should not be offended by it since the list is not sacred. It serves the same purpose in project review as a financial ratio does, i.e., to signal where further study and investigation are required. A deviation signaled by the checklist could have significant meaning to the company, or it could mean nothing, depending upon what the investigation discloses.

We feel that the project manager will need to use a checklist or other similar device to periodically review the status of his project. Therefore, we recommend that the technique be formalized to the degree required to facilitate project control.

Summary

In this chapter, we have examined the main tenets of control as well as some of the more subtle factors affecting it. We have reviewed the philosophy of control, some prerequisites for control, and some of the documentation that facilitates control of the project. We have reviewed the requirements of an information system. Our view has been that the project information system is that complex of communications which provides intelligence about the project.

In the next chapter, we shall discuss some of the techniques for portraying information which is used to evaluate project status, including milestone charting, PERT, CPM, and related means.

Recommended readings

Davis, Ralph C.: *The Fundamentals of Top Management*, Harper & Row, Publishers, Incorporated, New York, 1951, pp. 620–662.

Evans, Marshall K., and Lou R. Hague: "Master Plan for Information Systems," *Harvard Business Review*, January–February, 1962.

Jones, William M.: *Decision Making in Large Organizations*, The RAND Corporation, RM 3968-PR, Santa Monica, Calif., 1964.

King, W. R., and T. A. Wilson: "Subjective Time Estimates in Critical Path Planning: A Preliminary Analysis," *Management Science*, vol. 13, no. 5, January, 1967.

"A Management System for Management Systems: The Pentagon Builds a Monster," *Business Week*, Feb. 18, 1967.

Marshall, A. W., and W. H. Meckling: "Predictability of Costs, Time, and Success of Development," in Richard Nelson (ed.), *The Rate and Direction of Inventive Activity: Economic and Social Factors*, National Bureau of Economic Research, New York, in press.

Martino, R. L.: *Project Management and Control*, American Management Association, New York, 1964, vol. I, "Finding the Critical Path"; vol. II, "Applied Operational Planning"; vol. III, "Allocating and Scheduling Resources."

Rosenzweig, James: "The Weapons Systems Management Concept and Electronic Data Processing," *Management Science*, January, 1960.

CHAPTER 12
Project Planning and Control [1]

And yet, the PM (Project Manager) must know cost-progress and cost performance status not only for the project as a whole, but also for tasks . . . in order to control the project. But this is only part of the problem confronting him; he should also be able to forecast where likely trouble spots may develop in each of these levels of effort. [2]

The techniques outlined in this chapter concern the planning and scheduling of projects having the following general characteristics:

An objective that is known and can be specified

An anticipated date of completion

Actions and activities to accomplish the objective that can be determined in advance

A desired or required sequence for performing the activities

The reader should keep in mind the relationship this chapter has to Chapter 5, where the role of systems analysis and a system of plans is discussed. Chapter 5 develops the theme of an overall strategy for the organiza-

---

[1] The main theme material in this chapter is based on a more comprehensive report—Thomas L. Healy, *Project Administration Techniques,* The National Cash Register Company, Dayton, Ohio, Apr. 1, 1963.

[2] John Stanley Baumgartner, *Project Management,* Richard D. Irwin, Inc., Homewood, Ill., 1963, p. 44.

tion and the development of the necessary supporting plans to support that overall strategy. In the present chapter, we are concerned with the creation of a plan for a particular project and the techniques for controlling that project.

It is difficult to separate planning and control—a good plan puts you well on the way to establishing standards of performance against which progress can be measured and in terms of which the necessary corrective action can be instituted. Even the use of PERT-associated techniques makes it difficult to separate planning and control. Indeed, it is a moot question as to where the greatest value of PERT techniques is found—in planning or in control. We do not propose to enter into such a debate; it is more important that the reader recognize the interrelatedness of planning and control and the utility of PERT-associated techniques in planning for and controlling the project.

The planning and scheduling techniques described in this chapter include the traditional Gantt, or bar, chart and the network plans such as PERT. We shall place primary emphasis on the network techniques because they provide significant advantages over the traditional Gantt chart.

Network planning and scheduling techniques have attracted considerable interest and are widely used in many different types of projects. The techniques were originally developed for R&D and engineering projects, but other applications have included the preparation of computer programs, plant maintenance shutdowns, construction programs, the preparation of bids and proposals, the marketing of new products, and the installation of data-processing systems. The techniques can be used in any project since the details are developed in accordance with the requirements of the particular project. For a large, integrated project where hundreds of separate tasks and jobs must be planned and scheduled, a computer is required to handle the many calculations required in the analysis procedure. For smaller projects, the analysis can be done manually.

Traditional methods for project planning and scheduling

The best-known and most widely used technique for project planning, scheduling, and control is the Gantt chart. This chart consists of a scale divided into units of time (e.g., days, weeks, or months) across the top and a listing of the project elements down the left-hand side. Bars, lines, or other symbols are used to indicate the schedule and status of each element in relation to the time scale.

Such charts usually entail a sequence of steps necessary to complete the project, together with the time available for completion and a summary reporting technique in terms of the total job. In the original Gantt charts, the governing factor in accomplishing activities and tasks was the capacity of the workers and machines. The progress chart, the man and machine record chart, and the load chart are examples of these early charts. A division on the chart represented both an amount of time and the amount of work to be done in that time. Horizontal lines across the time divisions on the chart showed the relationship between the amount of work accomplished in a specific time span and the amount scheduled.

Project planning chart

In extending the applications of these techniques, Gantt's associates recognized that for some project-type efforts, time, rather than resources, was the governing factor. In such cases, resources would be made available within practical limitations to complete the project in the shortest possible time. The chart developed for these projects was called the *project planning chart* and was based on the progress chart developed by Gantt. Figure 12-1 is an example of a project planning chart for the development of an electronic device. The elements of the project (in this case, functional units) are listed on the left-hand side, and the units of time in workdays are shown at the top. The light horizontal lines indicate the schedule for the project elements, with the specific tasks or operations written above the schedule line. The starting and completion times are indicated by opening and closing angles, ⌐ and ⌐. Work accomplished is indicated by a heavy line below the schedule line.[3] The large V's on the time scale at the top of the chart mark the time to which progress has been posted. Progress is posted at regular intervals.

The system line in Figure 12-1 indicates that the project as a whole is six days behind schedule. At the last posting, the receiver video amplifier unit was the furthest behind schedule. The display and antenna units were ahead of schedule. If the work on the video amplifier and available personnel skills permit, therefore, the project manager should consider transferring personnel temporarily from the display and antenna units to the video amplifier unit. Other elements are behind schedule, too, but not as much as the video amplifier. Thus, bringing the video amplifier up to schedule should have priority.

---

[3] Project planning charts often use open bars (hence the name "bar charts"), with the ends indicating the start and completion times. Accomplished work is indicated by filling in the bar.

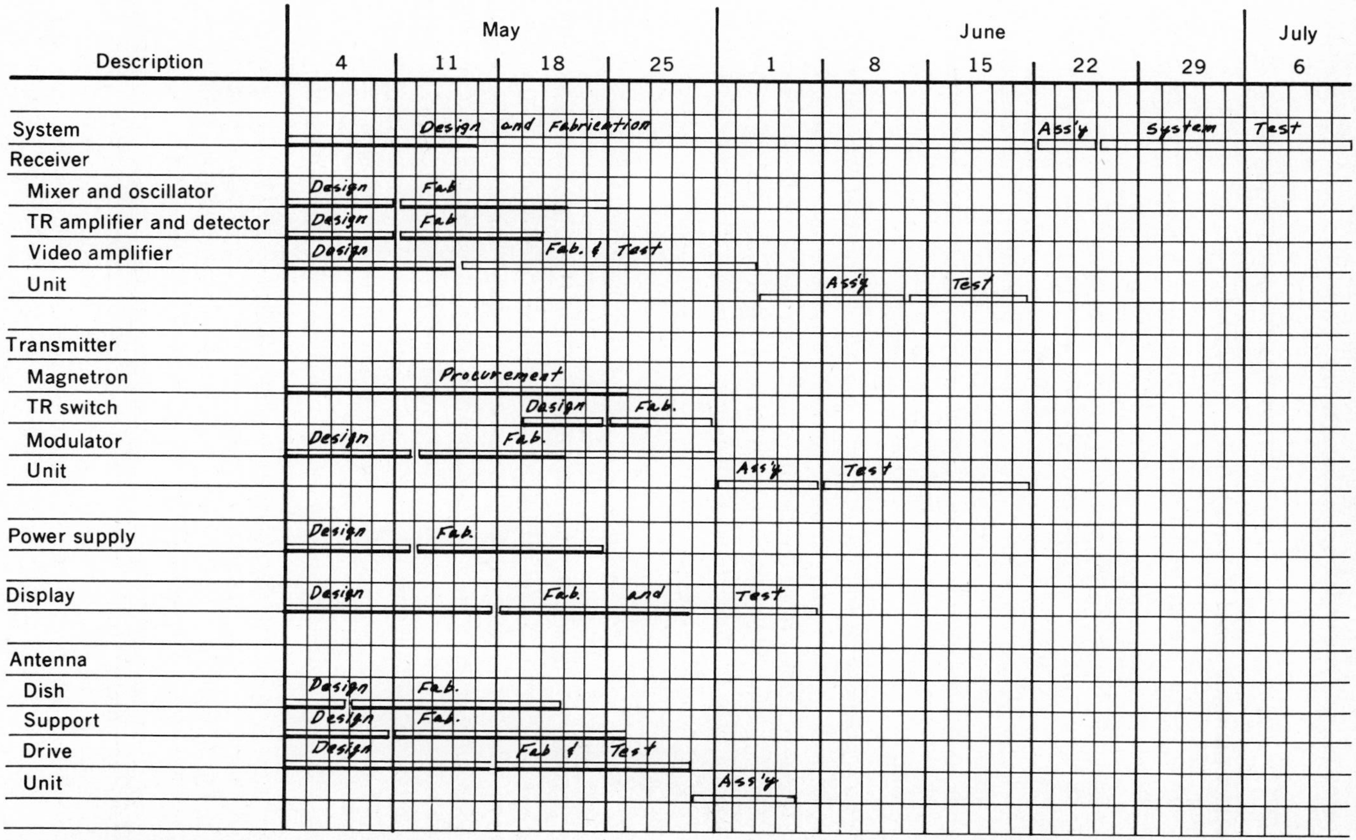

Description	May 4	11	18	25	June 1	8	15	22	29	July 6
System		Design and Fabrication						Ass'y	System	Test
Receiver										
Mixer and oscillator	Design	Fab								
TR amplifier and detector	Design	Fab								
Video amplifier	Design		Fab. & Test							
Unit					Ass'y		Test			
Transmitter										
Magnetron		Procurement								
TR switch	Design		Design	Fab.						
Modulator	Design		Fab.							
Unit					Ass'y	Test				
Power supply	Design	Fab.								
Display	Design		Fab.	and	Test					
Antenna										
Dish	Design	Fab.								
Support	Design	Fab.								
Drive	Design		Fab & Test							
Unit				Ass'y						

Figure 12-1 Project planning chart.

Preparing the project planning chart

A project planning chart is usually prepared as follows:

> Analyze the project to determine the method and approach to be used.
>
> Break the project down into elements to be scheduled.
>
> Estimate the time required to perform each element. (Time estimates should be made by the persons who will accomplish the work, or in conference with them.)
>
> List the elements down the left-hand side in sequence of time, considering those which must be performed sequentially as well as those which can be performed simultaneously. (If the completion date has been specified, the elements can be sequenced by working backward from the completion date.)

To post progress on the project, the amount of time that was estimated to accomplish that portion of work completed is determined, and a heavy solid line is extended from the left margin to represent that time increment. The span of time between that work-accomplished line and the charted completion date for that element, therefore, represents the amount of time required to complete that element.

Advantages and disadvantages of the bar chart

The primary advantage of the bar chart is that the plan, schedule, and progress of the project can all be portrayed graphically together. It is particularly effective in showing the status of the project elements and identifying the elements that are behind or ahead of schedule. The time the project is behind the schedule is usually determined by the maximum delay of any element from the schedule.

The bar chart has some disadvantages when applied to projects:

> Planning and scheduling must be considered simultaneously. The time dimension associated with the chart requires alternative plans to be evaluated in terms of the schedule established when the plan is originally chartered. Thus, the course of action must be selected almost entirely on the basis of the adopted schedule; little or no opportunity is provided for considering alternative plans with different schedules.
>
> It provides no means for assessing the impact of an element's being behind or ahead of schedule. Simply because a project element is behind schedule does not necessarily mean that the project is behind schedule by that amount. For most projects, only a few dates are critical in the sense that any delay in them will delay the project by a corresponding amount. The impact of slips in schedule dates depends upon the interrelationships between elements, which are not easily portrayed.

It does not present sufficient detail to enable the *timely* detection of schedule slippages.

Since it is usually maintained manually, the chart tends to become outdated.

The chart's simplicity precludes the portrayal of schedule-progress information for large and complex projects; its greatest value is in depicting gross progress (or lack of it) in the major elements of a project and in communicating the overall status of the project to top management.

Network plans

Introduction

Network plans enable the manager to separate planning from scheduling. This separation enables project planning to center around the technological aspects and time requirements of a project; the interference of other projects and the availability of resources then become the concern of scheduling. This separation of planning and scheduling permits alternative plans as well as alternative schedules to be considered. Separation is achieved through the use of a different graphic method and a new analytic procedure.

With traditional techniques, a linear calendar format is used. This forces the schedule to be prepared simultaneously with the project plan. The technological and time-requirement aspects of project planning become intermingled with the resource-allocation problems of scheduling. As a result, alternative plans are usually evaluated on the basis of their schedules. Furthermore, because planning and scheduling proceed in a step-by-step fashion, trade-offs between planning and scheduling cannot be determined so as to arrive at a preferred course of action.

Only a small percentage of the tasks and jobs are critical to the overall time requirement for completing most projects. Furthermore, tasks which are critical in one plan may not be critical in another, and noncritical tasks may become critical because of the way they are scheduled. Knowing which tasks are critical to a project plan facilitates scheduling the project and allocating the resources necessary to accomplish it. Scheduling the critical jobs first will usually permit considerable latitude in scheduling the remainder.

In network planning and scheduling techniques, the plan is prepared in the form of a network or flow diagram. Using a network rather than a bar chart alleviates many of the problems associated with planning and scheduling, since the analysis of the network enables the criticality of each task to be determined in a quantitative and objective manner. In addition to the criticality, a network also provides the following benefits:

A disciplined and logical basis for planning a project that helps to include essential jobs and eliminate unnecessary ones

A clear picture of the scope of the project

Identification of responsibility for performing specific tasks

Composition of network plans

Network plans are developed by first studying the project to determine the approach, methods, and technology to be used and then breaking it down into elements for planning and scheduling purposes. The elements of a project can be classified as follows:

Project objectives. These are the goals to be accomplished during the course of the project. In most cases, the project objectives are specified before the plan is prepared; the plan merely prescribes the course to be followed in achieving the objectives.

Activities, tasks, jobs, or work phases. These elements identify and describe the work to be performed in accomplishing the project objectives. They normally utilize time and other resources.

Events or milestones. These are points of significant accomplishment— the start or completion of tasks and jobs, the attainment of objectives, the completion of management reviews and approvals, etc. They are convenient points at which to report status or measure and evaluate progress.

After the elements of the project have been determined, they are arranged in the sequence preferred for their accomplishment. This is a synthesis process that must consider the technological aspects of the activities and tasks, their relationships to one another and to the objectives, and the environment in which they will be performed. A network is used to reflect these factors as it portrays the sequence in which the project elements will be accomplished.

Networks are composed of events which are represented by points interconnected by directed lines (lines with arrows) which represent activities. Constraints are also represented as directed lines. Elements of the network correspond to elements of the project as follows: Points in the network represent project objectives, events, and milestones; the lines between the points represent project activities, with the direction of the line indicating a precedence or sequential relationship; and directed solid or dashed lines indicate constraints.

Activities are the jobs and tasks, including administrative tasks, that must be performed to accomplish the project objectives; activities require time and utilize resources. The length of the line representing an activity has no significance (in contrast to Gantt charts, where it is the significant factor).

The direction of the line, however, indicates the flow of time in performing the activity.

Events are usually represented by circles or squares. Numbers are inserted in these circles and squares, which are used to identify the events and the activity that connects two events. Events represent particular points or instances in time, so they do not consume resources; the resources to accomplish an event are used by the activities leading up to it.

Constraints in network plans represent precedence relationships resulting from natural or physical restrictions, administrative policies and procedures, or management prerogatives, and they serve to identify activities and events uniquely. Constraints, like activities, are represented in a network plan by directed lines. However, constraints indicate precedence only; they do not require resources and normally do not require time. Those constraints which require neither time nor resources are represented by broken directed lines, which are often referred to as "dummy" activities.

Preparation of network plans

The network plan is constructed by drawing directed lines and circles in the sequence in which the activities and events are to be accomplished.[4] The network begins with an event called the *origin*, which usually represents the start of the project and from which lines are drawn to represent activities. These lines terminate with an arrow and a circle representing an event, which may be the completion of a project element or an activity. All activities that are to be performed next are then added to the network plan by drawing a directed line from the previous event. For example, suppose activities B and C are to be simultaneously performed upon completion of activity A. These three activities and their precedence relationship would be represented in the network plan as indicated in Figure 12-2. Activities and events are then added until the project is complete. Constraints are added where required. The network plan terminates with one or more events, called *terminal* events.

To progress from one event to the next requires that an activity be performed. Each activity begins and ends with an event. The event at the start

---

[4] There are two general methods which are used in actual construction of a network plan. This section describes the *forward* method, where construction begins with the start event and activities and events are added in sequential fashion to reach the end event. In the *backward* method, construction begins with the end event and proceeds backward to the start event. The backward method of network construction is often preferred to the forward method because attention is directed to the project objectives. With the objectives firmly in mind, the activities and events required to accomplish those objectives are often more easily determined.

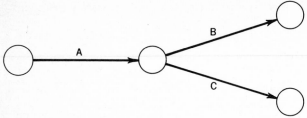

Figure 12-2   Simple network plan.

of an activity is called a *predecessor* event, and that at the conclusion a *successor* event. Time flows from a predecessor event to successor event, as indicated by the arrow, and is normally from left to right throughout the network. As each activity is added to the network, its relationship to other activities is determined by answers to the following questions:

> What activities must be completed before this activity can start? Activities that must be completed first are predecessor activities.
>
> What activities can start after this activity is completed? Activities that can start after are successor activities.
>
> What activities can be performed at the same time as this activity? Those activities are *concurrent*, or parallel, activities.

In preparing the network plan, administrative activities must be included, such as the preparation of contracts, the procurement of parts, and the preparation of test procedures, specifications, and drawings. Technical work often cannot begin until a contract has been awarded or long-lead-time articles have been procured. A test cannot be started until test procedures have been written, and tooling cannot commence until specifications and drawings have been prepared and approved.

Two activities with a predecessor-successor relationship are called *sequential* activities. Performing activities in sequence requires that the start of the successor activity depend upon completion of the predecessor activity. Activities performed concurrently must be independent of one another. However, activities independent of one another cannot always be performed concurrently; for example, if one activity creates a safety hazard for the other, they must be performed in sequence. Independent activities may have a common predecessor event or a common successor event, but not both.

Suppose, for example, that activities B and C can be performed concurrently but that both are dependent upon the completion of activity A; activity D can be started after both B and C are completed. The relationships would then be represented as illustrated by Figure 12-3. The constraint, or dummy activity, is needed between activities B and D so as to identify ac-

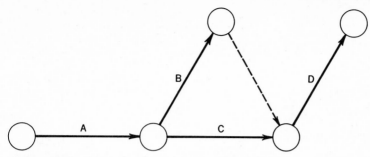

Figure 12-3   Network plan: correct predecessor-successor relationship.

tivities B and C uniquely by their predecessor and successor events. The constraint could just as well have been added between activities C and D.

AN ILLUSTRATION OF A NETWORK PLAN   To illustrate the preparation of a network plan, let us consider as a project the servicing of an automobile at a service station. This example will be slightly exaggerated in order to emphasize the interrelationships between project activities that must be considered. The project situations is described as follows:

Automobiles arrive at a service station for gasoline. Services provided by the station include cleaning the windshield and checking the tire, battery, oil, and radiator. Sufficient personnel are available to perform all services simultaneously. The windshield cannot be cleaned while the hood is raised. Customers are charged only for gasoline and oils.

Figure 12-4 shows the network plan. Events 1 and 9 are the origin and terminal events, respectively, representing the start and completion of service. Three constraints, or dummy activities, are used to sequence the activities properly.

The constraint between events 3 and 5, denoted as activity 3–5, is used so that the activities "check radiator" and "check battery" will not have common predecessor and successor events. The dummy activity 4–5 is used for the same reason. The constraint 4–6 is used to indicate that the activity of computing the bill cannot start until the activities "check oil" and "add gas" have been completed. Suppose that the dummy activities had been sequenced as shown in Figure 12-5a. This implies that computing the bill also depends upon completing the check of the battery and radiator, which is not true since there is no charge for servicing the battery or the radiator. On the other hand, suppose that the dummy activities had been sequenced

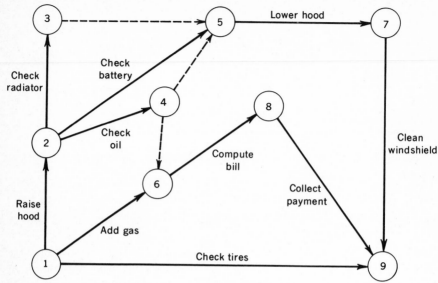

Figure 12-4   Network plan for servicing an automobile.

as shown in Figure 12-5b. This implies that the hood cannot be lowered until the gas has been added, which obviously is an improper relationship unless the gas-tank cap is under the hood. This simple case illustrates the care that must be exercised in sequencing and constraining activities.

Guidelines for preparing network plans

Only a few practical guidelines can be given for general use in preparing network plans, and most of these apply to the construction of the network only after the project activities and events have been determined. One question that invariably arises in preparing a network plan is: "What level of project detail should be contained in the network?" By this is meant the magnitude and scope of the events and activities to be shown. Obviously, if the network is to serve as an adequate plan, it must contain sufficient detail for scheduling the project and measuring progress against the plan.

The quality of a plan is often evaluated in terms of the amount of detail it contains. Network planners sometimes become obsessed with this precept and go to great effort to incorporate the smallest details. Each activity, regardless of its nature, can be divided into small activities. The correct procedure is to consider carefully which activities are required, which are not clearly defined, which are not essential, and how they are interrelated. The

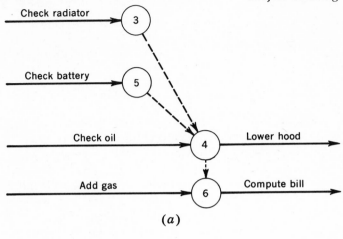

(a)

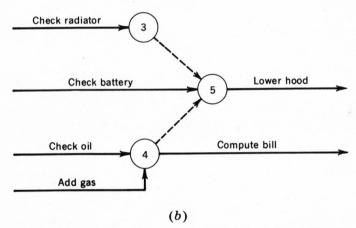

(b)

Figure 12-5   Two cases of improper sequencing of activities in Figure 12-4.

primary emphasis during the preparation of a network should be on planning the project, that is, developing a sound approach to how the project should be carried out and determining what must be done to accomplish the objectives. Once this is done, the network becomes a means for depicting the project plan.

Some of the guidelines suggested for establishing the correct level of detail for projects of substantial size and duration are:

Activities should represent efforts requiring four to six weeks to complete.
The level of detail should be one level below the level of responsibility; for

example, the network for the design of a system should contain activities and events pertaining to the design of each subsystem.

Standardized activities and events should be included in network plans prepared for similar projects.

None of these guidelines can be universally applied effectively. Determining the correct level of detail for a network plan is a matter of experience and judgment. The logical manner in which a network plan is prepared leads to incorporating more detail than is normally provided in other planning techniques. This happens frequently in networks for large projects where many people from different organizations participate in the preparation. In such cases, it is best to set an arbitrary level to use in preparing the initial network. After this initial network has been reviewed, a second networking session will usually produce a network with the appropriate amount of detail. Network preparation for large projects is facilitated by the following:

A project organizational chart with a description of the functions and responsibilities of the groups

A functional breakdown of hardware-oriented projects showing subsystems, assemblies, subassemblies, components, etc.

Analysis of network plans

The project network plan displays the activities, events, and constraints, together with their interrelationships. For the network to be useful in planning and controlling the project, time estimates must be made for the various activities which constitute the project.

In order to facilitate understanding of the ideas of network analysis, we shall for the moment assume that single time estimates have been obtained for each of the activities in a project network. Later, we shall discuss some of the ways which have been devised for obtaining these estimates. Here, our emphasis is on the *use* to which time estimates are put. The time estimates for each activity are typically expressed in terms of workdays or workweeks.

A *network path* is a sequence of activities and events traced out by starting with the origin event and proceeding to its successor event, then to another successor event, etc., until the terminal event is reached. The *length* of a network path is the sum of the time estimates for all those activities on the path.

After activity time estimates have been made, an earliest and latest time for each event may be calculated. The *earliest time* for an event is the length of the longest path from the origin to the event. Thus, it indeed represents the earliest time at which the event can occur (relative to the timing of the origin event). The earliest time for the terminal event is the length of the longest network path. It therefore represents the shortest time required to complete the entire project.

The *latest time* for an event is the latest time at which the event can occur relative to the timing of the terminal event. If one imagines that the direction of each activity is reversed, the latest time for an event is determined by the length of the longest path from the terminal event to the event in question.

In calculating earliest event times, the general practice is to consider that the origin event occurs at time zero. The earliest time for each event is the sum of the earliest time for the predecessor event and the time for the predecessor activity. If an event has more than one predecessor event, this calculation is made for each of them, and the largest sum is selected as the earliest time for the event. This is so because the earliest time is the length of the longest path from the origin to the event.

To calculate the latest time for an event, the latest time for the terminal event is usually initially set equal to the previously computed earliest time for the terminal event. Then, for each event, the time for its successor activity is subtracted from the latest time for its successor event. The result is the latest time for that event. If an event has more than one successor event, this calculation is made for each, and the smaller result is used as the latest time for the event. This is compatible with the view of the latest time for an event as the longest path from the terminal event backward to the event in question.

Using these basic activity, event, and path measures, a number of network measures may be developed to aid in network analysis.

Event slack is the difference between the latest time and the earliest time for an event. The slack for an event is the difference between the length of the longest network path and the length of the longest network path through the event. Hence, event slack is a property of a particular network path. Consider Figure 12-6, which shows the last three events of a network plan, time estimates for the activities (the numbers on the lines representing each activity), and earliest and latest event times (the pair of numbers in parentheses at each event). The slack for event 31 is 6 ($34 - 28$). This can also be determined from the lengths of the network paths. The length of the longest network path is the earliest time of terminal event 32, which is 42. The length of the longest network path through event 31 to 36 ($25 + 3 + 8$). The difference between the length of the longest network path and the length of the longest network path through activity 31 is therefore 6 ($42 - 36$), which is the event slack.

The most important use of event slack is in identifying the critical path.

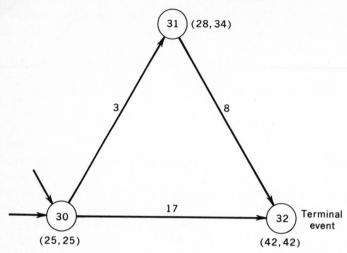

Figure 12-6   Portion of network illustrating computation of event slack.

The *critical path* is the longest network path. Thus, its length determines the minimum time required for completion of the entire project. *Critical events* are those events on the critical path. To identify critical events, one need only determine those events with the smallest amounts of event slack. Their identification is usually sufficient to identify the critical path; however, it need not uniquely identify it.[5]

The operational significance of the critical events is that they are the pacing elements of the project. If the project is to be expedited, the accomplishment of at least one of the critical events must be expedited. If there is a delay in the actual accomplishment of *any* critical event, the completion of the project will be delayed.

Using network plans in planning and controlling a project

As we have already pointed out, the construction of a network plan is a part of the planning function of project management. Network analysis makes use of the project plan to aid in scheduling a project.

Whether one is planning, scheduling, or controlling a project, the central idea involved in using network plans is the principle of *management by exception*. Stated simply, this means that it is the exceptions which require the attention of management. In the case of a project, the exceptions are the

[5] See Thomas L. Healy, *Project Administration Techniques*, The National Cash Register Company, Dayton, Ohio, Apr. 1, 1963, for details of those special situations in which this may be the case.

activities on the critical path, for it is they which pace the completion of the project.

If a project is to be expedited, some way must be found to hasten the accomplishment of critical events. Moreover, if the project is under way and the events on the critical path are not being accomplished according to plan, the project will be delayed if no way is found to hasten the completion of other critical events.

The application of the principle of management by exception in such projects usually takes the form of reallocating resources from noncritical activities to critical ones. This may be accomplished in either the planning or the control phase of the project; i.e., it may be done so that an earlier project completion date can be set up, or it may be done because the project is falling behind schedule. Presumably, such reallocations will permit faster accomplishment of critical activities and hence, faster completion of the project itself.

A number of techniques have been developed for accomplishing these ends. Among them CPM (Critical Path Method), PERT-Time, and PERT-Cost are the best known and most widely used. It is not our purpose to discuss these in detail here. Ample references to accessible writings on these techniques are given at the end of the chapter. As a conclusion to this discussion, we shall explore in some detail the basic ideas of PERT, one of the major methods by which activity time estimates are obtained.

Program evaluation review technique (PERT)

Introduction

The network plan depicts the interrelationships between the activities and events and the sequence in which they are to be accomplished. For the network to be useful in project scheduling and evaluation, time estimates must be assigned to the activities and a time analysis of the network performed. This section discusses the principles of one method for doing so—PERT.

In managing the Polaris missile, the Navy became concerned with techniques for evaluating its progress. A schedule had been established for its development, and a system was set up for reporting status, progress, and problem areas in terms of accomplishment or slippage (actual or forecasted) of important program milestones. Major components were also evaluated and their status indicated by one of the following terms: "in good shape," "minor weakness," "major weakness," or "critical." These evaluations provided no measure of the impact on the overall program made by accomplishing a milestone or changing the forecast for its accomplishment. Tight schedules had been established for the program, so it was necessary to know the significance of a slip in schedule date, its impact on future scheduled dates, and the prospect for future slippages so that corrective action could be taken. As the slips in schedules and the prospects for future slips were studied, ". . . it appeared that the capacity to predict future progress was more limited than desired." [6]

An operations research team was formed of representatives from the special projects office; Booz, Allen, and Hamilton, Inc., a management consulting firm; and Lockheed Missile Systems division, the prime contractor for the missile. This team was to study the application of statistical and mathematical methods to the planning, evaluation, and control of the Polaris program. The following objectives were established:

> To develop methodology for providing the integrated evaluation of progress to date and the progress outlook, changes in the validity of the established plans for accomplishing the program objectives, and effects of changes proposed for established plans
>
> To establish procedures for applying the methodology, as designed and tested, to the overall FBM (Fleet Ballistic Missile) program

The team felt that the two major requirements for a program-evaluation methodology were (1) detailed, well-considered time estimates for future activities and (2) precise knowledge of the required or planned sequence in which the activities were to be performed. Since the time required to perform development activities is often uncertain, a procedure for quantitatively expressing this uncertainty was desired; this led to the statistical estimation technique, which is a primary feature of PERT. The sequence requirement was fulfilled by use of network plans.

PERT, therefore, was originally developed as a technique for evaluating established plans and schedules, but its utility is not limited to this. PERT can also be used as a planning and scheduling technique. The PERT technique for estimating elapsed times provides a way of handling some of the uncertainties in estimating the time required to perform many types of activities.

Time estimates

After the network is prepared, the PERT planners obtain three elapsed time estimates for each activity: the shortest, the longest, and the most probable.

---

[6] D. G. Malcolm, J. H. Rosebloom, C. E. Clark, and W. Frazer, "Application of a Technique for Research and Development Program Evaluation," *Operations Research,* vol. 7, no. 5, September–October, 1959, pp. 646–669.

These three estimates are used to compute the expected times required to perform each activity and a measure of the probability of accomplishing the activity in that time. The expected time estimate for each activity is used in analyzing the network. Variabilities in activity times are accumulated along the network paths in the same manner as activity times are accumulated, and they provide a measure of variability for each event. The variability associated with an event can be used to make statistical inferences about the occurrence of the event at a particular time, such as "The likelihood that the project will be completed by its scheduled completion date is 34 percent."

The PERT approach requires obtaining the activity time estimates from the people who are responsible for performing or for supervising the performance of the activities. The person directly responsible for the activity should be asked to make the estimate because he is most knowledgeable concerning its inherent difficulties and the variability in its accomplishment. Scheduled times cannot be used because they are not adequately responsive to changing conditions, contain no information on variability, and are often made under conditions and in an environment that do not reflect the technical aspects of the activity. A single elapsed time estimate would not, by itself, provide a measure of the variability in the time; this requires a range of estimated elapsed times. Estimates of the extreme times, reflecting the optimistic and pessimistic times, can usually be given with some degree of reliability, however, and it is felt that the most likely time estimate lies somewhere within this range.

The three elapsed time estimates, referred to as the *optimistic*, the *most likely*, and the *pessimistic* times, are defined below.

OPTIMISTIC TIME   This is the shortest time in which the activity can be accomplished. There should be practically no hope of completing the activity in less time than this, but if everything goes exceptionally well, it should be possible to accomplish it in approximately this time.

MOST LIKELY TIME   This is the normal or most realistic time required to accomplish the activity. If the activity were to be repeated numerous times under the same conditions and without any "learning-curve" effects, it would be accomplished most frequently in this time. (The most likely time is not the expected time, but an estimate based on experienced judgment; the expected time is a mathematically computed value.)

PESSIMISTIC TIME   This is the longest time required to accomplish the activity assuming unusually bad luck (e.g., major redesign or major reshuffling of planned action). The pessimistic time estimate should include such possibilities as initial failure and a second start, but not major catastrophic events such as strikes, fires, tornadoes, etc.

The range between the optimistic and the pessimistic time estimates is used in PERT as a measure of the variability or uncertainty in accomplishing an activity. If there is no uncertainty, all the time estimates will be the same, and the range will be zero. If there is considerable uncertainty, the range will be large. The time estimates must necessarily be based on planned assumed resources. The most likely time estimate must be based on the same level of resources that is used for estimating the optimistic and pessimistic times. For example, the optimistic time estimate must *not* be based on an extra shift or additional personnel, while the most likely time estimate is based on a normal shift and fewer personnel.

The most likely time estimate should be made first so that the estimate considers the available or planned level of resources and appraises the technical aspects of the activity realistically. The optimistic estimate can then be made, based on the same resources but with the assumption that everything goes exceedingly well. The pessimistic time estimate is made last, assuming that problems arise. The time estimates for each activity must be made independently and should not include a pad to cover possible delays. The possibility of padding is reduced by skipping around through the network when developing the time estimates.

Analysis of the network plan

The first step in analyzing the network is to convert the three elapsed time estimates to a single expected time estimate. This estimate, called the *expected activity time* (not to be confused with the most likely time estimate), is designated by t_e and calculated by the following formula: [7]

$$t_e = \frac{\text{optimistic time} + 4 \times \text{most likely time} + \text{pessimistic time}}{6}$$

To illustrate, suppose the optimistic, most likely, and pessimistic time estimates for accomplishing an activity are 3, 5, and 9, respectively. The expected time for accomplishing the activity would be

[7] The deviation of this formula is based on the following assumption: The model for the probability distribution of an activity time is a beta distribution whose standard deviation is one-sixth the range between the pessimistic and optimistic time estimates and whose mode is equal to the most likely time estimate. K. R. MacCrimmon and C. A. Ryavec discuss the implications of all of the basic PERT assumptions in "An Analytic Study of the PERT Assumptions," *Operations Research*, vol. 12, no. 1, 1964.

$$t_e = \frac{3 + (4 \times 5) + 9}{6} = \frac{32}{6} = 5.3$$

With PERT, the measure of uncertainty or variability is called the standard deviation, σ, and is estimated by the following formula:

$$\sigma = \frac{(\text{pessimistic time}) - (\text{optimistic time})}{6}$$

For optimistic, most likely, and pessimistic time estimates of 3, 5, and 9, respectively, the standard deviation associated with the expected time would be

$$\sigma = \frac{9 - 3}{6} = 1$$

The uncertainty associated with the earliest time estimate for an event is determined by combining the uncertainties associated with the expected times for all the activities on the longest network path leading to the event. The network path that determines the earliest time for an event, therefore, also determines the uncertainty associated with that time.

The probability of accomplishing an event on, before, or after its scheduled date can be computed by using the earliest event time, the scheduled time, and the uncertainty associated with the earliest event time. If the scheduled time is prior to the earliest event time, the probability of accomplishing the event on or before its scheduled date is less than 50 percent. If the scheduled time is later than the earliest event time, the probability of accomplishing the event on or before its scheduled date is greater than 50 percent. As the scheduled date moves further away from the earliest event time, the probability of accomplishing the event on or before the scheduled date approaches an upper value of 100 percent. The following criteria are suggested for using the computed probabilities in program evaluation.

If the probability of meeting a scheduled date is less than 25 percent, the amount of risk associated with it makes it infeasible. In this case, the allocation of resources, the performance requirements, or the planned sequence of activities should be revised to obtain a probability greater than 25 percent, or the event should be rescheduled. With probabilities between 25 and 60 percent, the risk is normal and the allocation of resources is reasonable. With a probability greater than 60 percent, the activities should be examined for excessive resource allocations.

An important property of the computed expected times is that they are added to calculate an earliest time, and this earliest event time is also an expected event time and has a probability of 50 percent. This probability would not hold if most likely time estimates were summed in a similar fashion.

Efficacy of PERT

PERT has attracted considerable attention, which, to date, has probably been more extensive than its range of applications. The following comments and criticisms provide a measure of understanding of the basic technique.

Many feel that because the three time estimates are subjective, the estimator's personal bias will be introduced.[8] A fundamental principle of PERT is that the three estimates are to be made by persons who are most familiar with the technical aspects of the activities and therefore are best qualified to make the time estimates reflecting uncertainties involved in technical activities. Asking for three time estimates tends to remove the psychological barrier often encountered when only a single estimate is given, since a time range does not imply a commitment such as a single estimate does, and allowing the estimator to make a pessimistic time estimate permits him to provide for unforeseen contingencies that would probably be included as a pad in a single estimate. The effects of personal biases are felt to be canceled in the analysis of the network, since estimates of optimists are offset by estimates of pessimists.

Another controversial aspect of PERT pertains to use of computed expected times for scheduling. It can be shown that PERT assumptions provide optimistic expected times. Therefore, many feel that scheduled times should be later than computed expected times. But some argue that automatically setting schedules later than expected times may increase the likelihood of schedule slippages and that expected times should not be automatically used for establishing schedules. The basis for this argument is that the computed expected times provide for slippage, and since roughly half the activities will be completed in less than their expected times and half will require more than their expected times, one will balance out the other. In actuality, however, R&D activities usually take as long as their schedules

---

[8] W. R. King and T. A. Wilson have hypothesized that a historical analysis of time-estimating behavior can lead to the development of adjustment models. Such models could be used to adjust time estimates on the basis of historical estimating behavior. The adjusted estimates would presumably be superior to unadjusted ones. See "Subjective Time Estimates in Critical Path Planning: A Preliminary Analysis," *Management Science*, vol. 13, no. 5, January, 1967.

permit and are seldom completed ahead of schedule. Thus, schedule slippages occur in R&D activities which were not contemplated when schedules were prepared.

The validity of PERT expected time is another controversial matter. Where PERT is applied to the early stages of weapons-system development programs, the critical path is frequently 1½ to 2 times as long as the originally planned program. No doubt the greater attention to detail that is necessary in applying PERT accounts for part of the additional time. A study of completed Air Force weapons-system development programs conducted independently of any PERT considerations, however, indicated that extensions of development time by one-third to one-half over the originally planned program were the rule rather than the exception.[9]

Summary

This chapter focuses attention on some of the major ideas which have proved useful in project planning and control. Traditional techniques are discussed and analyzed, but the newer techniques of network analysis are given primary attention.

Recommended readings

Archibald, R. D., and R. L. Villoria: *Network-based Management Systems (PERT/CPM)*, John Wiley & Sons, Inc., New York, 1967.

Bigelow, C. G.: "Bibliography on Project Planning and Control by Network Analysis: 1959–1961," *Operations Research*, vol. 10, no. 5, pp. 728–731, September–October, 1962.

Burgess, A. R., and James B. Killebrew: "Variation in Activity Level on a Cyclical Arrow Diagram," *Journal of Industrial Engineering*, vol. 13, no. 2, pp. 76–83, March–April, 1962.

Camp, William E.: "Executive Direction of Projects," in Carl Heyel (ed.), *Handbook of Industrial Research Management*, Reinhold Publishing Corporation, New York, 1959.

Carruthers, J. A., and A. Battersby: "Advances in Critical Path Methods," *Operational Research Quarterly*, vol. 17, no. 4, pp. 359–380, December, 1966.

[9] A. W. Marshall and W. H. Meckling, *Predictability of the Costs, Time and Success of Development*, RAND Corporation, Paper P–1821, Santa Monica, Calif., Dec. 11, 1959.

Childs, Marshall R.: "Does PERT Work for Small Projects?" *Data Processing*, vol. 4, no. 12, pp. 32–35, December, 1962.

Clark, Charles E.: "The PERT Model for the Distribution of an Activity Time," *Operations Research*, vol. 10, no. 3, pp. 405–406, May–June, 1962.

Clark, Wallace: *The Gantt Chart*, 3d ed., Sir Isaac Pitman & Sons, Ltd., London, 1952.

Clark, Mrs. Wallace: "The Gantt Chart," in Harold B. Maynard (ed.), *Industrial Engineering Handbook*, McGraw-Hill Book Company, New York, 1956.

Cosinuke, Walter: "The Critical-path Technique for Planning and Scheduling," *Chemical Engineering*, vol. 69, no. 13, pp. 113–118, June 25, 1962.

Davis, E. W.: "Resource Allocation in Project Network Models: A Survey," *Journal of Industrial Engineering*, vol. 17, no. 4, pp. 177–188, April, 1966.

DOD and NASA Guide: PERT Cost Systems Design, Office of the Secretary of Defense and National Aeronautics and Space Administration, Washington, D.C., June, 1962.

Dooley, A. R.: "Interpretations of PERT," *Harvard Business Review*, pp. 161–172, March–April, 1964.

Federal Electric Corporation: *A Programmed Introduction to PERT*, John Wiley & Sons, Inc., New York, 1963.

Glaser, L. B., and R. M. Young: "Critical-path Planning and Scheduling," *Chemical Engineering Progress*, vol. 57, no. 11, pp. 60–65, November, 1961.

Hansen, B. J.: *Practical PERT*, American Aviation Publishing, Washington, D.C., 1964.

Jodka, John: "PERT (Program Evaluation and Review Technique): A Control Concept Using Computers," *Computers and Automation*, vol. 11, no. 3, pp. 16–18, March, 1962.

Kelley, James E., Jr.: "Critical-path Planning and Scheduling: Mathematical Basis," *Operations Research*, vol. 9, no. 3, pp. 296–320, May–June, 1961.

—— and Morgan R. Walker: "Critical Path Planning and Scheduling," *1959 Proceedings of the Eastern Joint Computer Conference*, pp. 160–173.

King, William R., and T. A. Wilson: "Subjective Time Estimates in Critical Path Planning: A Preliminary Analysis," *Management Science*, vol. 13, no. 5, January, 1967.

——, D. M. Wittevrongel, and K. D. Hezel: "On the Analysis of Subjective Time Estimates in Critical Path Planning," *Management Science*, November, 1967.

Kushnerick, J. P.: "How Dynasoar Managers Used PERT," *Aerospace Management*, vol. 7, no. 1, pp. 20–23, January, 1964.

Lockyer, K. G.: *An Introduction to Critical Path Analysis,* Pitman Publishing Corporation, New York, 1964.

MacCrimmon, K. R., and C. A. Ryavec: "An Analytic Study of the PERT Assumptions," *Operations Research,* vol. 12, no. 1, pp. 16–37, 1964.

Malcolm, D. G., J. H. Rosebloom, C. E. Clark, and W. Frazer: "Application of a Technique for Research and Development Program Evaluation," *Operations Research,* vol. 7, no. 5, pp. 646–669, September–October, 1959.

———, ———, ———, and ———: "Application of a Technique for R and D Program Evaluation (PERT)," *Operations Research,* vol. 10, no. 6, pp. 808–817, 1962.

Marshall, A. W., and W. H. Meckling: *Predictability of the Costs, Time and Success of Development,* RAND Corporation, Paper P–1821, Santa Monica, Calif., Dec. 11, 1959.

———: *Finding the Critical Path,* American Management Association, New York, 1964.

Martino, R. L.: *Applied Operational Planning,* American Management Association, New York, 1964.

———: *Finding the Critical Path,* American Management Association, New York, 1964.

———: *Allocating and Scheduling Resources,* American Management Association, New York, 1965.

Miller, Robert W.: "How to Plan and Control with PERT," *Harvard Business Review,* pp. 93–104, March–April, 1962.

———: *Schedule, Cost and Profit Control with PERT,* McGraw-Hill Book Company, New York, 1963.

Moder, J. J., and C. R. Philips: *Project Management with CPM and PERT,* Reinhold Publishing Corporation, New York, 1964.

Nevill, Gale, and David Falconer: "Critical Path Diagramming," *International Science and Technology,* October, 1962, pp. 43–49.

O'Brien, James J.: *CPM in Construction Management,* McGraw-Hill Book Company, New York, 1965.

Paige, H. W.: "How PERT-Cost Helps the General Manager," *Harvard Business Review,* November–December, 1963, pp. 87–95.

Pocock, J. W.: "PERT as an Analytical Aid for Programming Planning: Its Payoff and Problems," *Operations Research,* vol. 10, no. 6, pp. 893–903, November–December, 1962.

Sadow, R. W.: "How PERT Was Used in Managing the X–20 (Dyna-Soar) Program," *IEEE Transactions on Engineering Management,* vol. FM–11, no. 4, pp. 138–154, December, 1964.

SergioLerda-Olberg: "Bibliography on Network-based Project Planning and Control Techniques: 1962–1965," *Operations Research,* vol. 14, no. 5, pp. 925–931, September–October, 1966.

Shaffer, L. R., J. B. Ritter, and W. L. Meyer: *Critical Path Method,* McGraw-Hill Book Company, New York, 1965.

Special Projects Office, Bureau of Naval Weapons, Department of the Navy: *PERT Summary Report: Phase 1,* Government Printing Office, Washington, D.C., 1961.

Special Projects Office, Bureau of Naval Weapons, Department of the Navy: *PERT Summary Report: Phase 2,* Government Printing Office, Washington, D.C., 1961.

Stires, D., and M. Murphy: *PERT/CPM,* Industrial Education Institute, Boston.

——— and ———: *PERT/COST,* Industrial Education Institute, Boston, 1964.

Woodgate, H. S.: *Planning by Network,* Business Publications Limited, London, 1964.

Young, Lewis H.: "How Industry Schedules by Computer," *Control Engineering,* vol. 9, no. 1, pp. 16–18, January, 1962.

APPENDIX 1

Specifications of the project plan

A project plan, or some such document outlining applicable plans and planning tasks, is an essential tool of project management. It provides the necessary guidance for all the participants in developing the project as it gains in maturity, and it forms the basis for the project operations. The project package plan will be described in detail in the following sections.

Part 1. Project summary
Part 2. Project schedules
Part 3. Project management
Part 4. Market intelligence
Part 5. Operational concept
Part 6. Acquisition
Part 7. Facility support
Part 8. Logistic requirements
Part 9. Manpower and organization
Part 10. Executive development and personnel training
Part 11. Financial support
Part 12. Project requirements
Part 13. General information
Part 14. Proprietary information

PART 1. PROJECT SUMMARY   The project manager originates this section. It will be short in length and is prepared primarily with sufficient information to ensure understanding by top-level organizational officials who are interested in the key features of the project and what the project is intended to accomplish.

It should provide a brief description of the project and of the management structure, a summary of the guidance or constraints applicable to the project, the master project phasing chart, and the overall requirements of the project. The master phasing chart (Figure A-1) will contain a summary of the major milestones or key events contemplated in the project.

PART 2. PROJECT SCHEDULES   The project manager prepares these schedules with the assistance of participating organizations. It is important that the project manager be party to the preparation of this section, since he is responsible for the overall compatibility and consistency of the participating organizations' roles and schedule requirements.

The project-schedules section should be prepared on a form similar to that shown in Figure A-2, using symbols illustrated in Figure A-3, and should provide a generalized picture of the major milestones, key events, or critical actions which the project manager deems vital to the execution of the project. Only the information required by participating organizations or agencies to determine the time periods or important dates applicable to their functional actions should be reflected. If detailed scheduling is required, event logic network techniques (PERT) or individual-action Gantt charts can be used. Judgment is required in deciding whether or not to put all these networks in section 2 of the package plan since they tend to become voluminous.

PART 3. PROJECT MANAGEMENT   The main purpose of this section is to provide the participating organizations a summary of the management structure and philosophy applicable to the project. This section includes:

> Details of how the project will be managed in terms of what is to be done, how it is to be done, who will do it, and when it is to be done
>
> Specific identification of the participants in the project and a specification of their roles in terms of authority and responsibility
>
> Identification of the advisory groups and committees that are required to support the project manager—their roles, functions, scope of activity, and relationships (authority and responsibility) to the other project participants
>
> A copy of the memorandums of agreement that have been negotiated to support the project
>
> Identification of all the parties that are participating on the project on a contractual basis, and the role these contractors play in managing some subsystem of the project

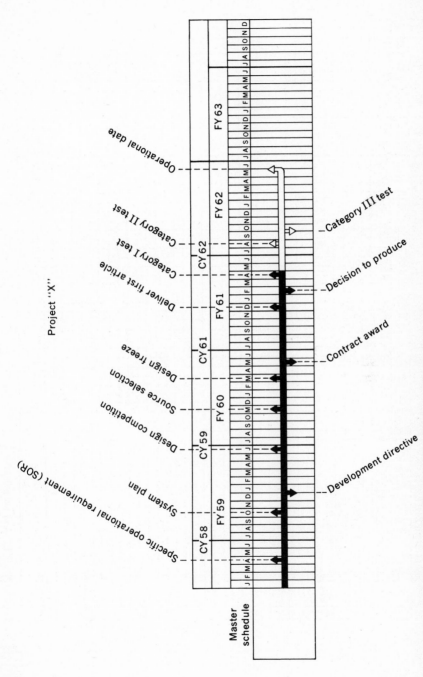

Figure A-1   Project master phasing chart for a weapons system.

PROGRAM SCHEDULE

SYSTEM (*Project*) NUMBER   SUBSYSTEM   TYPE OF SCHEDULE — MASTER SUMMARY SCHEDULE   AS OF DATE

LINE		PRIOR SCHEDULE DATES	FY 1961 CY 19	FY 19 FY 1962 CY 19	FY 1963	1964	1965	1966	COMPLETION DATES	LINE
1	Special operational requirement No. 2								1
2	PSPP approved								2
3	System program directive No. 3								3
4	Contract award								4
5	Preliminary model specification								5
6	Development engineering inspections								6
7	Make-up inspection								7
8	Contractor technique compliance inspection								8
9	First significant achievement								9
10	Start category I testing								10
11	End category I testing								11
12	Start category II testing								12
13	Start category III testing								13
14	Operational data								14
15									15
16									16
17									17
18									18
19									19
20									20
21									21
22									22
23									23
24									24
25									25
26									26
27									27
28									28
29									29
30									30
31									31
32									32
33									33
34									34
35									35
36									36

AUTHENTICATION

Figure A-2 Project schedules.

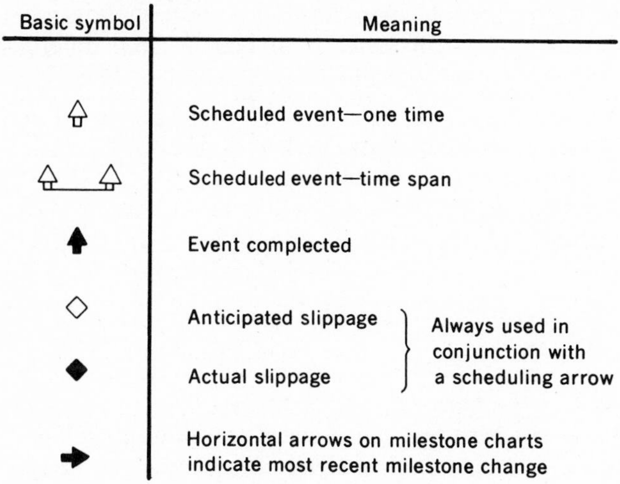

Basic symbol	Meaning
⌂	Scheduled event—one time
⌂ ⌂	Scheduled event—time span
▲	Event complected
◇	Anticipated slippage ⎫ Always used in
◆	Actual slippage ⎬ conjunction with ⎭ a scheduling arrow
➡	Horizontal arrows on milestone charts indicate most recent milestone change

Figure A-3   Project milestone symbols.

Specification of the management reports (the management information system) that are to be provided by the participants and used by the project manager in tracking the project

Organizational locations and functional breakdown of the project participants

A summary of measures to be taken for the protection of proprietary information

Any unusual management agreements or conditions which are required to sustain the project

Specification of the control policy and procedures to be used in delivering the project on time, within cost limits, and with the desired performance characteristics

A charter for any special task teams that are to be organized for the project

Citation of management philosophy to be followed for the contingent or "withdrawal" conditions in the project activities

Procedures to provide for a periodic review of the project by all the participants used in the project

The project-management section is probably the most important section since it is the focus of the project actions. The section can propose the *modus operandi* to be followed in the project and define the interdependent roles of all the participants. It will be the most difficult to write; a considerable amount of negotiating is required to develop an understanding of the reciprocal roles that the participants have in the endeavor. While the technical aspects of the project can be demonstrated, the patterns of interpersonal relationships between the human sources can be critical; a well-thought-out plan to create the proper environment for the people can do much to alleviate the conflict that can arise when people from different parent units are working together on a common objective.

PART 4. MARKET INTELLIGENCE Traditionally, a market is defined as the place where buyers and sellers exchange goods. In our view of project management, we must take certain liberties with that definition in order to make it meaningful and compatible with the definition of a project. Since we have held that a project can range from a product development effort to an *ad hoc* study of a corporate merger, the market for the product or services of a project can range widely. In other words, the objective of a project can be to provide a certain service to an organization. Presumably, the organization that is to receive the service has a need—or, perhaps better stated, a *demand* —for such service. If this is the case, we can proceed to reason as follows: *A market for the project is that environment where the product or service of the project is demanded.* Thus, the demand for specific recommendations regarding a corporate merger may stimulate the formation of a project group to study the feasibility of the merger. The project group that is created studies the project in terms of the cost (financial and opportunity), the schedule (when is the best time to effect the merger and on what types of time phasing), and the performance (what corporate performance, profitability, organizational continuity, etc., will result).

If we accept this definition, the market-intelligence section takes on added significance because the project manager and his team must be as knowledgeable as possible about the environment in which the project is being conducted.

This section is an analysis of the environmental conditions which led to the project requirement, together with any special intelligence which would affect the project design and operation. In preparing this section, proprietary or sensitive information will be used, and it should be safeguarded carefully. It serves as a means of identifying the need to review or alter the requirement for the project as the environment changes.

This section will include a current analysis of the competitive situation in the market (e.g., the competition to be faced by another company's product) and an estimate of all such potential capabilities to be encountered in the future. The basic forecasts which try to portray the environment at some future period of time will be contained in this section. The section on market intelligence is of prime importance to the project. It provides the master information file about the expected conditions under which the project is expected to survive.

PART 5. OPERATIONAL CONCEPT The operational concept will be originated by the project manager and contains in summary form the objective and a clear identification of the project or capability that it will replace or enhance. To be included are conceptual statements covering:

Objective
Limitations
Expected use
Readiness
Support
Organizational structure
Manpower
Personnel
Training and education
Facilities
Availability dates

PART 6. ACQUISITION   Section 6 portrays the development-test-production plan to achieve the project objectives as described in section 1. This includes:

Project description and performance, reliability, and maintainability. Describes the utility capability, anticipated performance, and design features and gives an illustration of the entire system.

Subsystem description. Essentially the same information will be shown here as for the above system.

Personnel area subsystem. A detailed explanation of the human factors of the project and how those factors integrate into the system.

Background, difficulties, and approach.

Test and evaluation data. Include test planning factors, test objectives, detailed test schedules, resources, test management, and test participants.

Production data such as manufacturing methods, processes, industrial facilities, tooling, special test equipment, quality-control procedures, plant layout, etc.

PART 7. FACILITY SUPPORT   This section gives a description of the real facilities (plant, access roads, easements) required to support the project. If new construction is required, this section should contain a detailed plan of action to acquire the property, through lease, purchase, sale-leaseback, or other arrangements.

PART 8. LOGISTIC REQUIREMENTS   This section will be originated by the organizational logistician and encompasses a comprehensive summary of the logistic support required for the project. It will include:

Logistic concepts, principles, and requirements in the areas of materials, supplies, spare parts, repairs, engineering, transportation, materials handling, quality control, test support, data-processing equipment, support facilities (e.g., terminal facilities), and medical services

Material and supply control procedure

Peculiar or unusual circumstances that affect material and supply support requirements

PART 9. MANPOWER AND ORGANIZATION   This section is concerned with the degree of manpower allocations for the project. It will become the basis for the recruitment action of the personnel department. This section will contain:

Assumptions and factors on which the manpower requirements are established

Projections of manpower requirements by type (salaried, wage-rated) and the skills required

Strategy for locating qualified people, e.g., through unsolicited applications, employment agencies, educational institutions, or professional meetings

Policies related to recruitment

PART 10. EXECUTIVE DEVELOPMENT AND PERSONNEL TRAINING   This section will be originated by the education and training office and is designed to provide a comprehensive summary of the personnel development and training required to support the project. It should be cross-referenced to other sections to reflect related actions and authorizations. The section contains:

Trained personnel requirements with specific identification of those peculiar to the project

Type, locations, and key dates of special courses that can be offered to increase the skills of the personnel

Specialized training equipment that is required

Planned management development program to include:

An analysis of manager requirement

An inventory of manager talent

A determination of individual needs

An appraisal of individual progress

A means for program evaluation

PART 11. FINANCIAL SUPPORT   This section, although compiled by the project manager, is a joint responsibility of all the project participants, and will be an integral part of the project package plan. The project manager, in collaboration with the finance officer, will be responsible for developing implementing instructions, ensuring overall consistency of data, and preparing and collating the section.

This section is designed to:

> Provide the basis for the accounting period for the presentation of the estimates of *direct costs* of the project. Such estimates of direct costs will serve as backup data for the organizational budget
>
> Provide estimates of *total costs* (direct and indirect) for the development, production, and (if required) operation of the project (or product)

Cost categories will include:

> Development. All resources (effort, material, facilities) for applied research, development, test, and evaluation directly associated with the project endeavor
>
> Investment. Additional one-time resources (capital and operating) which are directly related to the establishment or buildup of a project, after an assessment of the usefulness of those assets which can be inherited from other organizations or activities
>
> Recurring. Those resources (capital and operating) required to maintain the project during its projected operational phase, period by period

PART 12. PROJECT REQUIREMENTS   This part will consist of a consolidation of the organizational requirements which generated the requirement for the project. Included would be such documents as a resolution of the board of directors, specific letters of authorization, approval of higher-echelon plans which this plan supports, unsolicited proposals, bid packages, etc. This section can be used as central source of the overall documentation which justifies and authorizes the project.

PART 13. GENERAL INFORMATION   There will be information which is not suitable for enclosure elsewhere in the project plan, but yet is vital to the plan documentation. This section should include a summary of the alternatives, such as trade-offs between costs and schedules considered in meeting the objective. A discussion of the variation in performance, schedule, and cost associated with each alternative should be included.

PART 14. PROPRIETARY INFORMATION   General matters relating to the security classification of the project should be included here. For example:

> Physical security requirements and personnel background clearance (particularly appropriate when working on projects for the government)
>
> A schedule to change the proprietary classification of the project as appropriate
>
> Policy regarding the public release of information about the project
>
> Instructions concerning any special handling of the equipment or documentation of the project

APPENDIX 2

The project manual

9.0   Financial management
     9.1   Budgets
     9.2   Internal reports—cost
     9.3   External reports—cost
     9.4   Cost account numbers

10.0   Meetings
     10.1   Weekly project meeting
     10.2   Internal meetings
     10.3   Meetings with other project participants

11.0   Quality assurance
     11.1   Requirements
     11.2   Procedure

12.0   Reliability, maintainability, supportability assurance
     12.1   Requirements
     12.2   Procedures

13.0   Field service and engineering
     13.1   Requirements
     13.2   Policy and procedures

APPENDIX 3

Project-management review, checklist

Authority and responsibility of the project manager

Are there any limitations on the project manager's executive authority? If so, identify and explain them.

Does the project manager exercise control over the allocation and utilization of all resources (men, money, material) approved in the project? If not, describe where control is lacking.

Are there any limitations upon the project manager's authority to make technical and business management decisions required by his project and authorized by his charter?

Does the project manager furnish information and requirements necessary for effective procurement planning and contract negotiation? Does he approve all proposed contractual actions for his project consistent with his charter?

Does the project manager approve the scope and schedules of his project effort? Does he approve the plans for accomplishing his objectives? If not, what limitations are placed upon him? Who imposes them and by what authority? Who does approve the scope of the project, the schedule, and the plans?

How does the project manager report on the progress of his project?

Did the initial project manager have a primary role in the selection of key subordinates? Does the current project manager exercise this responsibility?

Does the project manager have a primary role in controlling the tenure of his key subordinates?

Did the initial project manager have a primary role in the determination of his organizational structure? Does the current project manager determine his organizational structure?

Does the project manager have a primary role in the assignment of tasks to his organization? Does he, in turn, control assignments to others?

Project charter

Does the project manager have a current and adequate charter approved by either the head of the organization having cognizance of the project or the head of the organization having dominant interest?

Is the project manager designated by name in the charter?

Does the charter designate the project elements or parts thereof for which the project manager will be responsible?

Does the charter define the interface relationships and the communication channels and identify the organizations which support the project manager in the following areas?

    a   Production
    b   Finance
    c   Marketing
    d   Contract administration
    e   Customer communication

Does the charter provide for the project manager to control the allocation and utilization of all resources approved for the financial program?

Does the charter indicate the organizational and physical location of the project office and the organizations to provide administrative support? If not, what is lacking?

Does the charter delineate any special delegation of authority or exemptions from corporate policy?

Is the charter approved and signed by the chief executive officer? If not, by whom? What is the date of the charter? Is it current?

Does the charter clearly define the scope of the project?

Does the project charter provide that the project manager will do the following?

    Organize, plan, and administer the project-management office
    Make authorized technical and business management decisions
    Establish initial and long-range objectives

Accomplish experimental test, engineering, and analytical studies

Delineate operational requirements, design specifications, performance specifications, technical approaches, etc.

Prepare a project master plan

Prepare, submit, and justify initial and long-range funding requirements

Exercise financial management controls over all allocated project funds

Define work efforts; approve plan of execution, scope, and schedule of work; and approve costs of work

Furnish information and requirements for contract negotiations

Approve, consistent with corporate policy, all proposed contractual actions

Establish and promulgate design interface specifications to ensure project integration

Respond to requirements of other project managers and head of functional activities in resolution of interface problems

Negotiate working agreements with organizations outside as appropriate

Develop and maintain the integrated logistic support plan for the project

Establish methods and procedures for project configuration control

Ensure that the quality assurance reliability, maintainability, and value engineering programs for the project are adequate

Ensure that technical documentation is prepared and available for concurrent delivery with hardware

Analyze project performance in relation to required performance specifications

Maintain a complete chronological history (significant events and decisions)

Institute appropriate management-control techniques (required by higher authority or selected) to provide status, progress, and forecasts

Report the current status and progress of the project to the appropriate people

Prepare a budget for and justify travel funds

Execute efficiency ratings for personnel

Does the project charter define the interface and operating relationships, between (1) project manager and other designated projects, (2) project manager and functional groups, (3) project-manager–interagency relationships, etc.?

Does the project charter identify supporting organizations to participate in work in support of the project?

Does the project charter specify adequately manpower to staff the project-management office?

Does the project charter provide a staffing schedule?

Does the project charter identify personnel in liaison offices and in field organizations tied exclusively to, and under the management control of, the project manager?

Does the charter identify the organization responsible for "public information"?

Does the charter provide for a review for project disestablishment or a date for project disestablishment?

Is the charter in the proper format?

> Introduction
> Mission
> Scope of project
> Specific authority and responsibility of project manager
> Specific interface and operating relationships of project manager
> Personnel staffing for project-management office
> Resources assigned to project
> Project administrative support
> Public information
> Project disestablishment

Project priority

Does the project have a priority? If so, what is the priority?

Project complexity

What is the project manager's opinion of project objectives; specifically, do they have a significant effect on the organization's fortunes?

Does the project manager manage a group of projects which are conducted substantially on a concurrent basis with each having significant technical problems?

Does the project involve unusual organizational complexity or technological advancement?

Does the project require extensive interdepartmental, national, or international coordination or support?

Does the project present unusual difficulties which need expeditious handling to satisfy an urgent requirement?

Historical data

Does the project manager maintain historical titles?

Project visibility

Is there any evidence that subcontractors have counterpart "managers" designated specifically and solely to manage their contractual efforts?

Project manager's rank

Does the project manager have sufficient executive rank to be accepted as the agent of the parent organization when dealing with outside organizations?

Project manager's staff

Is there evidence that the project-management staff is composed of persons with a high degree of technical and business managerial competence?

Is there evidence of recent experience in project management among the key subordinates of the project manager's staff?

What evidence is there of formal training in the special requirements of project management among the project manager's key subordinates?

Will any of the key subordinates of the project manager's staff (that he desires to keep) be available for the duration of the project?

Are all members of the project-management office assigned to the office on a full-time basis?

Communication channels

Does the project manager have direct two-way communication between his office and key participants involved in support [contractors and(or) bureaus, etc.] of his project which assures timely and effective direction and interchange of information?

Reporting

Does the project manager provide formal written and(or) oral briefings to top management on the status and progress of his project, including the identification of the problems?

Does the project manager attend formal briefings held by other company project managers?

Project reviews and evaluations

What procedure does the project manager use to identify his problems and review the status of his project?

Personal contact with key subordinates?
Conference?
Formal, scheduled briefings by key subordinates?
Review of outgoing progress reports?
Combination of the above?
Other?

How frequently does the project manager review the status and progress of his project? How?

Does the project manager's procedures for program reviews and evaluations provide coverage for schedule accomplishment, technical performance, cost and logistic support, etc.?

Management information systems

Has the project manager applied management control techniques and developed information systems for effective control?

Financial management

Does the project manager assess and document the effect of proposals to increase or decrease the resources authorized for the execution of his project upon cost, schedule, and performance objectives? How? Does he reassess requirements? How?

Planning

Does the project manager have a project master plan? What is its station?
Does the project master plan include the following?

Project summary
Project schedules
Management and organization plan
Market intelligence
Operational concept
Acquisition procedures
Facility support requirements
Logistics requirements
Manpower requirements
Executive development and personnel training requirements

Financial support strategy
Policy for protection of proprietary data

Technical direction

How does the project manager ensure the integration of schedule, performance, and cost considerations to manage his project?

Can the project manager issue technical instructions directly to prime contractors? To subcontractors? To others? If not, what are the limitations upon this authority?

Who in the project manager's organization exercises configuration change control?

How does the project manager ensure the adequacy of the following?

Space equipment
Training facilities and equipment
Documentation
Test equipment
Containers
Safety
Security (technical)
Failure analysis
Calibration of test equipment
Cost effectiveness
Reliability and maintainability

General

How has the project manager provided for ensuring an adequate implementation of the following?

Value engineering
Subcontractor information system(s)
Subcontractor performance evaluation

Does the project manager attend top-level policy meetings with the customers?

Has the project manager been overruled by his seniors under customer pressure? If so, why?

Has the project been given sufficient publicity in the company paper?

Does the project manager encourage the primary project contributors to attend technical meetings or symposiums on related topics? Has the project manager arranged a visit by officials of the customer's organization?

Have procedures been established whereby outstanding contributions to the project by some of the participants can be recognized?

What assurance does the project manager have that the project contributors have developed a full understanding of the problem (as through the possession of a detailed statement of work)?

Have administrative procedures been set up in the project whereby creative groups are free from administrative paper work?

Have schedules been set up to conduct design reviews to assure in-process design adequacy?

Index

Index